# Psychoanalytic Centrism

### By Gerald Schoenewolf

ISBN-13: 9781481155410
ISBN-10: 1481155415

Copyright 2010 by Gerald Schoenewolf
LIVING CENTER PRESS
207 East 15th Street
New York, NY 10003

# Acknowledgements

For many years I hesitated to publish this book, knowing full well that it violates several current taboos and indeed confronts those very taboos. However, several people to whom I showed all are part of the manuscript believed that I should publish it, and I wish especially to thank Eva Pappas and James Phalen for their gracious support. Neither of them agreed with all I have say, but they thought it was important for me to have the right to say it. I am also indebted to my lifelong editor, Jay Aronson, who believed in me when nobody else did.

All but two of the papers in this volume have either been published in journals or presented at professional conferences. The first paper, "The Death Trauma and Its Consequences" was never published or presented, but I still have faith in it. I have placed it first because I think it is one of my best. "Perverse Sexuality and Perverse Mothering" was written especially for this volume. Of the rest, "The Persistence in the Belief that Schizophrenia is Hereditary" and "The Scapegoat and the Holy Cow in Psychotherapy" originally appeared in the *Journal of Contemporary Psychotherapy*. "Schizophrenia in a Dysfunctional Family" and "Towards a Viable Theory of Female Psychology" were first published in *Changes: An International Journal of Psychology and Psychotherapy*. The chapter, "The Psychology of Hate" originally appeared in *The Encyclopedia of Human Behavior*; "Psychological Factors in Cancer" first came out in *Clinical Issues: The International Journal of Psychoanalysis; and* "Child of the Full Moon" was in *Voices: The Art and Science of Psychotherapy*. "Dealing with Character, Sex and Race in Psychotherapy" originally appeared, in a much different form, in *Psychoanalysis and Psychotherapy*, where it was entitled, "Analyzing Audrey: Dealing with Character, Sex and Race in Psychotherapy." "Vampire Coupling" was first seen in *The Journal of Couples Therapy.* "Gender Narcissism and its Consequences" was first presented at a conference of the National Association for Research and Therapy with Homosexuals.

# Contents

# Introduction

Psychoanalytic Centrism

# 1.

# Principles of Psychoanalytic Centrism

A healthy individual is an individual who has a strong ego that can mediate between the id and the superego. As Freud put it, "Where id was, there ego shall be." Thus, a healthy individual is centered. He or she is not dominated by the id or the superego. Such an individual is neither all work nor all play. Such an individual is not plagued by impossible standards, religious beliefs or compulsions; nor is such an individual driven by impulsive desires or sentimental beliefs. A healthy individual is a grounded individual who respects the urges of the id and pleas of the superego but does not necessarily give in to them. This individual is open-minded, but not to the point of being unrealistic. This individual is spontaneous, but not to the point of being without boundaries. This individual seeks pleasure, but not at the expense of responsibility; nor seeks responsibility at the expense of pleasure. First and foremost, a healthy individual is a balanced individual, leaning neither too far to the left nor to the right.

A healthy group (i.e., culture) is a group that has a strong center that can mediate between the left and right. It is not dominated by the left or the right. It is neither all work nor all play. It is not plagued by impossible standards, religious beliefs or compulsions, nor is it driven by impulsive desires or sentimental beliefs and ideals. A healthy group is a grounded group that respects the pleas of the left for equal rights and the demands of the right for responsibility but does not necessarily give in to them. The healthy group is open-minded but not to a point that it invites danger. The healthy group seeks pleasure without disregarding responsibility and is responsible without disregarding pleasure. It wants rights for all people, not for selected people.

With regard to psychoanalytic research, the centrist leads toward a neutral and unbiased view. Freud was a centrist and so were all of the early pioneers of psychoanalysis. Freud did not want either religious or political sentiments to becloud psychoanalytic research. Instead, he strove for neutrality. I also consider myself a psychoanalytic centrist and have attempted to take a neutral point of view. Throughout this book I have used theories and concepts from many schools of psychoanalysis, trying to blend them into a centrist thesis, and I have sought a balanced viewpoint with an underpinning of reason rather than moral righteousness. Because a dogmatic form of liberalism has become the trend today, I have been most critical of these leftist tendencies that I believe have taken over the field and have suppressed and censored all other points of view, including the centrist view.

The bottom line is that I believe centrism to be the healthiest attitude. It is the most objective and least biased way to look at life. It is the kind of centrism found in the most ancient and time-tested philosophies, such as Taoism or Buddhism in the East and Socrates in the West. And it is this centrism that has the potential of leading humans out of our aggressive, competitive and destructive mode towards a more viable future.

# 10 Principles of Centrism

1. *There are two or more sides to every question.* The more extreme one's ideas are—whether extreme right or left, the more one-sided they will be on every issue. A centrist considers all sides of a question and everything in between. An extremist is convinced that only his/her side matters and negates the other side and all that is in between.

2. *Human situations are complex.* A centrist considers the complexity of each situation, understanding that humanity and human life is ruled by contradiction. Every individual and every group operates on the basis of a plethora of causes and effects, and therefore is driven by a mixture of thoughts, feelings and motivations. Religious and political people look for moral answers. The more extreme they are, the more they apply a simple point of view and a simple solution to all situations.

3. *It is important to make distinctions.* A centrist understands that there are various shades of gray, and only by considering all the shades can we make sound decisions that lead to resolution. Extremists see what they want to see; they see only black and white and insist that black and white is the only truly important thing to see. They demand that all people stop making distinctions and accuse those who make distinctions of waffling, and of not having the courage to take a stand, which leads to strife.

4. *Moderation is the key.* Centrists use constructive language and make reasonable decisions that avoid provocative and manipulative words and actions; hence they resolve rather than inflame a situation. Extremists use provocative words, make manipulative decisions and engage in actions that inflame a situation and worsen it.

5. *Prejudice is often in the eye of the beholder.* Prejudice exists, but it exists universally. There is no one group that has a monopoly on being a victim. Everybody victimizes someone, and everybody has been victimized by someone. Extremists look for prejudice everywhere. Centrists seek what's there.

6. *The truth will set you free.* Centrists face reality, even though that reality may be unpleasant. Extremists believe in religious or political dogma and do not look any further than that. When an alcoholic accepts the truth—that he is an alcoholic—he begins to be freed from his alcoholism. When a person accepts reality, whatever it is, he is then free of the myths than entrap him. When a group accepts reality, it is free of the group myths that entrap it.

7. *Calm rational discussions lead to real solutions.* Centrists engage in calm, rational discussions and negotiations that lead to compromise solutions. Such solutions, in which there is give and take, lead to peace and harmony. Extremists, ruled by their emotion, believe in forcing their views on others, as these views are considered either sacred (handed down by God) or politically correct (handed down by group consensus). Forced views do not lead to peace and harmony.

8. *It is best to be open-minded.* The centrist open-minded and not wedded to any idea or stance. If you start by being open-minded to each situation, you will find the solution that works. If you start by being closed-minded, you will only find the solution that works for you but negates other solutions. This leads to constant strife.

9. *Healthy relationships require mutual respect and cooperation.* Centrists have an attitude of mutual respect and cooperation toward all, no matter what their point of view; this leads to constructive communication. Extremists have an us-against-them attitude and only respect and cooperate with those who are seen as allies. They idealize their allies and demean their opponents, and they insist on having their way; this leads to conflict.

10. *The search for right and wrong is a sickness.* Accept yourself and be compassionate toward your darker parts, and you will be compassionate toward all others. Hide your darker parts, and you will look for the darker parts of other and be quick to accuse and condemn them of high treason.

Psychoanalytic Centrism

# Part 1 - Theory

Psychoanalytic Centrism

# 2

# The Death Trauma and Its Consequences

Freud looked at death and its effect on personality formation in terms of denial and in terms of the death drive. This paper attempts to extend Freud's theory and the theories of others by positing a death trauma. The death trauma refers to a human being's first awareness that he or she has to die. According to the author's and other people's research, there seems to be a period lying somewhere between the Oedipal and latency stages during which children first have this awareness. This initial awareness can have a profound effect, contributing to superego formation and the onset of latency, causing one of several defensive attitudes that affect personality.

> *Death is here and death is there,*
> *Death is busy everywhere,*
> *All around, within, beneath,*
> *Above is death and we are death.*
> --Shelley (Davidoff, 1942, p. 58)

Poets have long pondered death and its meaning to human beings. In Western literature, the theme of death permeates the works of romantic poets such as Shelley, Keats, and Byron, the sonnets and plays of Shakespeare, and the verses of Robert Browning, T. S. Eliot, and Dylan Thomas. Indeed, popular anthologies of the classic poems of then and now contain a high percentage of reflections on death, afterlife, and the ephemeral quality of existence. Considerations of death are also prominent in Eastern literature although in a different way; they are often subtly implied through observations of nature. Chinese poets, from ancients such as Li Po, Tu Fu, and Han Yu, to the modern voices of Lin Ya-tzu and Mao Tse-tung, often talk about the sadness of seeing the petals of flowers falling down or chill of a rainy afternoon. In Japan, Haiku poets are likewise noted for their indirect allusions to death.

Indeed, in reading the poets, one senses that death has had a major impact on the shaping of the poet's personality. For example, the poems of Dylan Thomas, from "Fern Hill" to "Go Not Gently into That Good Night," as well as his life history of suicidal alcoholism, demonstrate a profound anger and regret about death that seems to lie at the root of the poet's personality (Tremlett, 1992).

Freud laid the foundation for a psychological theory about the impact of death on human development; indeed, his concept of a death instinct not only in human beings but also in all living matter is one of the cornerstones of his psychodynamic theory. However, Freud's concept is as much about biology as it is about psychology, using biological analogies to explain the death instinct. Writing about the relationship between Eros and the death drive, he compares it to biology, noting that what eros is aiming at "by every possible means is the coalescence of two germ cells which are differentiated in a particular way. If this union is not effected, the germ cell dies along with the other elements of the multicellular organism" (1919, p. 45). He sees a struggle between these opposing forces in all living matter. On one hand, there is the instinct toward sexual union and life (eros), and on the other hand there is the instinct to return to the nonliving matter from which life erupted (thanatos). As he succinctly puts it, "The aim of all life is death" (p. 36).

One of Freud's followers, Stekel, made a significant contribution to the death instinct theory. It was Stekel who first used the term "thanatos", and who outlined a theory of the death instinct during meetings of the

Vienna Psychoanalytic Society that took into consideration death anxiety. According to Stekel, anxiety was the result of "the reaction to the advance of the death instinct, caused by a suppression of the sex instinct" (Nunberg and Federn, 1967, p. 395). Stekel later examined death symbolism in dreams and, according to Freud, claimed that "the idea of death will be found behind every dream" ( Freud, 1917, p. 237), a notion that Freud found confusing. Stekel, unfortunately, did not flesh out his theory, although it seems to be a prelude to the one presented here.

Freud also considered the psychology of death in connection with his thoughts about World War I, observing that in general people are inclined to deny the fact of death, particularly their own death.

> Our own death is indeed unimaginable, and whenever we make the attempt to imagine it we can perceive that we really survive as spectators. Hence the psychoanalytic school could venture on the assertion that at bottom no one believes in his own death, or to put the same thing in another way, in the unconscious every one of us is convinced of his own immortality. (1915, p. 304-295.)

Freud goes on to state, "This attitude of ours towards death has a powerful effect on our lives" (ibid, p. 296). Freud only hinted at what that powerful effect is, noting that when death is denied, life becomes impoverished. When we are not in touch with the reality of our own death, we are also not in touch with the deepest wellsprings of life. Instead of participating in life, we read about it in novels or watch it in the theater. In the theater, Freud notes, "We die in the person of a given hero, yet we survive him" (ibid, p. 298). Only during times of war, when tens of thousands die in a single day, are we forced to acknowledge the existence of death, and, ironically, that acknowledgement heightens our sense of being alive, but only temporarily.

### The Death Trauma and Its Consequences

Freud and Stekel hinted at the impact on human development of the fact of death, and Stekel implied that human beings differ from all other animals in that they are aware of their own existence and at some point become aware of their own mortality. Wainrib (1996) a Jungian psychoanalyst, refers to the "vanishing of one's being," asserting that every individual has experienced it; while it leaves no memory traces, it plays a major role in the organization of the unconscious self. He associates "vanishing of one's being" to Freud's "Hilflosigkeit" ("Helplessness"), the original distress without recourse that one experiences as an infant. Wainrib perhaps hints at what I call a *death trauma* at a point in infants' lives when they first understand that they must die, when they first become aware of their own body's inexorable tendency toward returning to inanimate matter. This death trauma, encapsulated in Wainrib's concept of the first awareness of helplessness, happens at a later period of time, as I will postulate.

Although Adler (1932) and others have written about a "birth trauma," nobody to my knowledge has written about a "death trauma" per se. The death trauma, as I see it, refers to that moment in a person's life when he or she realizes they have to die and all that such an awareness implies. Many of my patients have talked about the moment they found out that life is finite and how that knowledge affected them personally. This awareness, which can be an earth-shattering recognition or merely a subliminal flicker in their train of thought, is in any case—I would conjecture—a major milestone in their lives. I would say it is probably the most disturbing awareness anyone can ever have. The death trauma happens to everyone to some degree or another and, according to my research, it generally happens from the end of the oedipal stage or the end of latency (but this can vary greatly and can sometimes happen much earlier or later). Something in a child's life will trigger it. The awareness may be set off by the death of a mother, father, sibling, or playmate. It may come on the heels of a suggestion made during a sermon at Church, or as the result of a lesson at school. It may be associated with an injury during rough play or from an automobile accident. It may be brought about by some devastating occurrence such as a war, hurricane, or volcano. It may be related to a child's oedipal thoughts about killing off a father or sibling in order to possess Mother, or getting rid of a mother to possess Father. It may be provoked by deprivation or by sexual or physical abuse. In any case, the death trauma brings on a period of preoccupation with death that can last days, weeks, months, or even a lifetime.

The severity of this death trauma would seem to depend on three variables. First, it depends on the intelligence and sensitivity of the child. Children who are more intelligent and sensitive are probably more likely to have a deeper personal understanding of death; hence, their trauma will be greater. Freud's (1909a) case history about Little Hans, a creative child who later became a director of operas, describes a horse phobia (a fear of being bitten by, and possibly killed by a horse) that was developed by a 5-year-old child. Freud connected this fear of being bitten by a horse to unconscious castration fear. However, it was also connected to the fear of losing his mother, and it seemed to indicate that Hans at this early age had recognized the possibility that he could die (be eaten by a horse). Children who are less sensitive or intelligent will not have as deep an understanding of death. Some children will have no conscious awareness of the fact of death; it will register only in their unconscious. For such children the trauma may be less, although the unconscious impact may still be strong.

Second, the death trauma depends on the context of the trauma. Does the child find out about death because his mother dies? Does the child find out because her father has to go to war? Does the child find out when someone tells him in an unfriendly way? Does the child find out because a volcano blows through his house and he himself almost dies? Does the child find out because her favorite pet dies and nobody cares? Naturally, the more overwhelming to the ego are the circumstances, the deeper the possible trauma. Another factor is the duration of the circumstances. A child may be caught up in a war that lasts for several years, in which case he or she must daily deal with the threat of death. This kind of circumstance is likely to leave a lasting imprint, regardless of other factors.

Finally, the severity of the trauma depends on how the child's family and other members of the immediate environment respond to the trauma. This last variable is perhaps the most crucial. If children feel loved and supported in their attempts to make peace with their own mortality, the trauma will be lessened. If not, the trauma will be increased. Obviously, parents who have themselves not come to grips with their immortality will not be able to be supportive to their children. If a boy goes to his father and asks, "Father why do we have to die?" and the father, due to his own inability to accept death, snaps, "We just have to, that's all!" that boy will not be soothed, and his death trauma will linger and fester within his psyche. Similarly, if a little girl goes to her mother and asks the same question, and the mother has dealt with the question for herself through faith in Judaism or Christianity, she may answer, "Because Adam and Eve ate the apple." This will not satisfy the girl's curiosity or calm her anxiety.? She will then say, "But *I* didn't eat the apple, why do *I* have to die?" The child will want a reasonable answer, but the parent won't be able to give her a reasonable answer, so the child must repress her feelings and "have faith" rather than resolve her feelings and achieve a mature acceptance of death.

Following are some case histories to illustrate my thesis:

One of my patients was confronted with death when she was seven years old and a playmate became sick and died. As her family was quite abusive, her bond with this peer was the strongest one in her life, and his death left her shaken. This event was further complicated when her parents refused to allow her to attend his funeral. In her therapy sessions she didn't consciously relate her playmate's death to her development, but there were indications that on an unconscious level her playmate's death affected her subsequent personality formation. Whenever she was sick after that she became very frightened without knowing why, and she developed a lifelong anger about death that remained a part of her personality. In addition, she had a tendency to devote herself to relatives or friends who were dying, as if to make up for missing out on the death of her playmate.

Another of my patients was emotionally abandoned by his mother at the age of five, when a younger brother was born. Until then he had been his mother's favorite. He went through several years of fighting for her attention, during which she made him the scapegoat of all her own frustrations with her abusive husband. Eventually the boy sank into a depression. When he was about nine years old and attending Bible

School he learned the words "mortal" and "immortal" with regard to the story of Adam and Eve, and he went through a period in which he felt horrified at the discovery of his own mortality. He began to fear he would die at any moment. He suffered his whole life from a regret about, and fear of death.

Another patient understood death when he lost his pet dog at age seven. He found the dog on the side of the road when he was on his way home from school. He picked up the dog and took it home and showed it to his mother, thinking the dog was sick. His mother explained that the dog was dead and wouldn't return to life. After they had buried it in the back yard, he continued to question his mother about death, and at one point asked her, "Will I have to die?" Her answer was to cry and hug him. From that point on he always had a core feeling of sadness inside him that welled up whenever he was stressed out about something. I saw this patient when he was in his mid-thirties, and he always entered my doorway with an expression of futility. He would continually read the obituaries and bemoan some celebrity's death. Underneath, I felt he was still bemoaning his pet dog's death, as well as the prospect of his own demise.

Yet another patient's father was murdered when he was ten years old. This patient told me that after this event he spent months in a dark melancholy, perhaps not too different than the melancholy of Shakespeare's Hamlet. He was not only full of a helpless rage towards his father's unknown assassin, but also became acutely aware of the possibility of his own death. As an adult he seemed to always be looking over his shoulder, expecting to be murdered. He went through phases of depression in which he contemplated suicide.

### Building on the Theory of Kubler-Ross

Kubler-Ross (1969) in a study of terminally ill patients observed that they went through stages in dealing with death. Their first reaction to the news that they had incurable cancer was denial. They would express disbelief that they could have such a disease or that they were going to die. Next they would verbalize anger about their situation and would often behave aggressively to those around them, manifesting an attitude of "Why me?" Next they would attempt to bargain with God, not yet convinced that the situation was hopeless. After no bargains could be made, they would sink into a depression. Finally, they would reach acceptance of the inevitability of death.

It seems that upon discovering their mortality, children go through stages similar to the ones Kubler-Ross observed in her patients: After the first glimpse that they themselves must die, children flip in and out of *denial* ("No, it couldn't be true!"); then they are *afraid* ("I don't want to die!"); then they are *angry* ("It's so unfair!"); then they try to *bargain* with God ("Let me live and I'll be good!"), then they are *depressed* ("What good is life?"); then *apathetic* ("Who cares?"), and finally they *accept* death. Like Kubler-Ross's patients, some children get to the last stage (acceptance), and some get stuck in an earlier stage. The stage at which they get stuck has a large influence on their personality development.

Indeed, Kubler-Ross's stages may well represent emergences into consciousness of attitudes that were already there in the unconscious. I would conjecture that the stage at which one of her patients gets stuck when facing a terminal illness is probably the stage at which the patient was fixated in childhood. The strength of the fixation and the stage of the fixation are related to the circumstances surrounding the child's discovery of death. The death trauma continues to have an affect on an individual's moral, emotional, and intellectual development. Depending on the stage in which the child is fixated, the child, and later the adult, will develop a particular attitude toward death and a particular way of dealing with death, which in turn will influence his or her personality formation. There are seven attitudes, that is, seven primary ways that people may deal with death and its ramifications, according to my clinical experience:

1. *Denial.* We refuse to acknowledge the reality of death or our deepest feelings about death; this can lead to superstition, religion, sublimation, and reaction formation.

2. *Anger.* We regard death as a major betrayer; this may lead us

to rebel against it by taking life-threatening risks.

3. *Fear/Dread.* We develop a fear of death and sometimes a particular kind of anxiety that Kierkegaard called "the sickness unto death" (1954).

4. *Bargaining.* We make deals such as doing good deeds for poor people or accomplishing "great" achievements designed to win immortality.

5. *Depression.* We ponder the meaningless of life; this may lead to despair and to contemplation of suicide.

6. *Apathy.* In some cases we give up completely, lose interest in life, and allow death to take us.

7. *Acceptance.* We resolve our feelings about death and come to an understanding that it is an inevitable reality.

I have observed each of these stages in my patients. One of my patients told of how he tried to bargain with God after he realized, at the age of nine, that he was mortal. Another related going through a dark period (a depression) that lasted about two years. Yet another reported that after trying unsuccessfully to talk about his fear of death to various adults without getting a comforting response, he fell into a state in which "I didn't care about anybody or anything anymore." He said he felt numb inside and had no feelings at all when he attended his grandfather's funeral. Some of my patients were still stuck in a stage and had not reached, in childhood or in the present, acceptance.

### Stages of Awareness of Death

Until the Oedipal stage or later, children cannot be aware of death in the deepest sense. They know about death and have fantasies about the death of parents, siblings, pets and the like, but this knowledge is more of an intellectual than an emotional thing. They don't yet understand that they really won't live forever and that nobody will. It hasn't registered.

According to Piaget (1952), until around the age of six, children view all objects in the world as alive; he refers to this as animism. Children have little ability to discriminate between the animate and inanimate: to the pregenital child, rocks are as alive as horses. As the child grows older, such animistic thinking begins to diminish, so that from the ages of six to ten it becomes limited at first to objects that move and then to objects that move spontaneously. According to Piaget, children don't have the ability to appreciate the finality of death until around the age of ten or eleven. Although they may be preoccupied with death before that age and express that concern through play or through more direct activities, they harbor the view that death is temporary and that it can be reversed.

Similar stages of awareness of death have been described in psychoanalytic literature. From the earliest months of life, the child is aware of separation from mother and experiences separation anxiety when she disappears. To a one-year-old child, a mother's disappearance from sight means she no longer exists: she is dead. Piaget termed the ability to realize that mother still exists even when she is out of sight "object permanence," which he believed develops toward the second year of life. If a mother creates too much separation anxiety, a child may begin to have murderous fantasies about her. Klein (1932) was one of the first to document the many aggressive fantasies of preoedipal children. Trude's mother gave birth to a younger sister when she was two years old, at which time she began to attack her mother by "wetting and dirtying herself," according to Klein. Trude had wanted to rob her pregnant mother of her children, "to kill her and to take her place in coitus with her father" (p. 5). Mastering separation anxiety requires that children learn to externalize aggressive and sometimes murderous feelings about separation to give themselves a sense of control.

Klein and Reviere graphically describe an infant's love and hate relationship with the mother's breast and its association with death. In the beginning, an infant is unaware of its dependency on the mother and her breast. However, if mother and her breast are withholding, the infant becomes painfully aware of the dependence. When the infant discovers that it cannot supply all its own milk and other needs, it explodes with hate and aggression. The authors describe such an infant as going through uncontrollable and overwhelming emptiness and loneliness accompanied by an aggressive rage that brings "pain and explosive, burning, suffocating, choking bodily sensations" (1964, p. 9). They assert, "This situation which we all were in as babies has enormous psychological consequences for our lives. It is our first experience of something like death, a recognition of the non-existence of something, of an overwhelming loss, both in ourselves and in others, as it seems" (p. 9). What Klein and Reviere may be describing is a body-ego version of the death awareness that will eventually deepen to a full-blown cognitive preoccupation later on during the first stage of latency.

In the anal stage, from about 18 months to 3 years, children deal with death through fantasies about magical powers. By their very wishes (Klein, 1932), they believe they can cause the death (temporary removal) of anyone who offends them. At the same time, they fear that others can do likewise to them. Just as feces can be flushed away, so also Mother can be flushed away and the child can be flushed away. (Movies such as the classic horror film *Carrie*, about people with magical powers to kill others with their thoughts hark back to this stage of development.) Also at this stage there begins to be a fusion of the libidinal and aggressive tendencies; children begin to take pleasure in aggression, as when they laugh with delight at aggressive cartoons on television. Traversing this stage successfully depends partly on learning to channel aggression into play and later, as an adult, into sublimated activities such as art, music, dance, athletics, or business.

During the oedipal stage, fantasies of death revolve around the oedipal triangle. Whereas earlier children's fears of death often concern animals that chase them, now the threatening figures are more human, witches, monsters, giants, robots, or men from outer space, often reflecting the figures they see on television. The threatening figures represent a parent or sibling who is a rival for either the mother or father's affection. The fear of death is connected with castration fear and the talion principle: if a boy has fantasies of getting rid of the father, then he will fear the father will get rid of him. The child's notion of death becomes more emotional during this stage, and gradually loses its sense of reversibility. Freud's case of Little Hans, alluded to earlier, documents a case of an oedipal-age boy whose horse phobia went on for several months and symbolized, according to Freud, the boy's castration fear

(fear of annihilation) linked to the father. He wanted to get rid of the father, so he feared the father also wanted to get rid of him. Based on the degree of Han's fear, it didn't appear that he believed this state of affairs was reversible.

Toward the end of the oedipal stage and the beginning of latency, it appears that many children go through a period of preoccupation with death. Hall (1964) and Yacoubian and Lourie (1973) have noted this phase of preoccupation with death and suicide. Yacoubian and Lourie state, "This phenomenon appeared during the course of interviews with "normal" school-age children and those with emotional problems" (p. 157). The authors conclude that thoughts of suicide during this stage are normal. It is during this phase, roughly between the ages of six and nine, when the death trauma would often appear to occur. However, depending on other variables, it can happen earlier or later. In my own research I have also noticed that this period occurs with regularity. During this phase children will be consciously or unconsciously concerned with death in its many guises; this concern may appear directly through questions about death and related matters, or it may show itself indirectly through dreams or play fantasies. Sometimes there is a preoccupation with suicide, while at other times there is a concern with, and fear of, sickness, accidents, or catastrophes. This period of death awareness may be quite subtle, and it may be hardly noticed by parents, if at all. However, for the elementary school child, it is a highly painful and meaningful period of life.

Bowlby (1961) asks the question: "At what stage of development and by means of what processes does the individual arrive at a state which enables him thereafter to respond to loss in a favourable manner?" (p. 323). He is referring to the fact that until a certain stage of development, when children lose a loved one, they tend to deny the reality of the loss. In their mind the loved one could not really be gone forever, and they are always expecting their return. In psychoanalytic terms, they are not able bring about the decathexis of the lost object. In normal development when a child has reached latency he can accept loss realistically and move on. However, sometimes he/she cannot accept a loss well beyond latency and into adult life. There may be many reasons why this happens. One reason may be that if people develop a fixation due to the death trauma and other traumatic factors, they may have problems in accepting loss for the rest of their lives. Wolfstein (1980) believes that children learn to decathect lost objects during adolescence, when they normally go through the process of separating from parents. The process of separating from parents, however, does not begin in adolescence, but evolves throughout early childhood and particularly during the end of the oedipal stage, when children must give up their desires for the opposite-sex parent and their aggressive impulses toward the same-sex parent. Therefore, the first decathexis probably happens then.

### Death Trauma, Superego, and Latency

The death trauma would seem to have an influence on superego development. The child's awareness of immortality has a sobering effect, giving way to a prolonged conscious or unconscious preoccupation with death that in turn leads to moral considerations. When Adam and Eve in the Bible learn that they are immortal, their shame and guilt is intensified; they realize they are naked and quickly get dressed; that is, they begin to have moral standards. This Biblical story can be seen as a symbolic telling of the beginning of each person's life and of the development of the superego. Adam and Eve become aware that they have had sinful sexual feelings (synonymous with a child's oedipal urges) and they connect the sinful sexual feelings with the fact that they now have to die ("returning to dust"). For Adam and Eve it was the birth of morality. For each child, it is the birth of the superego: of self-consciousness, shame, guilt, and standards (i.e., the ego-ideal). Incidentally, Freud did not consider his death instinct as having an impact on superego development, but rather, saw the superego as an agency that might obtain mastery over the individual's instinct of aggression and thereby help to sustain civilization (1930).

Regarding the development of the superego, Freud states it is "most intimately linked with the destiny of the Oedipus complex, so that the superego appears as the heir of that emotional attachment which is of such importance for childhood" (1933, p. 57). He goes on to explain that when children give up their intense sexual and aggressive impulses for their parents, they are compensated for this loss of important objects by an intensified identification with them. Hence on the heels of the object loss, and through this identification with parents, the superego is formed. However, before children get to the point where they give up their oedipal wishes, they go through the vicissitudes of the castration complex. For boys this entails the threat of castration (death). For girls, it entails actual castration (in their minds), and also loss of mother's love (a kind of death). Hence, the reason children give up their intense sexual impulses towards parents is that they are scared off by fears of annihilation; these fears, in turn, prod them towards morality.

The element in Freud's theory that is perhaps implied but not directly stated is that the fear of death (symbolized by castration fear) motivates the child to become moral, that is, to identify with the parents rather than seduce or oppose them, and to adapt the parent's conscience and standards. The boy's fear of castration and possible annihilation by the father, and the girl's fear of rejection and abandonment by the mother (another form of annihilation) scare them away from the id-impulses, which have no morality but are tied to the pleasure principle, and catapult them toward a concern for others (their parents). This initial fear of annihilation, on the cusp of castration fear, is then reinforced during the later period of death awareness at the end of the oedipal stage and the beginning of latency.

Incidentally, it should be mentioned that other psychoanalysts do not share Freud's contention that superego formation primarily occurs during the oedipal stage. Klein (1932) believes that it starts in infancy, when a child responds to the "good" and "bad" breast of its mother, and adopts either a depressive or paranoid attitude. Ferenczi (1925) asserts that superego formation begins during the anal stage, when the child's anal and urethral identification with parents brings about a physiological forerunner of the ego-ideal. "A severe sphincter-morality is set up which can only be contravened at the cost of bitter self-reproaches and punishment by conscience" (p. 267). More recently, Shengold (1988) points out that the child's toilet training is accomplished both out of love and fear; the child wishes to master the sphincters in order to be like the idealized parents, but also fears and feels aggressive toward the parents and devaluates them. This leads to the formation of the ego-ideal and the primitive superego. Shengold then points to a connection between anality and death: "Death is *the* open door. Anality, the involvement with *things*, denies death as it scants life in its insistence on the fixed and the eternal" (p. 38).

Regardless of when the superego starts to form, the fact of death appears to contribute to its formation all along. During the oral stage, separation anxiety leads to fears of mother's death and frustrated dependency to fears about one's own death; during the anal stage, death becomes evident in fantasies about flushing people away and in fantasies of magical powers; and in the oedipal stage death is associated with castration fear or with the loss of a parent's love and approval. In each instance, the awareness of death deepens and results in an increasing sense of morality.

The death trauma may also exert an influence on the child's transition from the oedipal stage to latency. Freud (1920, 1930) associated latency to the development of the superego, which, as previously stated, arises in connection with the resolution of the Oedipus and castration complexes. The child gives up libidinal pleasure due to the threat of losing the opposite-sex parent's love and the threat of castration, and this leads to the asexual attitude of the latency stage. However, it also seems likely that the death trauma adds to the child's avoidance of sexuality during the latency period. When children go through the period of death awareness that is often accompanied by a preoccupation with suicide, it is a sobering rite that turns the child away from libidinal thoughts. When we are most in touch with feelings about death, we are least in the mood for sex. This holds true for children perhaps even more than for adults.

Yacoubian and Lourie studied forty children aged three to fourteen who had attempted suicide. They also interviewed controls who had not attempted suicide but who had gone through a period of suicidal ideology. They found that all children went through a period of preoccupation with death, and they noted, "These suicidal preoccupations are as common at six as they are at fourteen" (1973, p. 157). At the same time, there is a often a spurt of religiosity during the latency years, sometimes leading to even more intense religious feelings in adolescence. For the first time, there is a great concern on the part of children about afterlife, and a child will typically wonder about the meaning of life, what happens after death, who goes to heaven, and who goes to hell. These concerns reflect their awareness of their mortality and their attempts to deal with it as best they can.

Erikson (1950) viewed the latency years as a period during which a child had to master the conflict between "industry" and "inferiority". During this stage, children either develop feelings of competence and confidence in their abilities or they experience inferiority, failure, and feelings of incompetence, while at the same time forgetting about sexuality. Just as adults often attempt to master various types of anxiety through busywork, so also the death trauma, coming on the heels of the Oedipus complex, may have the effect of motivating children to become more industrious during the elementary school years so as to avoid thinking about death. And if the death trauma is too severe due to an inappropriate response by parents, teachers, and others, it may contribute to feelings of inferiority.

### Death Attitudes in Personality

Fixation leads to repression, and repression leads to a permanent defensive attitude toward death. Fenichel (1945) was one of the first to succinctly point out that in certain cases when people suffer from what we nowadays call anxiety disorders, the fear of death is an omnipresent part of their personality. He cites the examples of the person who becomes obsessed with death because of an unconscious wish to join a dead spouse, parent, or other loved one. Such people are usually diagnosed as suffering from *depression.* Then there is the person who harbors a *fear* of death because of an unconscious fear of castration or fear of loss (of love)—an indication perhaps of how fear of death informs personality. There is the person who *denies* death as a way of compensation for an unconscious death wish against another. And finally, there is the person for whom the *dread* of death represents an unconscious fear of excitement (sexuality). Often these latter conflicts are found in cases of histrionic personality disorder or in phobic disorders, and they can be overwhelming and all consuming. Fenichel further notes that in cases of obsessive-compulsive disorder, the *fear* of death takes the form of a fear of infection, which covers a deeper fear of castration, impregnation (for females), or reingulfment. Freud (1909b), in his case about the Rat Man, interprets the patient's obsessive fear that some fatal accident will happen to his ladylove as an unconscious wish for her death. However, in other cases of obsessive compulsion, *bargaining* about death may lie beneath the compulsive rituals such as never stepping on a crack (and never breaking Mother's back).

Binswanger (1944) describes a young woman who suffers from anorexia nervosa and has a preoccupation with thinness. Toward the end, the theme of suicide becomes prominent and she begins to exult in thoughts of death. "I'd like to die just as the birdling does,/That splits his throat in highest jubilation,/And wildly be consumed in my own fire" (p. 246). Binswinger interprets this in existential terms: "The existential exultation itself, the festive existential joy, the 'existential fire' are placed in the service of death" (p. 285). Putting aside Binswinger's existential psychoanalytic terminology, which serves to glorify rather than clarify West's condition, it appears that she suffered from both hysteria and masochism and that both have a defensive function with regard to the dealing with death: for her, death was a triumph over her controlling father. There was both *apathy* and *acceptance* in her attitude toward death.

## Conclusion

In explaining my theory of the death trauma, I have borrowed from different schools of psychoanalysis, psychology, and sociology. As such, my terminology may at times seem mixed and old-fashioned. This terminology reflects my view that these schools, both past and present, are still relevant.

As I have noted previously, there is no greater shock than that of first discovering one's own mortality. Freud wrote about the shock of a child's first discovery of the difference in sexual anatomy. This shock pales in comparison with the larger shock of death. The discovery of our own mortality literally changes everything. Whereas before this shock, children can think only of an infinitely extended here and now, afterwards they can only think about the end of here and now. Whereas before they harbored a magical belief in their own indestructibility, afterwards they must become preoccupied with how vulnerable they are, how tenuous life is, how easily they can become ill, and how easily they can be stabbed, choked, poisoned, shot, beaten, or injured. This great shock that only humans (and perhaps dolphins and other higher animals) must go through, cannot help but have a profound effect on our personality formation. Indeed, it may be the most profound effect of all, underpinning all that we think, feel and do. It also affects superego develop and translates into a variety of traits that manifest themselves in adulthood.

*References:*

Abrams, M. H., Ed. (1962). *The Norton Anthology of English Literature*. New York: W. W. Norton.

Adler, A. (1932). *The Myth of the Birth of the Hero*. New York: Alfred A. Knopf.

Binswanger, L. (1944). "The case of Ellen West." In *Existence, a New Dimension in Psychiatry and Psychology*, R. May, E. Angel, and H. F. Ellenberger, Eds. (pp. 278-364). New York: Basic Books.

Bowlby, J. (1961). "Processes of mourning." *International Journal of Psychoanalysis*, 42:317-340.

-- (1969). *Attachment*. New York: Basic Books.

Erikson, E. (1950). *Childhood and Society*. New York: W. W. Norton.

Fenichel, O. (1945). *The Psychoanalytic Theory of Neurosis*. New York: W. W. Norton.

Freud, S. (1909a). "Analysis of a phobia in a five-year-old boy." *Standard Edition*, 10:3-152.

-- (1909b). "Notes upon a case of obsessional neurosis." *Standard Edition*, 10:153-318

-- (1915). "Thoughts for the times on war and death." *Standard Edition*, 14:275-302.

-- (1917). "Introductory lectures on psycho-analysis, part III" *Standard Edition*, 16:243-484.

-- (1920). "Beyond the pleasure principle." *Standard Edition*, 17:3-122.

-- (1930). "Civilization and its discontents." *Standard Edition*, 21:59-148.

-- (1933). "New introductory lectures on psycho-analysis." Standard Edition, 22:3-184.

Goodwin, F. K., and Jamison, K. R. (1990). *Manic-Depressive Illness*. New York: Oxford University Press.

Klein, M. (1932). *The Psychoanalysis of Children*. New York: Delacorte Press.

Klein, M. and Reviere, J. (1964). *Love, Hate and Reparation*. New York: W. W. Norton.

Kubler-Ross, E. (1969). *On Death and Dying.* New York: Collier Books

Nunberg, H. and Federn, E. (1967). Minutes of the Vienna Psychoanalytic Society, Vol. 2. New York: International Universities Press.

Piaget, J. (1952). *The Origins of Intelligence in Children.* New York: International Universities Press.

Shengold, L. (1988). *Halo in the Sky: Observations on Anality and Defense.* New Haven: Yale University Press.

Spitz, R. (1965). *The First Year of Life.* New York: International University Press.

Thompson, C. (1950). *Psychoanalysis: Evolution and Development.* New York: Grove Press.

Tremlett, G. (1992). *Dylan Thomas: In the Mercy of His Means.* New York: St. Martin's Press.

Wainrib, S. (1996). Anxiety of annihilation, fascinations of self-destruction. Revue Francaise de Psychanalyse, 60:65-76.

Wolfstein, M. (1980). "How is mourning possible?" In *New Directions in Childhood Psychopathology: Vol. 1: Developmental Considerations,* Edited by Harrison and McDermott, Jr. (358-382). New York: International Universities Press.

Yacoubian, J. H. and Lourie, R. S. (1973). "Suicide and attempted suicide and children and adolescents." In *Behavior Pathology of Childhood and Adolescence,* Edited by Sidney L. Copel (149-165). New York: Basic Books.

# 3

# A Viable Theory of Female Development

---

Ever since Sigmund Freud explained his theory of female development, those theories have come under attack. They were criticized from the moment he wrote them, but in the years since his death they have been almost completely discarded; yet the theories offered to replace Freud's theory are flawed. This paper reexamines his theories and the views of his critics, primarily feminists, and attempts to point the way to a viable theory of female development.

---

When I wrote this paper two decades ago, psychoanalysts were still debating Freud's theories of female development. Nowadays, that debate is no more. After years of emotionally charged complaints about his theories, thousands of articles assailing them, and wide-spread repudiation of the man and his theories, the debate is over. The feminists have won, and any man who invokes Freud's name or defends his theories about women is dismissed with a shake of the head and a roll of the eyes, indicating that such a person must be incredibly backwards to still be carrying on about Freud.

Several years earlier, I wrote a book called *Sexual Animosity between Men and Women* (1989). It was described by one reviewer as "a book for misogynists" (Sauzier, 1990). When I made a presentation of the book at the Washington Square Institute in New York, I received a similarly hostile reception. A woman psychoanalyst read an angry response to my presentation that chided me for drumming up theories, including Margaret Mahler's, that were no longer acceptable. At that time, the feminists had not completely won; there was still scattered resistance to their take-over of psychoanalytic theory; I was allowed to present, but only in order for a "party member" to immediately repudiate me. What was the thesis of the book and presentation that was so repellent? For the most part, I was reiterating Freud's views on female psychology—on male and female castration complexes and how they contribute to the animosity between men and women. Yet, the repudiation of my thesis was overwhelming. Indeed, one might safely argue that, of all the repudiations of Freud's theories over the years, those leveled at his theories about women have been the most intense and complete. Therefore, anybody who still sees Freud's theories on women as mostly valid, as I do, will likewise be repudiated.

It is clear that many women do not accept Freud's theories about women, but it is not clear how they would replace them. A recent paper by Young-Breuhl (1994) entitled, "What Theories Women Want," sheds light on this phenomenon. Young-Breuhl observes that there has been a shift in theories about women since Freud—from Oedipally focused drive theory to pre-Oedipally focused relational theory. Seen in a larger social context, she sees a change from the "rejecting mother" causal theory of neurosis of Freudian psychoanalysis to the "abusive masculinity theory" of the new feminist psychoanalysis. This new system, Young-Breuhl contends, serves to valorize rather than analyze female pathology, making women's psychic illnesses into heroic endeavors at rejecting masculine bias and oppression.

Her point is well taken. A sizable majority of female psychoanalysts has insisted that women psychoanalysts—and not Freud or his followers—should decide which theories about women are acceptable and which are not. However, they have often repudiated Freud's theories not by offering new research or by debating the issues he raised in calm, reasoned tones, but by *ad hominem* criticisms.

Meanwhile, they have suggested substitute theories of female development that do not adequately explain female psychopathology or sexual development.

Psychoanalytic theorizing from the outset has been a complicated business. As long as Freud was alive, he remained the final judge of whether or not new theories were valid. Those who strayed too far from his own view, such as Adler and Jung, were ostracized. Since his death, new schools of psychoanalysis have emerged, and differences in the theoretical framework of these schools have widened. Feminist psychoanalysis is one that has emerged most strongly, if not as a separate school, at least as a distinct perspective, particularly with regard to female psychology. How do we determine in these post-Freudian days whether the theories of feminist psychoanalysts or other schools are valid?

Determining the validity of theories in psychoanalysis will continue to be complicated. However, as with any scholarly or scientific endeavor, there are certain rules that should be followed: (1) theories should be based on clinical research, consisting of either direct observations of parents and children (Mahler, 1968; Roiphe and Galenson, 1981) or reconstructive analyses of child and adult patients that can be replicated by other psychoanalysts; (2) investigations should be an open-minded search for the truth, not biased towards a particular finding; (3) investigators should not be prohibited from a particular finding because it may be deemed religiously, ethically or politically incorrect; (4) theories should be validated through objective replication of research and calm debate.

These are not my rules, but the rules passed on from generation to generation since the scientific era began. Abandoning them now would mean, I think, the end of psychoanalysis as a cohesive body of social science and the beginning of psychoanalysis as a belief system, such as communism. Using these criteria, it is possible to look at both Freud's theories and those of feminist psychoanalysts in an effort to determine which aspects of each are convincing, and to move beyond them in formulating a viable theory of female sexual development.

### Feminist Psychoanalytic Theories

Although I can understand Young-Bruehl's view of a shift from Oedipally focused drive theory to pre-Oedipally focused relational theory, I disagree with her in characterizing classical Freudian theory as a "rejecting mother" causal theory of neurosis. Freud looked at many factors—mother, father, siblings, biology and society. The Oedipal triangle, the cornerstone of the Freudian theory of neurosis, involves many variables, among which are: the child's innate wish to get rid of the parent of the opposite sex and marry the parent of the same sex; the child's relationship with both mother and father, and the relationship of siblings. I do agree that more recent feminist psychoanalytic theories of female development have shifted to an "abusive masculinity theory" of female neurosis—attributing neurosis to male oppression. However, I would characterize the shift that has occurred since Freud a bit differently: I see it as a shift from a psychodynamic causal theory (women's mental disorders are caused by complexes and fixations engendered during early childhood) to a sociodynamic causal theory (women's mental disorders are either trumped up by male bias or caused by male social oppression).

One of Freud's earliest supporters, Adler (1929), became one of the first to cast aspersions on his theories of women. He denounced Freud's libido theory as well as the concept of penis envy and replaced it with his theory of "the masculine protest". Even though Adler himself coined the term "Organ inferiority," describing individuals who due to some physical defect develop feelings of inferiority about themselves, he did not apply this term to women and their feelings about their genitals. Women's problems were not due to a complex about their sexual organs, he decided, but were the result of their inferior status in society. Adler seems to have been influenced by the philosopher Nietzsche, using phrases such as "will to power" as the underpinning of his new theory of women's development. Horney (1926) joined Adler in attacking penis envy, contending that the term was a "male concept." She was the first woman to resort to polemical arguments, the first to use the term "male bias," in her writings. Although she did not go as far as Adler in substituting a different theory, such as the "masculine protest," she also cited social conditions as partly responsible for female psychopathology. By using polemical arguments, Horny set an example for all subsequent writers to follow. From that time on, psychoanalytic writing about women's theories began to take on an imperious and uncivil tone.

It is not penis envy, many feminist psychoanalysts have since contended, but men's privileged position in society, which women resent. "I believe," Thompson states, "that the manifest hostility between men and women is not different in kind from any other struggle between combatants, one of whom has a definite advantage in prestige and position" (1943, p. 53). Like Horney and Adler, she dismisses the concept of penis envy, asserting that it is a "male conceit" stemming from phallic narcissism. She concludes: "Characteristics and interiority feelings which Freud considered to be specifically female and biologically determined can be explained as developments arising in and growing out of Western woman's historic situation of underprivilege, restriction of development, insecure attitude towards the sexual nature, and social and economic dependency. The basic nature of women is still unknown" (1942, p. 84). This argument attacks Freud's maleness and does not adequately address his theoretical discussion of the issue. She contends that the male role in society involves more privilege and status, and that women's envy of men is caused entirely by that fact, but she offers no alternate theory of development and suggests that female psychology remains unknown. It is as though she is saying only women can know women, and maybe even they do not know. And while alluding to phallic narcissism, she does not consider the possibility of "vaginal narcissism." I believe this comes about from penis envy, and represents a narcissistic injury to women resulting in repression of the original injury and the formation of a shell of female pride; so that in adult life women no longer remember the primary envy but are aware only of the secondary envy of the male role.

Miller (1973) was in the vanguard of women who objected to the classical psychoanalytic "cultural stereotyping" of women, which held that a normal women should embrace the role of wife, mother and nurturer of children and that any deviation from this role was a sign of feminine psychopathology. "The belief that women could or should accept and adjust to the stereotyped role has been a cause, not a cure, of their problems" (p. 381). She sees this attempt to fit women into a stereotypical mold as a kind of social oppression in and of itself. While Freud regards a woman's fulfillment of this traditional role as the road to mature development, Miller regards it as a road to neurosis. Hence, her theory of development again suggests that women's neurosis stems from social oppression—that is, being forced into a stereotypical role. Mature development revolves around women shrugging off this social oppression and rejecting the traditional female role.

Although penis envy has been the most controversial aspect of Freud's theory of female sexual development, other concepts such as female masochism and female superego development—as contrasted with male superego development—have also been attacked and dismissed. In an interview, Chasseguet-Smirgel (1985) takes issue with both these concepts. Differing with those who label Freud as Victorian, she suggests instead that his writings on female psychology were influenced by his cancer. In particular, she alludes to Freud's assertion that penis envy leads women to have a less developed sense of justice and fair play: "I cannot escape the notion (though I hesitate to give it expression) that for women the level of what is ethically normal is different from what it is in men" (1925, p. 257).

Citing this passage as well as his theories of the life and death instincts, Chasseguet-Smirgel observes, "I believe that he introduced this particular theory of the instincts because of his cancer and that his theory about female sexuality is connected to his cancer and his concern about his own death." Asked to elaborate on this idea, she explains that Freud saw female sexuality as something mysterious, a "dark continent" to be feared. "This could be seen as a disguise, a reaction-formation against his fear of femaleness as something that is linked with death, for all of us" (pp. 534-535). Again, although Chasseguet-Smirgel's interpretation of Freud may or may not be correct, this represents a continuation of ad hominem refutations of Freud and does not engage Freud's assertions or offer a substitute theory of superego formation.

Klein does provide an alternate theory of superego development.

She places the beginning of the masculinity complex, penis envy and superego development in the oral-sadistic stage. Her theories, unlike those of others, is based on her observations of children during play theory. She notes: "Not only do the envy and hatred she feels toward her mother color and intensify her sadistic phantasies against the penis, but her relations to the mother's breast affect her subsequent attitude towards men in other ways as well" (1932, p. 207). Klein's theory retains the castration complex but maintains that an oral-sadistic envy and hatred of the breast precedes the envy of the penis, and that both factors affect the girl's superego formation. I agree with Klein that superego development starts earlier; in my own research I have found that superego development begins during the anal stage, when children first hear the words "good" and "bad" applied to their behavior. Klein's breast-envy theory does not seem valid to me. When an infant gets its first teeth, it bites the breast, not out of envy, but to try out the new teeth.

Sulloway (1979), Masson (1984) and Kroll (1986) are among the many who criticized Freud's abandonment of the seduction theory and saw it as proof of Freud's male bias. Masson concludes that Freud dropped the seduction theory in order to cover up the "crimes of the fathers," as well as to gain acceptance in the patriarchal scientific community of Victorian Europe. In other words, Freud's abandonment of the seduction theory was an attempt to make mothers and not fathers culpable, and to deny the "abusive masculinity" etiological factors in female sexual development. This argument is not only ad hominem, but is also a distortion of what Freud said. In fact, although Freud abandoned the notion that all cases of hysteria were due to childhood sexual abuse, he never doubted that sexual abuse exists. He fully believed the memories of incest by Katherine, Rosalia H., Elisabeth von R., and the Wolf Man, maintaining that the abuse was crucial to their development. "You must not suppose…that sexual abuse of a child by its nearest male relatives belongs entirely to the realm of phantasy" (1916, p. 460).

To restore the seduction theory, as these writers suggest, while dismissing Freud's other theories about female development, would again be a way of attributing female psychological disorders to male oppression—in the form of sexual molestation. But Freud discarded this theory for a good reason; he found that most cases of hysteria were not precipitated by father-daughter incest. In my own experience, I have found that hysteria is often engendered by a hostile or competitive response by a maternal caretaker during the girl's period of sexual discovery. One patient was severely chastised by her stepmother when she was caught masturbating at the age of six, which included a spanking in front of the whole family. She grew up to be rebelliously sexual as a young adult, as though she were constantly saying, "You see, my sexuality is just fine." At times hysterical patients recall vague memories of incest but are, in actually, bringing up fantasies they once had at an early age and then repressed because they were of a forbidden nature. Freud was always willing to change theories when new ideas or information came to light. Theory building, as Freud noted, must be done cautiously, taking into consideration the complexity of human psychodynamics.

Gilligan is another who addresses Freud's theories and finds them flawed by a masculine bias. Unlike her predecessors, she offers a new theory to replace them. She takes to task for its bias not only Freudian psychoanalysis but virtually all theories about women in all fields of social science. In the place of Freud's theories, she espouses a developmental line that "delineates the path not only to a less violent life but also to a maturity realized through interdependence and taking care" (1982, p.9). She argues that "Freud's negative and derivative description of female psychology," with its emphasis on the rejecting, close-binding mother, should be replaced with a "positive and direct" account of female development that stresses "the positive aspects of the attachment to mother" (ibid). If looked at through men's eyes, she posits, "women's failure to separate then becomes by definition a failure to develop," but when looked at through women's eyes, it can be seen instead as a strength, a capacity for attachment which leads "to loving relationships, empathy and altruism," while male tendencies toward separation "lead to disruption and violence" (ibid).

Gilligan does not flesh out her "attachment theory" of women's development, but seems in agreement with Miller and others that abnormal development is somehow connected with women attempting to live up to male standards. At the same time, she dismisses Freud's theories by branding them as "negative views of women" or "products of male bias." Her contrasting of a male developmental line in which separation fosters "disruption and violence" with a female developmental line in which attachment leads to "loving relationships, empathy and altruism" is first of all a misinterpretation of Freud. Freud's (1925; 1931)—and later Mahler's (1968)—emphasis on separation and individuation was based on Freud's analyses of many patients and on Mahler's observation of many mothers and infants. To suggest that attachment to mother leads solely to loving relationships while separation leads to disruption and violence shows a lack of understanding of their research and of the complex process of separation and individuation. Moreover, Gilligan's theory seems to be exactly what she accuses Freud's theory of being: it is a "negative and derivative description" of male development and a rather idealistic depiction of female development. Finally, although she points to a new account of female development that stresses the positive and direct aspects of the attachment to mother, she does not provide us with details that would enable us to understand abnormal development. The implication is that abnormal development occurs if women separate from their mothers, but she does not back this implication up with any hard data.

Clower is one of several feminist psychoanalysts to cite research in other fields to disprove Freud. She points to research in endocrinology by Gadpaile (1972), which shows that in the beginning of fetal life both sexes are under the influence of female sex hormones and both have female sex characteristics. This evidence, she suggests, invalidates Freud's contention that females at first have a masculine orientation. "The clitoris is not, as Freud thought, an inferior substitute for the penis" (1979, p. 307), she concludes, since both men and women have clitorises before men have penises.

She is referring to Freud's assertion that "The sexual life of the woman is regularly split up into two phases, the first of which is of a masculine character, while only the second is specifically feminine" (1931, p. 230). He theorized that until the phallic stage little girl think of their clitorises as little penises, and fantasize that they are little boys trapped in a girl's body. However, Clower, like others, misinterprets Freud's language. He does not believe that the clitoris is an inferior substitute for the penis or that little girls are inferior to little boys. When he writes that upon discovering that differences in the sexual anatomy of males and females the girl "acknowledges the fact of her castration, the consequent superiority of the male and her own inferiority (1931, p. 238), he is using a figurative style to convey the internalization that occurs in the girl. In her mind she views her clitoris as inferior and herself as inferior. Freud did not actually believe that the anatomy of either sex was inferior, only that the differences led to a differing interpretation and developmental line.

Clower's attempt to connect the events of fetal life with those of a toddler's sexual development does not make sense. The fact that both sexes are influenced by female sex hormones and bear female sexual characteristics in fetal life does not nullify the observation that little girls, during a certain stage of development—the stage of auto-eroticism— think of themselves as little boys. Those are two separate processes, one biological, the other psychological. But, even if you see them as parallel, the fact that in fetal life girls are always girls does not mean that in infantile life they might not go through a stage in which they want to be boys and, in fact, act as if they are boys. Humans often imitate those whom they envy and admire, so it stands to reason that if they envy boys having a penis they would want to be like them.

Similarly, Clower points to research by Masters and Johnson (1966), which could find no distinction between a vaginal and clitoral orgasm, using it to refute Freud's assertion that the mature female denounces the clitoris in favor of the vagina and accepts the traditional role of heterosexual intercourse and motherhood. "Neither as a woman nor as a scientist have I ever been able to believe that femininity is derived from castrated maleness," she states (p. 230). Again, Clower misinterprets Freud's language, taking it literally rather than the figurative way it was meant. And her argument misses the point. The fact that Masters and Johnson could not find a difference between the vaginal and clitoral orgasm does not really detract from Freud's theory.

The main point of Freud's theory was not about whether a vaginal or clitoral orgasm was more important or prevalent among women, but about how, for both males and females, mature sexual development involves traversing the stages of autoeroticism, resolving gender narcissism and developing fulfilling and genuine object relations with persons of the opposite sex.

Clower refers to research by Stoller (1968), Money (1965), and Money and Ehrhardt (1971) to support claims that gender identity is shaped by parental attitudes and expectations. Therefore she argues against Freud's claim that anatomy is destiny, contending that there is no biologically determined masculine or feminine identity role. This argument has been taken up by other feminists writers (see Miller, 1973; Mitchell, 1974). While it may be true that gender identity can be, some extent, shaped by parents, this does not preclude biologically determined sexual traits. Innate mating and nurturing rituals have long been noted in lower animals (Montagu, 1976), so would it not follow that some aspects of human sexuality are innate as well? Moreover, when Freud said that "anatomy is destiny," he did not mean that anatomy and only anatomy is destiny, but that anatomy helps to shape destiny in concert with environmental factors—as when a brother is favored by a parent over a sister (Freud, 1925). For sure, Freud somewhat neglected object relations for drive theory, but he did manage to describe them to some extent. (Incidentally, I have noticed that feminist writers will argue for genetics when genetics proves their argument, but will cite environmental factors, as Clower does above, when that is convenient. For example, Gilligan uses genetics when she implies that men are born with a masculine bias.

Although Clower sets herself apart from feminists who distort Freud, she herself misinterprets him again and again. She also spends several pages recounting a feminist history of male oppression of women, which implies that she too, like the feminists she sets herself apart from, considers women's abnormal development has more to do with "abusive masculinity" than with classical women's theory. Taken together, her criticisms of Freud suggest that she is in agreement with those who believe that the cultural stereotyping of women lies at the root of many of their problems.

More recently, Prozan has written a book that takes the feminist psychoanalytic theories to another step. *Feminist Psychoanalysis: Theory and Practice* (1993), recapitulates all the cited arguments against Freud and supplants them with theories of women's development based on their being victims of male stereotyping, bias and oppression. In her view, nearly all the psychological and organic ailments of women are the result of masculine social oppression (i.e., the sociodynamic point of view). "Feminists believe that women have been prevented from developing their full potential by social mores and not by their anatomy, because society has confined them to roles of wife and mother, subordinate to and financially dependent on their husbands" (1993, p. xvi). Like Thompson and Gilligan, she asserts that only females can understand female psychology and therefore only they should write about it. "Just as psychoanalysis has been subject to revision, so too feminist theory is being debated *among feminists*" (p. 336). She also implies that only female psychoanalysts understand females and should therefore treat female patients (whereas either female or male psychoanalysts may treat males).

Obviously, in writing this paper demonstrates that I disagree with this last point. To say that only females can understand females and that only females should treat females implies, first of all, that males are biased but females are not. I would argue that both have their particular biases, including biases resulting from gender narcissism. Nearly all psychotherapists have had patients who have told them, "You can't understand me because you're too conventional and I'm an artist," or "You're Christian and I'm Jewish," or "You're white and I'm black." In actuality, I would contend that due to the gender narcissism that inhibits insight into one's own sex, males may be more objective about females, and females may be more objective about males.

In nearly all of the feminist papers I have detected an implied rejection of the concept of the unconscious mind, another cornerstone of psychoanalytic thought. For example, Clower states, "Neither as a woman nor as a scientist have I ever been able to believe that femininity is derived from castrated maleness." So if she has not experienced it and doesn't believe it (the feeling of castrated maleness), then it doesn't exist. If she doesn't remember ever having had the feeling, then the concept must certainly be invalid. Yet, if she calls herself a psychoanalyst, then I would think she should always consider how the unconscious works.

## Psychodynamic Theory and Sociodynamic Theory

At the core of the debate between Freudian and feminist psychoanalysts is whether or not women's abnormal development derives from psychological factors (the castration complex, separation) or from societal forces (cultural stereotyping, male oppression). This debate parallels a broader public dispute stirred up by the feminist movement that began in the Victorian era and has grown to the point where it has now wrought wholesale changes in standards of normality.

The traditional roles of women have not been accorded the same prestige as the traditional roles of men. All societies from the beginning of recorded history have been patriarchal in nature, beginning with the male-dominated tribes of the cave men, up to the present, in which men still hold most leadership roles in government. Whether this constitutes oppression of women, or is a natural evolution of civilization from agrarian to industrial to technological modes in which the roles of males and females have changed according to the situation, is a matter of continued debate. Likewise, it is questionable as to whether such societal factors are entirely, or mostly responsible for women's problems, as many feminist psychoanalysts would maintain.

This debate reminds me of the nature-nurture controversy that has existed in the behavioral sciences for some times. The answer to this question seems obvious when you study the available information: both genetics and the environment contribute to the formation of personality and behavior—it is not one or the other. Likewise, a combination of genetic, psychological and social factors undoubtedly contribute to the development of both male and female sexuality.

This is not a new idea. Many psychoanalysts, including Freud, have devised theories of female psychology that attempted to consider genetic and social; factors.  Among them are Mahler (1968), Kestenberg (1968), Nagera (1975), Buxbaum (1979), Socarides (1979), Kernberg (1980), Roiphe and Gallenson (1981), and McDougall and Siegel (1988).  However, these voices have been largely disregarded when it comes to debate about women's psychology.  Indeed, Socarides acknowledged recently that he can no longer get his papers published in most journals that had formerly welcomed them (Socarides, 1995), and his developmental theories, which combine genetics with environmental factors, no longer count.

Politics has devalued Freud while research has validated his theories.  Two major studies validated the theory of the castration complex.  In observing 38 children and 22  mothers over a period of four years, Mahler and colleagues (1975) confirmed the existence of penis envy in girls (as well as castration fear in boys).  During the rapprochement  subphase (beginning at about 15 or 16 months of age), girl discover the difference in anatomy between themselves and boys.  Upon this discovery, according to Mahler, girls tend to masturbate desperately and aggressively.  The discovery "coincides with the emergence of the affect of envy" (p. 105).  Mahler describes how various girls acted out their feelings of envy and anger, noting that they "tended to turn back to mother, to blame her, to demand from her, to be disappointed in her, and still to be ambivalently tied to her.  They demanded from mother that she settle a debt, so to say" (p. 106).

Roiphe and Galenson (1981) also confirmed the existence of penis envy in their intensive study of about 70 infants.  Like Mahler, they point to a definite genital awareness at the beginning of a of the second year and a sense of gender identity by the end of the second year and assert that girls universally react strongly to the discovery of the difference in sexual anatomy, noting that it brings about the "recrudescence of fears of object loss and self-disintegration" (p. 272).  They supply numerous case histories of the reactions of little girls to their sexual discovery.  One of them, Suzy, first showed an  interest in her genital area at about 15 months—at the time when she first saw a boy's penis.  With her eyes "riveted on his penis," she pointed at it and then touched her own genital area.  For the next few months she  often tried to lift the skirts of the women in the nursery (looking for penises). She did the same thing at home with her mother, who became upset at her behavior. The authors speculated that she might also have tried to touch her father's penis during showers with both parents. When she was 20 months old, after touching a little boy's penis upon following him into the bathroom, she went through a period of intense masturbation and lifting of her skirt and the skirts of women around her. At the same time there was a complete deterioration of her toilet control, which persisted over the next few months. "Michael has a pee-pee. I have no pee-pee. Why?" she asked her mother. This was accompanied by a general behavioral regression and negativism. When she was brought to the nursery, she refused to leave her stroller. "Sitting there for a considerable time looking sullen and distressed, she screamed if any of the children tried to touch her (pp. 144-145). They conclude that "penis envy and the feminine castration complex exert crucial influences upon feminine development" (p. 285).

My own research, reconstructing the memories of adult patients, has also confirmed the existence of the castration and Oedipus complexes and a difference in female and male superego development. However, I am aware that numerous psychoanalysts claim they have never encountered evidence in their own practices of the castration complex. Since a number of psychoanalysts confirm it and a number do not, how can we resolve the issue? It is my contention that enough research has been done to confirm the theory. Psychoanalysis is not a hard science in which research can be replicated precisely. We must rely on whether the available arguments or case histories are convincing, whether the investigator demonstrates an open-minded search for the truth (rather than a bias), and whether others who show the same scientific objectivity have replicated it. Moulton, like many feminist psychoanalysts, suggests that the concept of penis envy is destructive to women. However, she admits that negative attitudes towards men, such as hostility, envy and competitiveness must be dealt with, "attributing them to biological inadequacy, which must be accepted as inevitable, perpetuates a vicious circle by enhancing women's rage at men, whose superiority is thus confirmed" (1970, p. 100). Like others, Moulton misinterprets Freud. I repeat, Freud did not believe that women's sexual organs are biologically inferior; only that little girls at first believe them to be inferior, just as some men feel inferior because they have small penises. Women are not doomed to inferiority by their anatomy; they are doomed only if they develop fixations at that stage due to inappropriate parental responses and are resistant to psychoanalysis or other reparative experiences. Penis envy is a psychological, not a biological phenomenon. A man's inferior feelings about having a small penis (the male castration complex) and a woman feeling of inferiority about not having one, can be worked through in psychoanalysis.

Referring to a comment Freud made at the end of a lecture on femininity, "If you wish to know more about femininity enquire from your own experiences of life" (1933, p. 135), Moulton concludes that Freud was suggesting that women themselves would have to develop a suitable theory of women's development. My own sense of that lecture was that Freud was feeling pressured by the questions of feminists, not only at the end of that lecture but toward the end of his life; he made such statements in order to appease the questioners. In essence, Freud held the line with regard to his theory of women. And I think it is essential that we also continue to hold that line. If we, as psychoanalysts, cannot stand up against pressures that would silence us and take control of certain of our theories, we no longer have a social science. We have a belief system.

## A Viable Theory of Female Psychology

A viable theory of female psychology might utilize ideas from the cultural realm as well as the psychological realm, without dismissing one or the other. Social factors play a role in the formation of sexual attitude, orientation and identity. The values and standards of a particular society influence the child-rearing practices of that society. If masculinity is given a higher value than femininity, as it is in many societies, then it will have an effect on feminine self-esteem and sexuality. If the standards of a society are excessively frustrating for one gender or another, due to restrictive designated roles, then those standards will likewise have a destructive effect. More research needs to be done in order to establish how and when social factors influence development of both males and females.

Yet, these factors in and of themselves are not enough to explain female psychology. Classical psychoanalytic theory must not be discarded through polemical arguments or because a consensus has found it to be "biased" or "Victorian" or "out of date. " Classical concepts about female development--drive theory, the castration and Oedipus complexes, and the importance of separation and individuation —have not been refuted by reasoned arguments. To say that a woman's envy of men is solely related to societal unfairness is too absolute and dispenses altogether with any notion that females may suffer from disorders related to traumatic situations in their childhoods having nothing to do with society's unfairness.

Development of the castration and Oedipus complexes has been observed with consistency in males and females by many convincing investigators. These consequences of these complexes have also been documented. Elsewhere (Schoenewolf, 1989) I have pointed out how male and female narcissism emerge out of these complexes. Males who have not resolved their castration complex (castration fear) may be driven both by an unconscious guilt that causes them to appease women or attempt to degrade them, and by a pride that causes them to focus on their size of their penis and on sexual conquest. Females who have not resolved their castration complex (penis envy) may be driven by a primitive envy that causes them to either idealize men or to attempt to compete with them and devalue them.

Freud's theory about the differences in male and female superego development has found less replicating research. Researchers differ with him about when moral development occurs, and it seems clear the it begins much earlier than the Oedipal period. However, even if we accept that moral development is different for males and females, we must not suggest that females are less moral than males (or the reverse, as some feminists seem to suggest). Milgram's (1975) experiment, in which an experimenter had subjects administer electric shocks to "actors" who pretended to be follow subjects, showed that both men and women were willing to be cruel, since about 65 per cent of both males and females went up to the highest level (450 volts). In the relations between the sexes, women may tend more towards emotionality and men more towards aggression. The difference in the male and female morality is a matter of style, not degree.

With regard to what constitutes normal sexuality, some modifications may be in order. The term *female masochism*, seems unfortunate and misleading. To denote mature development as masochistic is inappropriate. Should we then call mature male development sadistic? Rather, we might say that the mature male give up the auto-eroticism of the Oedipal stage and becomes active in seeking intercourse with a female; and the mature female's journey toward giving up auto-eroticism and becoming receptive to vaginal intercourse and motherhood should be retained—recent views about homosexual rights notwithstanding. This does not mean that all women must be mothers; only that it is normal for them to want to be. This view of women's development is in harmony with animal behavior in general, where it is the role of the female to give birth to and nurture children. However, neither Freud nor any other classical psychoanalyst ever meant to suggest that women might not do other things in life—as was demonstrated by the number of women Freud encouraged to be psychoanalysts.

Masters and Johnson (1966) perhaps led the way to establishing a more viable theory when they concluded that there were not one but three variations of the female sexual response, each considered a normal variation. Similarly, there could be more than one normal developmental line for females. The classical psychoanalytic developmental line, ending in marriage and motherhood, would be one line, whereas another line might be that of women who eschew motherhood and opt instead to have a career. A third option could and would be women who choose to have both a family and a career. Humans are much more complicated than animals, so that the range of what might be considered normal development should be wider.

However, whatever the theories end up being, they should be verified on the basis of their viability, not because of their perceived religious, ethical or political correctness.

**A Final Comment**

I showed this paper to a woman acquaintance and her comment was, "It's feels irrelevant to me. Dated. People aren't writing about that anymore." However, another woman acquaintance liked the paper and recommended it should be published. "I think there are still questions that haven't been answered," she said.

Along with the Feminist Movement of the twentieth century have come sweeping changes in sexual roles, values and morality. These changes have also influenced psychoanalytic theory. Indeed, the influence is now so great that in many quarters Freudian theories of female psychology are seen not only as passé, but also as an offence to women. They are no longer tolerated, and people shake their heads and smile at anybody who still mentions them. In a sense, we have come full circle since the early days when Freud ostracized those who strayed from his theories. Freud was wrong and feminists are wrong.

Censorship has no place in any scientific or scholarly pursuit. Censorship negates our attempt to develop a theory of female psychology or any other theory. Rather than censorship, a calm, open-minded discussion of the issues is most likely to produce a theory that is finally acceptable. As far as I am concerned the contest is not over. It is ongoing. Theories that link psychopathology solely to psychodynamic factors and neglect completely the sociodynamic or genetic factors are not viable. And theories that consider only the sociodynamic or genetic factors and disregard the psychodynamic factors are likewise not valid. Only by considering all factors can we develop a theory that works.

*References:*

Adler, A. (1929). Problems in Neurosis: a Book of Case Histories. P. Mairet (ed.). New York, Harper & Row, 1964.

Buxbaum, E. (1979). Modern woman and motherhood. In T. B.

Karasu and C. W. Socarides (eds.) *On Sexuality.* New York, International Universities Press.

Chasseguet-Smirgel, J. (1985). Feminine sexuality: an interview With Janine Chasseguet-Smirgel by Honey and Broughton. *Psychoanalytic Review*, 4, 527-548.

Clower, V. (1979). Feminism and the new psychology of women. In T. B. Karasu and C. W. Socarides (eds.). *On Sexuality.* New York, International Universities Press.

Freud, S. (1916). Introductory lectures on psychoanalysis. *Standard Edition*, 15, 3-488.

-- (1925). Some psychical consequences of the anatomical distinction between the sexes. *Standard Edition*, 19, 243-259.

-- (1931). Female sexuality. *Standard Edition*, 21, 223-246.

-- (1933). New introductory lectures on psychoanalysis. *Standard Edition*, 22, 3-180.

Gadpaile, W. J. (1972). Research into the physiology of maleness and femaleness. *Archives of General Psychiatry*, 26, 193-207.

Gilligan, C. (1982). *In a Different Voice: Psychological Theory And Women's Development.* Cambridge: Harvard Press.

Horney, K. (1926). The Flight from Womanhood: the Masculinity Complex in Women as Viewed by Men and Women. *International Journal of Psychoanalysis*, 7, 324-339.

Kernberg, O. (1980). *Internal World and External Reality.* Northvale, NJ, Jason Aronson.

Kestenberg, J. S. (1968). Outside and Inside, Male and Female. *Journal of the American Psychoanalytic Association,* 16, 456-520.

Klein, M. (1932). *The Psychoanalysis of Children.* New York, Delacorte, 1975.

Kroll, M. (1986). *Freud and his Father.* Trans. A. UJ. Pomerans. New York, Norton.

Mahler, M. S. (1968). On Human Symbiosis and the Vicissitudes of Individuation. New York, International Universities Press.

Mahler, M. S., Pine, F. and Bergman, A. (1975). *The Psychological Birth of the Human Infant: Symbiosis and Individuation.* London, Maresfield.

McDougall, J. (1984). Eve's reflection: on the narcissistic and homosexual components of female sexuality. Paper presented at symposium, The many phases of Eve: beyond psychoanalytic and feminist stereotypes, Los Angeles, Feb. 25.

Masson, J. M. (1984). *The Assault on Truth: Freud's Suppression of the Seduction Theory.* New York, Farrar, Strauss & Giroux.

Masters, W. H. and Johnson, V. E. (1966). *The Human Sexual Response.* Boston: Little Brown.

Milgram, S. (1975). Obedience to Authority. NY: Harper & Row.

Miller, J. B., ed. (1973). Psychoanalysis and Women. Harmondsworth, England: Pelican.

Mitchell, J. (1974). *Psychoanalysis and Feminism: Freud, Laing and Women.* New York, Vintage Books.

Money, J. ed. (1965). *Sex Research: New Developments*. New York: Holt, Rinehart, Winston.

Money, J. and Ehrhardt, A. A. (1972). *Man and Woman, Boy and Girl*. Baltimore/London, Johns Hopkins Press.

Montagu, A. (1976). *The nature of human aggression*. New York: Oxford University Press.

Moulton, R. (1970). A survey and re-evaluation of the concept of penis envy. *Contemporary Psychoanalysis, 7*, 84-104.

Nagera, H. (1975). *Female Sexuality and the Oedipus Complex*. Northvale, NJ: Jason Aronson.

Prozan, C. K. (1993). *Feminist psychoanalysis: Theory and Practice*. Northvale, NJ, Jason Aronson.

Roiphe, H. and Galenson, E. (1981). *Infantile Origins of Sexual Identity*. New York, International Universities Press.

Sauzier, M. (1990). Review of Sexual Animosity between Men and Women. *Readings, 5*, 30.

Schoenewolf, G. (1989). *Sexual Animosity between Men and Women*. Northvale, NJ, Jason Aronson.

Siegel, E. (1988). *Female Homosexuality, Choice without Volition*. Hillsdale, NJ: Analytic Press.

Socarides, C. W. (1979). *A unitary theory of sexual perversions*. In T. B. Karasu and C. W. Socarides (eds.) On Sexuality. New York, International Universities Press.

Socarides, C. W. (1995). How America went gay. *America,*

November 18, 20-22.

Stoller, R. (1968). *Sex and Gender: the Development of Masculinity and Femininity.* Vol. 1, London, Maresfield.

Sulloway, F. J. (1979). Freud: Biologist of the Mind. New York, Basic Books.

Thompson, C. (1942). Cultural pressures in the psychology of women. In J. B. Miller (ed.) *Psychoanalysis and Women.* New York, Penguin, 1977.

Thompson, C. (1943). Penis envy in women. In J. B. Miller (ed.) *Psychoanalysis and Women.* New York, Penguin, 1977.

Young-Bruehl, E. (1994). What theories women want. *American Imago,* 51, 373-396.

# 5

# Gender Narcissism and Its Manifestations

---

Narcissus was the name of a young man in Greek mythology who fell in love with his own reflection. Thus, falling in love with one's self has become a cornerstone in defining narcissism. I have taken this one step further to try to define and understand the phenomenon of gender narcissism, inferiority about one's gender or one's gender anatomy and compensation for that inferiority by erecting a bubble of gender pride. This pride and the underlying inferiority feelings and rage, leads to various manifestations.

---

The term narcissism was originally taken from the Greek myth about a beautiful young man who fell in love with his own reflection in a pool of water, jumped in after it, and drowned. The term was used to denote the attitude of a person who takes his own body as an object of attraction and desire, and focuses primarily on the practice of masturbation. Since then psychoanalysis has broadened the definition of narcissism to mean an excessive self-love or concern for the self and lack of concern for others.

The first, narrower definition of narcissism might now more aptly be termed gender narcissism. Gender narcissism develops in reaction to feelings of inferiority about one's gender and might be defined as excessive love or concern for one's gender, one's genitals, or one's gender identity, and negative feeling about the opposite sex--generally involving fear, disgust, resentment or competitiveness. It leads to the formation of gender-narcissistic alliances rather than libidinal unions, and it is primarily rooted in the anal-rapprochement phase, during which time an individual's sexual orientation and identity are shaped.

In psychoanalyzing a number of individuals over the years that had gender-narcissistic features, I began to get a first-hand understanding of how gender narcissism is formed and manifested. Recently I decided to conduct a more systematic study. A search of my files found 30 patients who had been in treatment for at least six months and possessed three or more gender-narcissistic features. Their cases were reviewed and contrasted with another group of 20 randomly selected patients. Personality types ranged from hysterics and obsessive-compulsives to borderlines and schizophrenics, and sexual types included heterosexuals, bisexuals, homosexuals, transvestites, transsexuals, pedophiles, and fetishists, as well as women who engaged in strip-teasing and prostitution. The study found that gender narcissism is fairly common, with all personality types showing degrees of it; however, gender-narcissistic features were less prevalent among heterosexuals than they were among other types. When gender narcissism is present to a high degree, it has a disturbing effect on relationships, sexuality, and sexual identity.

## Psychoanalytic Theories and Research

In his writings on narcissism, Freud (1914, 1916) postulated an early stage of primal narcissism during which time an infant is preoccupied with its self and with its own pleasure while being oblivious of the needs of others. Various circumstances could result in fixations at that stage which could persist into adulthood. He noted that narcissism could be seen in various character types, and described how it involved the investment of libido in the ego, or in objects similar to the self (alteregos). Homosexuals fall into the category of those who invest their libido in persons who are like themselves. The hypochondriac withdraws both his interest and his libido from the objects of the external world and displaces them on the organs in his own body. Megalomaniacs, prone to the highest grandiosity, withdraw libido from frustrating objects and return it to their own ego.

Freud theorized that an ego ideal is formed by the ego (becoming part of the superego), its function being to compensate for the repression of primal narcissism. "This ego ideal is the target of the self-love which was enjoyed in childhood by the actual ego" (1914, p. 94). Along with this ego ideal, a sexual ideal is also formed as an auxiliary to the ego ideal. The ego ideal and sexual ideal run parallel to one another.

Although Freud did not use the term gender narcissism, he pointed to the narcissism that was associated with both male and female sexual development. He saw homosexuality as being a prototype of narcissistic development, and he linked this narcissism with the male and female castration complexes. With regard to male homosexuals, he noted that until puberty they were generally strongly fixated to their mothers, and hence identified with her instead of their with their fathers, and looked for love objects in whom they could rediscover and reclaim their masculinity, and toward whom they might relate as their mothers related to them. "The choice is towards a narcissistic object which is readier at hand and easier to put into effect than movement towards the opposite sex" (1923, p. 233). He observed that in taking a love object that is similar to himself, the homosexual can symbolically actualize his narcissistic fixation, and he added that the avoidance of sexual relations with the opposite sex was a way of not only of remaining loyal to their mothers, but also of avoiding the incestuous feelings that might be aroused in the transference.

Studying a case of female homosexuality, Freud (1920) observed that it grew out of the girl's castration complex (penis envy), which in turn led to the formation of a masculinity complex. Like male homosexuality, he linked female homosexuality to narcissism--in particular, to a narcissistic protest regarding femininity. "Psychoanalytic research has recognized the existence and importance of the masculine protest, but it has regarded it, in opposition to Adler, as narcissistic in nature and derived from the castration complex" (p. 92). Elsewhere he writes that the castration complex begins before the age of three and is "more closely allied to primal narcissism than to object-love" (1918, p. 204). Thus, the wellspring of female homosexuality (and consequently of gender narcissism) is the girl's discovery toward the end of the stage of primal narcissism, that she lacks an organ that others have. This becomes a major narcissistic injury.

Males and females traverse separate routes on their way to developing gender narcissism, yet there are also certain similarities. For both, the crucial period for the development of gender narcissism, sexual orientation, and sexual identity, seems to be the anal-rapprochement phase. Mahler and colleagues (1975) note that during this phase, falling roughly between the ages of one-and-a-half to three, a fear of re-engulfment can be observed in boys and girls, as the discovery of the difference in male and female anatomy exacerbates the anxiety of separation from Mother. These fears are often displaced onto the bathroom, where fantasies of being sucked into the toilet are common. This fear of re-engulfment is related to a disillusionment with Mother's omnipotence and was believed by Mahler to lead, when left unresolved, to the formation of the castration complexes of both boys and girls. For girls, this disillusionment centers around disappointment that Mother doesn't have a penis, and a resentment of her (and corresponding fear of re-engulfment); for boys, it centers around guilt about having a penis and subsequent fears of re-engulfment. Both then translate, later, into fears of castration (for boys) or annihilation (for girls).

Winnicott (1964) also observed this fear, noting that every male and every female is born of "Woman" and that each retains a fear of Woman, a fear of being lured back into a state of infantile dependency. He pointed out that both genders dealt with this fear through identification with Mother. He linked this fear to the development of feministic sentiments in women, and to the disparagement of women by men (since men cannot successfully identify and merge with Mother).

Mahler lists three stressful and possibly traumatic events that occur during this period: (1) the child must master toilet-training, which means giving up the complete freedom of infancy and submit to the demands of another person; (2) the child begins to walk, and hence becomes independent of mother, requiring the working through of separation anxiety; (3) the child discovers the difference in sexual anatomy, which for girls arouses envy and a feeling of having been cheated of some coveted "toy" and ultimately betrayed; and which for boys arouses a feeling of guilt and ongoing fears of castration.

Stoller (1968), Money and Ehrhardt (1972), and Socarides (1979) have also identified the anal-rapprochement phase as a critical period for the establishing of gender identity and sexual orientation. Stoller, for example, places the beginnings of feminine identification among transsexuals in this phase, explaining that mothers of such individuals have the common psychological feature of having treated their sons in a way that interrupts the formation of "core gender identity." Money and Ehrhardt designate the eighteenth month or so as the critical age beyond which successful "sex reassignment" is not possible. Socarides, concludes that the nuclear conflicts of all sexual deviants derive from the preoedipal period, especially the years between one-and-a-half and three. This period falls roughly at the end of the stage to which Freud attributes primal narcissism.

The implication is that narcissism about one's gender and gender anatomy (gender narcissism) develops during this stage and is related to unresolved castration complexes. It seems to hinge on the extent to which both males and females can successfully separate from, and de-idealize the omnipotent and omniscient mother of the stage of primal narcissism. In those instances when a mother herself is narcissistic and therefore resists this normal progression of events (i.e., does not want to hear the little girl's complaints about not having a penis or the boy's boasts about having one), the child will develop a narcissistic fixation.

To the problems of this pregenital stage, Freud added the problems of the oedipal stage. In the oedipal stage, separation from mother and bonding with father is a key. A boy who is too closely attached to his mother and cannot bond to a father because the father is either too passive, hostile, or absent, will not be able to resolve his Oedipus or castration complexes; a girl who is too closely attached to her mother and fails to bond with her father for similar reasons will likewise fail to resolve her castration complex and often develops a negative Oedipus complex. The failure to resolve both the castration and Oedipus complexes becomes further bedrock upon which gender narcissism is built.

Another difference in the routes traveled by boys and girls during the Oedipal phase, according to Freud, was that boys may develop an envy of the womb (corresponding to penis envy). In his case history of Little Hans (1909), Freud explained that "in phantasy he was a mother and wanted children with whom he could repeat the endearments that he had himself experienced" (P. 93). He saw this identification with Mother and her gender role as a normal phase in boys; however, like all phases, if it is not resolved it can interfere with development--i.e., impede male gender role identification--in which case we might say (although Freud did not use this term) that the boy develops a "femininity complex" and clings to the desire to be a woman. On the other hand, a girl who cannot resolve her castration or Oedipus complex may develop a masculinity complex during this phase and, according to Freud, cling obstinately to clitoral masturbation and to the hope of one day getting a penis; in which case "the fantasy of really being a man, in spite of everything, often dominates long periods of her life" (193 1, p. 23 0).

With regard to boys, a number of psychoanalysts have cited the experience of urination with the father as crucial to the formation of a healthy masculine identity. Roiphe and Galenson (1981) note that urination while standing with the father represents a turning point, a "ceremony" that serves to bolster the boy's healthy masculine pride and bond with the father. Tyson (1986) emphasizes that urination with the father is an important step toward the establishment of "core gender identity elaboration and consolidation" (p. 8).

For girls, separation from Mother and bonding with father seems to be a bit more difficult than for boys, according to many researchers, due to the fact that girls can more easily identify with Mother; this identification make them less able to truly separate and  establish their own sense of self. Roiphe and Galenson (1981), in a long-term observation of the interactions of mothers and children, document a number of cases in which girls with hostile  mothers and distant fathers clung even more tightly to their mothers. "In those girls with severe castration reactions the hostile ambivalence to the mother becomes very intense, the maternal attachment is heightened, and the turn to the father does not occur" (p. 275). Freud (1931) asserted that little girls have "the dread of being killed by the mother--a dread which on its side justifies the death-wish against her, if this enters consciousness" (p. 237). McDougall (1984) observes that while punishment for masturbation and sexual wishes is fantasized by boys as castration, the same punishment is fantasized by girls as death. Kemberg (1975) states that in borderlines with severe penis envy, who have been unable to separate from Mother, the consequent rage aroused by fear of the mother is displaced onto the father. All of these factors mitigate against the de-idealization of Mother and the resolution of castration and Oedipus complexes and therefore reinforce the development of gender narcissism.

Incidentally, narcissism of children has been demonstrated by Piaget's early studies (1923) of the decentering process of children and young adolescents. Based on studies in which children are interviewed at length about their ideas during various ages, Piaget's work documents that until the age of eight a child does not attempt to take another's point of view to make himself understood; in fact, the child is egocentric, behaving as if everyone shares the same view as himself. From the age of nine to eleven, that egocentricity gradually gives way to a form of verbal and conceptual syncretism, which serves to gain acceptance for his point of view. Only in adolescence does the normal individual truly consider other points of view. Hence, from Piaget's work one might deduce a broadened stage of early narcissism, perhaps divided into two parts: primal narcissism (up until two-and-a-half) and normal narcissism (up until eight). Both primal and normal narcissism would be convertible into gender narcissism in the event that a fixation occurred at either of those periods.

Homey (1950), was among the first to write of gender narcissism, using the term "male narcissism" to describe the phallic pride exhibited by some men, although she did not use the same term in describing the female pride that is exhibited by some females. Such masculine pride, according to Horney, is often linked to "phallic narcissism" and alludes to the phallic narcissistic stage. Perhaps, I would add, the term "clitoral narcissism" might be apt for girls with a fixation at the earlier stage of corresponding female sexual development.

## General Characteristics of Gender Narcissism

Although I had written previously about gender narcissism (1989, 1991), I had not systematically studied the topic. In reexamining the psychoanalytic literature and reviewing the histories and psychodynamics of a group of gender-narcissistic patients, I was able to corroborate the basic theories of classical psychoanalysis, including the much-debated theories of female development, as well as delineate the characteristics and manifestations of gender narcissism.

In selecting patients for the study, I looked for the following features:

(1)Inferiority/superiority feelings about one's gender;

(2)Excessive concern about one's genitals;

(3)Envy of or disgust toward the genitals of opposite sex;

(4)Resentment of one's gender role and envy of the role of the opposite sex;

(5)Bitterness about feeling castrated or cheated (females), or rage about feeling psychologically castrated (males);

(6)Fears of castration (males) or annihilation (females);

(7)Oedipal guilt;

(8)Idealization (grandiosity) about one's own gender and devaluation of opposite gender;

(9)Idealization of mothers and devaluation of fathers.

One of the first things I noticed, upon selecting 30 patients for the study--16 males and 14 females--was a link between gender narcissism and sexual psychopathology. All 30 reported severe problems in their sexual relationships. In contrast, those 20 patients selected at random for the control group (10 males and 10 females) reported fewer sexual problems and showed much less gender narcissism. Among this second group were cases whose narcissistic issues generally revolved not around gender but other issues such as intelligence, height, or basic self-worth.

## Female Narcissism

All of the 14 females in the study voiced resentments about being female, about the female role, or about their female reproductive organs, which I traced to castration and masculinity complexes. In contrast, the control group of females expressed considerably less resentment about gender issues. Typically, gender-narcissistic females would complain that their femininity was a "handicap," the role of wife and mother was "demeaning," and their reproductive organs were "disgusting" or "a monthly pain." One borderline stated angrily about her genitals: "I wish I could just have them cut out of me and be done with it."

These negative attitudes had apparently been introjected from their parents. If their mothers had harbored similar feelings of resentment about their femininity, these attitudes were passed along to the daughter through verbal and nonverbal messages (i.e., devaluing the daughter's looks, discouraging her sexual curiosity or masturbation, bemoaning femininity and the feminine role, or favoring a son over the daughter). The daughters then unconsciously devalued their own femininity but did not blame it on their mothers, with whom they were too attached, but on their fathers, who were often passive or distant. All maintained intense relationships with their mothers, more intense than with any other person.

They reported a generalized anger about what they saw as "men's attitudes toward them," which contrasted with the more positive reports about relations with men of women in the control group. Some of the former made no distinctions between "good" and "bad" men, while others, utilizing the defense mechanism of splitting, saw some men, generally heterosexual men, as all-bad (inherently sexist) and some men, generally homosexual men, as all-good (nonsexist). At the same time, they generally idealized women, citing their moral superiority. I interpreted this as their projecting negative judgments about their femininity onto men while erecting a narcissistic armor of female grandiosity. Many gender-narcissistic women made men the scapegoats for their inner conflicts about their femininity, vocalizing sentiments that have become common among militant feminist circles such as, "Men are the cause of all the problems of women." Thus, they were competitive with men, rather than cooperative, wielding the attitude expressed in the song lyric, "I can do anything better than you can."

Five of the gender-narcissistic females were homosexual, three were bisexual, two were heterosexual, two were prostitutes, one was a strip-teaser, and one was abstinent. All maintained intense friendships with women. In contrast, all of the females in the control group were heterosexual. The former tended to have relationships of the narcissistic varieties described by Kohut (1971)--idealizing or twinship models. Either a younger woman would idealize an older one, particularly her aggressive femininity, and thus feel special by being close to her, and have the experience of being initiated by her into the realm of womanhood; or two women of equal age would idealize one another and feel as though they were two superior and special women (in particular, superior to men). There was often a vengefulness in their exclusion of men from their intimate lives (one noted that she had fantasies of her father jealously and angrily watching her make love to another woman), and a resentment of traditional women who were openly receptive to men and to the roles of wife and mother. I had the sense that since they were prevented by their mothers from bonding with their fathers and men, they did not want any other women to do so.

Those who had sexual relations with men often chose passive men whom they could control, only to complain about their passivity. I interpreted this as a way of reversing roles and enacting resentments stemming from their castration and masculinity complexes. If they had lesbian relationships, each could likewise act out her masculinity complex, one by playing the masculine role and the other by identifying with the one who was playing it. Their sexuality, whether oral or manual, consisted primarily of mutual clitoral masturbation, which had the symbolic meaning of asserting their clitorises, and thereby gratifying their clitoral narcissism. This symbolism could be traced back to memories, fantasies, and dreams about discovering the differences in male and female anatomy and feeling deeply cheated and disappointed, without getting adequate soothing from either parent; of being discouraged from masturbating (hence becoming fixated in such masturbation); and of having their femininity disparaged by both parents (as when a father, feeling excluded by mother and daughter, reacted by constantly teasing the daughter about her body). There was an additional aspect of their relationships of wanting not only to exclude men but to make men feel jealous of them (left out) and show them that their penises and their masculinity were unneeded. This represented a reversal of the envy they felt toward men.

Some women could only relate to men in conditional ways. One used strip-teasing to elevate her low female self-esteem. She could show off her body while keeping men at a distance, thereby asserting her femininity and receiving affirmation from men while acting out rage by emotionally castrating them. This vocation also represented an act of spite at her mother, who had called her a "slut" whenever, as a child, she had made infantile sexual overtures to her father. Prostitution served a similar purpose for two females, enabling them to make men pay for sexual services while emotionally rejecting them. Another woman, whose religious views prevented her from being lesbian, acted out her penis envy and female grandiosity by retreating from sexual relations entirely, rationalizing that it was a "dirty business" and she was above it all. A therapist by profession, she worked primarily with younger women, whose complaints about their husbands served to reinforce her rationalization for remaining abstinent. Invariably, she would encourage her patients to leave marriages rather than try to resolve them.

All female narcissists voiced sentiments of penis envy, while only three of 10 control cases did so. Penis envy could be deduced from a resentment of men, envy of their roles, and revulsion toward penises. Penises were seen not as attractive objects of pleasure and procreation, but as unattractive and frightening. One obsessive-compulsive had an obsessive fear of men's penises and of rape that took the form of agoraphobia. Along with this penis envy was an accompanying aversion to playing the traditional female role of giving birth to and nurturing children. This role was seen as making them subservient to a man, of forcing them to be penetrated by "his arrogant cock," to bear and nurture "his" children, which would symbolically mean submitting to their fathers and competing with their mothers. Any such thoughts aroused primitive fears of maternal annihilation.

Gender-narcissistic females also generally had more painful menstruations. Twelve of 14 reported severe cramps and/or headaches accompanied by feelings of resentment about their femininity. The severe menstruations were related to their resentment about playing the female role of giving birth and nurturing "his" children. Only four of the ten control cases reported menstrual pain, and only occasionally. I interpreted severe menstrual problems as a somatization of gender narcissism.

Whatever their sexual orientations, all had histories that matched the profile described by Freud and others with regard to the development of castration and Oedipus complexes. Their mothers had bound them to themselves and prevented them from forming relationships with their fathers or other men. Sometimes these mothers were overly affectionate, so that there was an undertone of incest in their relationships with their daughters. Sometimes they were anxiously protective, masking an underlying animosity and competitiveness (the result, perhaps, of their own unresolved Oedipus complexes). Sometimes they were openly hostile or competitive. Invariably they were controlling of their husbands and their daughters.

When fathers were in the picture, they were generally passive men or hostile. When the girls turned to Father (or surrogate) during the oedipal phase, Mother, through verbal or nonverbal cues, interrupted that turn. Mothers would draw the daughter to themselves and confide in them about problems with Father ("All men care about is using you for sex.") Father would retreat passively or angrily from the field of competition, yielding to Mother. Hence, there was an unspoken barrier between Father and daughter. The daughters would end up despising the fathers for allowing this to happen, while repressing their anger at their mothers (sometimes developing reaction formations). I note here that a number of feminist psychologists have stressed that separation from mother is not necessary, even harmful (see Gilligan, 1982), a position with which I strongly disagree.

In a many cases siblings figured into the equation. An older or younger brother would be favored by one or the other parent. He would, of course, have an organ that the girl did not have, and he would be given favored treatment. If he was older and he was competitive and rejecting of her, she might then grow up hating him and displacing that hatred on men in general. If he was younger, she would feel resentful that he had taken her mother's attention away, and conclude that it was because he was a male and had an organ she did not have.

Nearly all of the gender-narcissistic females either had rejected entirely the role of motherhood and opted instead for a career, or had waited until after they had established a career to have children. Their resentment of the motherhood role was transformed into an obsession with "equality" in their relationship with their husband, and a demand that he share in the childrearing. In the case of lesbians, one woman usually played the masculine role and the other the feminine role. The one who played the feminine role did not resent nurturing a child since she was not doing it for a man but for a woman (symbolic of Mother).

In their relationships with me, father, mother, and sometimes sibling transferences were prominent. The mother transference was evident in their fear of being controlled by me. The father transference was demonstrated in an extreme ambivalence toward me as a sexual object. One day they might be seductive, the next they would eye me in a fearful way. Upon analysis, they often admitted that they feared that I was going to use or rape them. Their ambivalence had to do with alternatively wanting to submit to the rape (and get it over with) or to repel it. It was difficult for them to conceive of a warm, trusting relationship with a man. This was related to a deep, infantile craving to bond with Father and equally deep fears of incest, maternal annihilation, and their own repressed animosity. When talking about their histories, it was much easier for them to talk of their anger at their fathers than at their mothers. They had a need to idealize their mothers (harking to fixations during the rapprochement stage), whom they felt they would be betraying by opening up to a male therapist. Many would struggle with all of this and be overwhelmed; then one day they would disappear.

Their female narcissism had the two components found in all narcissism--grandiosity and rage. In working with them, I had to be very careful to serve as a self object, mirroring and joining them with regard to their idealization of their own femininity and their feeling that they were victims of male oppression. If I said or did anything to the contrary, it would arouse the deepest wellsprings of rage and bitterness. I would suddenly find myself in the "enemy camp" and unable to dig my way out of it. In that case, the patient might quit therapy in a huff, castigate me, or threaten to report me for violation of ethics, sexism, harassment, etc. My few successful cases involved women with a lesser degree of gender-narcissism. Generally gender-narcissistic females avoid male therapists and instead look for female therapists who suffer from a similar gender narcissism to whom they can form collusions.

### Male Narcissism

Like their female counterparts, gender narcissistic males also voiced inferior feelings about their gender, and in specific, their penises (they were small or disgusting). In contrast, the 10 control cases reported lesser inferiority feelings about their penises or no concerns. The inferior feelings of the former came from negative judgments about their masculinity that had apparently been introjected from their parents. These introjections were the result of mothers who directly or indirectly disparaged their genitals or masculinity, or of fathers who had inferiority feelings about their own masculinity or were competitive or rejecting toward their sons. At any rate, the sons learned to devalue their own masculinity and to develop a compensating narcissism.

Because of their identificational bonds with their mothers, some tended to identify with their mothers and possess strong feminist views. In some cases they incorporated their mother's defense mechanism of splitting, dividing men into two categories, viewing their fathers and all traditional, assertive, or heterosexual men as menacing, oppressing, and disgusting, while regarding nontraditional, passive, or homosexual men as sensitive and caring. In such cases their own impulses of male aggression were disowned and projected onto "masculine" (conventional or heterosexual) men. There was also an envy and resentment of such men, related again to the identification with Mother and with Mother's unresolved castration complex. In other cases, where phallic narcissism was high, there was a reaction against feminism, and an identification with "masculine men." In yet other cases, such as with the transvestites and transsexual, their male aggression was converted to female aggression.

Their relationships, like those of female narcissists, were also of the narcissistic kinds described by Kohut. There were six homosexuals, three fetishists, two heterosexuals, two transvestites, one bisexual, one transsexual, and one pedophile in the experimental group. In contrast, all of the control cases were heterosexual. Male narcissists, regardless of their sexual orientation, placed more emphasis on relationships with men. Younger homosexual or bisexual men sought out older men who represented to them an ideal of masculinity. They would form an idealizing transference to such a man and submit to him anally, thereby hoping to be initiated into the world of men and masculinity. The older man could meanwhile play and identify with the aggressor--the "masculine" role as modeled by his father or some other man. This act would also serve to assuage their tremendous amount of Oedipal guilt (having symbolically knocked off their fathers). Men of the same age would form twinship transferences in which they could mirror each other as two superior men--imbued with all the positive traits valued by their mothers (sensitivity, artistic appreciation, refined tastes, respect for women) while lacking the negative traits their mothers despised (male pride and sexual assertiveness).

Three of the six homosexuals and one of the heterosexuals were prone to promiscuous sexuality, but none of the control cases. The promiscuous sexuality of gays consisted of a series of one-night rituals designed to maintain distance from the tabooed father while bolstering their masculinity through contact with an externalized masculine ego ideal and assuaging oedipal guilt. In these encounters they could each identify with the aggressor-father as they took turns playing the father-aggressor role. Meanwhile the sexuality was usually sadomasochistic and emotionally distant. Even homosexuals who had longer lasting relationships had problematic sexual relations due to narcissistic interferences such as self-consciousness about their penises, bodies, etc.

The sexuality of the homosexuals in my study was centered

on anality and on the phallus. Three control cases showed anal or phallic-narcissistic features. This factor was traced back to their fixations in the anal-rapprochement phase, during which time anal-eroticism is at its highest and anal narcissism begins. Anal fixations were often brought about by a mother who pampered her son during toilet training and a father who wanted to impose discipline but was prevented from doing so by the mother, and hence felt frustrated. The boy then became beholden to his mother and guilty and afraid of his father, which in turn aroused a great deal of castration fear, covered over by more gender narcissism. Phallic and anal narcissism, related to such frustrations, was evident in the emphasis these men put on the size and beauty of their genitals and, by extension, their physiques; the size and beauty of their buttocks; and on the glories of anal penetration and mutual masturbation. This emphasis went beyond the normal idealism that accompanies sexual passion; it was an obsessive preoccupation permeating all relations, tied to fantasies, dreams, and early memories of anal masturbation, and conquering or being conquered by their fathers.

Of the heterosexual gender narcissists in my study there was one whose sexuality combined both gender and anal narcissism, who could only have emotionally distant relationships with women in which rough anal sex was the primary mode of sexual expression. His gender narcissism was evident in his contemptuous attitude toward women (defending against a fear of reengulfinent and womb envy) and his male chauvinism. The gender narcissism of a foot fetishist manifested itself in a feeling that he had a feminist (reverent) attitude toward women which was therefore superior to the attitude of straight men. A bisexual who enjoyed phallic voyeurism and exhibitionism, was fixated in the phallic-narcissistic stage, when his infantile masturbation was harshly attacked by his mother and his older brother. His sexual relations were with women but his fantasies were mostly about muscular, dominating men with huge penises or about witches who permitted him to masturbate all he wanted but warned him that the consequence of masturbation was that his penis would grow to several feet in length. Peeping and showing off his phallus to other males was a way of affirming his masculinity and feeding his gender narcissism. Two transvestites and a transsexual in the study harbored a gender narcissism in which not their masculinity, but their femininity was idealized; they had strong femininity complexes, viewing themselves as more feminine than most women, and proud of it, while denigrating masculinity as menacing and disgusting.

The male narcissists, like the females in my study, had histories that confirmed the observations of classical psychoanalysts. Their mothers had bound them to themselves and prevented them from becoming pals with their fathers, often even preventing them from playing with other boys and later from taking part in athletics. Sometimes an undertone, and sometimes an overtone, of emotional or actual physical incest permeated their relationships. Sometimes the mothers were hostile but close-binding. The fathers, when they were present, were passive or hostile. There was often a barrier between gender narcissists and their fathers, and the sons would end up resenting the fathers and displacing all their anger, both at their mothers and at their fathers, onto their fathers. Mother, to whose allegiance they were sworn, had to be protected from their anger. This anger at fathers was then further displaced and transferred onto conventional or heterosexual men in general.

As with female narcissism, siblings also figured into the equation. An older or younger sister might be favored by one of the parents. She would have an organ that the son did not have, and she would be given special treatment. If she was an older sister and was competitive and rejecting of her younger brother, he might then grow up hating her and displacing that hatred on women in general. If she was younger, he would feel resentful that she had taken his mother's attention away, and conclude that it was because she was female and had the same organ as her mother. This reinforced masculine inferiority and womb envy.

Fourteen of 16 reported severe castration fear, particularly those with hostile fathers. In contrast, only three of ten control cases voiced castration fears. Castration complexes of gender narcissists were manifested in a fear of competing with traditional (or heterosexual) men for the favor of women or in attitudes of appeasement or disparagement toward women. One man had a compulsive need to dominate both men and women. Since most male narcissists are Oedipal conquerors, they feel they have already won their mothers (in fact, have gotten more familiar than they wanted) and do not wish to compete for other women. Such competition arouses oedipal castration fears. At the same time, they display an attitude of bitterness related to memories of having already been psychologically castrated; the source of this bitterness is repressed while the bitterness itself is converted into womb-envy, resentment of the male role, envy of the female role, and an aversion to female sexuality.

In their treatment, the father transference had to be worked through first, then the mother and sibling transferences. The father transference was apparent in an ambivalence comprised of alternately idealizing and distancing behavior. Either they would try to please me--if homosexual, seduce me--or they would keep me at a distance as their fathers had done to them. "You're straight (or, you're conventional) so you won't understand me." Underneath this pose was a frightening unconscious desire to be initiated by me into the world of masculinity, often by being taken anally. When they flipped into their mother transferences, they became submissive and idealizing and our relationship took on the quality of the idealizing, idealized, or twinship dyad they once enjoyed with their mothers.

A number of both female and male homosexuals had politicized their feelings about homosexuality. Not only their gender was idealized, but also homosexuality as well. Homosexuals, they held, were more sensitive, more humane, more refined, and more moral than heterosexuals. "If straights were as peace-loving as gays, the world would be a better place," was an often expressed sentiment. Underpinning this grandiosity was the narcissistic rage, which viewed the world in terms of a gender war between straight males and victimized gays. If I did not mirror their idealization or their view of the world, I would quickly experience this rage in the form of character assassination, threats, or hasty terminations. I also had to mirror their idealization of mothers or face similar consequences.

Incidentally, it is this idealization of mothers and the almost complete and unquestioning identification with them--traceable to the inability to de-idealize mothers and separate from them during the anal-rapprochement phase--that lies behind the intractability of most forms of gender narcissism. The success of the therapy with them seems to hinge on the degree to which we can resolve this mother fixation. I had very limited success with my group. Most left therapy after a short time, often after getting in touch with repressed material about their mothers. De-idealization of the mother represents maternal castration, the threat of their own castration, and the extinction of their own grandiose selves. Still stuck in a primitive narcissistic, symbiotic merger with her, their fate is inexorably bound with hers, as when one identical twins follows another to the same sickness. Those in the control group, in contrast, were usually able to overcome such fixations.

## Case Histories

*Case #1.* Nancy's parents filed divorce papers when she was not yet two years old. At the time, she was in the midst of the anal-rapprochement stage. Separation from her father was difficult, but since he continued to see her every weekend, the trauma of separation was at first apparently not so severe. However, her mother was bitter about the divorce, and this bitterness had both immediate and long-term effects on Nancy's developing femininity. The immediate effect was that it caused her mother to cling to her all the more, which interrupted the separation from her.

For the mother, the loss of her husband represented a narcissistic injury and aroused her rage. Resentful of her ex-husband and jealous of her daughter's blossoming Oedipal relationship with him, she began to interfere. Quite frequently she would promise her ex-husband he could visit on a certain day, then cancel at the last minute. When the husband became angry about this, she would lambaste him, telling him he was getting what he deserved. A year after the divorce she met another man, a widower with a daughter a year older than Nancy, and quickly married him. She then began demanding that her ex-husband allow her new husband to legally adopt Nancy, contending that it was destructive for him to stay in her life. "We have a new family now," she would say. After he refused, she stepped up the pattern of promising and then reneging on visitation rights. Much pressure was put on Nancy not only by her mother but also by her stepfather and stepsister; all were denigrating her real father and discouraging her from seeing him.

When Nancy was five an event happened that was of central importance in shaping her personality and her sexual development. Until then her father had not taken her for a vacation, even though he had been granted a month's vacation each summer as part of his visitation agreement. That summer he informed Nancy's mother that he was going to take her to visit his family in a nearby state. At first the mother agreed. Plans were made and airline tickets were purchased. At the last minute she changed her mind and would not let Nancy go, protesting that Nancy was too young to be away from her mother for that long a period. The father, enraged, pretended to give in to the mother but then, upon picking Nancy up for what was to be a weekend visit, whisked her away to the airport, whereupon he called the mother and told her that he and Nancy were flying to his family after all, "because I have a legal right to do so!" They were on an airplane within half an hour and stayed for two weeks with Nancy's grandparents. When they returned, Nancy's mother and stepfather were waiting with vengeful arms.

For many days Nancy's mother and stepfather interrogated, lectured, and chastised her for having gone away without their permission. They drilled it into her that they and only they had custody of her, and that it was wrong of her to do what she had done and that her father had committed a criminal act. They made her feel ashamed of her formerly loving and idealistic Oedipal feelings toward her father. In addition, her stepfather's daughter used the occasion to act out feelings of sibling rivalry by ridiculing Nancy's trip and her father. "If he loves you so much, why did he leave you?" she kept saying. The result of this assault was that Nancy refused to see her father for a few months. Each time he called for his weekly visit, her mother informed him that Nancy did not want to talk with him.

Caught in this battle between her parents, she had become a sacrificial pawn. All the mother's rage at the father was taken out on her. She was given the message that her father was bad and that positive feelings for him were misguided and a betrayal of Mother and Family. She was made to understand that if she wanted to stay in her mother's good graces she was expected to have complete allegiance to her. Her new stepsister and stepfather backed her mother up completely, lecturing her about being loyal to her "real family." She was surrounded and overwhelmed.

Her mother was herself gender-narcissistic. The mother's childhood, in which an older sister had been favored by her father over her, had left her insecure about her own femininity and sexuality; she had erected a narcissistic bubble of feminine pride that reflected her mother's token idealization of her and defended against her father's ridicule. When she married Nancy's father, he was expected to overvalue her the way her mother had, not devalue her as her father had. Instead, he devalued and left her, and she had flown into a narcissistic rage. Before the forbidden vacation, she had pampered Nancy as her mother had pampered her. This pampering fed into Nancy's primal narcissism and served to foster dependency on her mother. After the vacation, the mother began ridiculing Nancy as her father had ridiculed her. She discouraged her infantile masturbation with statements such as, "That's dirty," and focused in an obsessive way on every aspect of her physical appearance. Under this severe scrutiny, Nancy developed asthma and later, during adolescence, anorexia. The aim of this assault by her mother was to keep Nancy's blooming sexuality under her control and prevent her from forming an alliance with her father.

Her father, meanwhile, compounded the problem by trying to convince Nancy that her mother was "sick" and that she should move out and live with him. The father had gone into therapy and, like many people in the early stages of therapy, tended to brandish interpretations like weapons. Hence he would analyze Nancy's mother and Nancy herself and advise them both to go into therapy. Although this advice may have been well-founded, it only served to make matters worse, since it was ego-dystonic and was viewed by Nancy as an attack. The father also exacerbated Nancy's Oedipus complex by parading an array of new girlfriends in front of Nancy and holding each forth as an example of what a healthy woman was like--in contrast to her mother. Many nights she recalled sleeping over at her father's apartment and hearing the sounds of sexual intercourse in the other room. As a result Nancy developed fixations in both the anal-rapprochement and Oedipal phases.

The main fixation was during the Oedipal stage when she had returned from the forbidden vacation with her father and had been, through no fault of hers, severely punished. This punishment had reinforced her castration and Oedipus complexes so that she developed unconscious conflict about her vagina and her attraction to her father. There were also fixations in the oral and anal stages, due to the mother's narcissistic indulging of and then spiteful clinging to her daughter; the indulging consisted of making her into a narcissistic extension of herself (the externalized representative of her mother's ego-ideal): she was the princess who would someday stand in her mother's stead. Upon her parents' separation, Nancy had gone from princess to pauper in her mother's eyes, and she had introjected both these judgments into a harsh superego.

Her ego-ideal reflected the overvaluation of her pregenital mother, but there was also an "ego-reject," if you will, that reflected the devaluation of the Oedipal mother. The ego-ideal and ego-reject were opposing parts of her superego. One set up an ideal image toward which she must strive; the other a rejected image that she should deny and project. Her personality showed signs of this battle, vacillating between periods in which she assumed a stance of pride in her femininity and saw herself as the princess who could outdo any man and would tolerate no criticism, to periods in which she sank into a pit of self-consciousness and insecurity about her femininity, devaluing her genitalia, and avowing, in an identification with her mother, that men had it better. During these times she was prone to somatizing these feelings through bouts of asthma and anorexia. The relationship with her mother was repeated by her relationship with her stepsister. The stepsister formed a twinship alliance with her mother and her attitude toward Nancy was similar to the mother's. She too harped on Nancy's deficiencies of character and femininity. Hence, Nancy could get nothing supportive from any mother or mother-surrogate.

In her twenties she had several relationships with men that rekindled her bitterness. On a transference level she saw all men as forbidden objects who (1) threatened to arouse forbidden incestuous Oedipal feelings that would (2) represent a betrayal of her mother and hence might result in her annihilation. In addition (3) there was a fear that men would abandon her as her father had done and (4) a concomitant fear of the accumulated rage she had repressed that was now directed almost entirely at her father and at men in the form of projections onto them of the judgments about her inferiority as a female. In her relations with men, she would attempt to defend against all these inner fears by idealizing herself and devaluating the men. By her late twenties, she had given up dating. She had a strained relationship with her father--who constantly gave her the message that she needed therapy and was becoming disturbed like her mother-- while maintaining an intense relationship with her mother. Although her relationship with her mother had contributed greatly to her problems, she needed to continue to protect and idealize her mother, since she had become dependent on her positive mirroring and terrified of her hostility and spite. Having given up men, she retreated into a coterie of women friends. Some were lesbians, others had simply retreated from the sexual arena, sublimating their libido by concentrating on their studies or careers. In her relationships with women she sought out older or more confident women with whom she could form a narcissistic bond, hoping to bask in their radiance. She hoped also that such a woman could initiate and accept her into the world of womanhood (as her mother and older sister had refused to do), and affirm her femininity. Inevitably, she formed alliances with women who were as narcissistic as her mother, demanded the same kind of allegiance, and could be just as vindictive if that allegiance was violated. Hence the relationships did not turn out to be reparative, but rather served to reinforce Nancy's fixations.

Within this milieu her defensive posture of feminine grandiosity was built-up even further, along with her tendency to disparage her father and men. This defensive trend found an outlet in militant feminism, which was rife in that coterie. Stuck in this mode, no man could possibly relate to her; her gender-narcissistic shell prevented it. Hence, she had come to fulfill her mother's unconscious aim of keeping her dependent on her by undermining her confidence in her femininity and preventing her from relating to her father and to all men, as well as her father's aim of making her feel bad and sick like her mother. She felt inferior to her mother, her sister, and most other women; felt women had it worse then men; felt that she had been cheated; felt that she was bad and disgusting; and felt that was emotionally ill. On top of it all, she could not endure therapy for therapy represented the ultimate betrayal of her mother. She had fulfilled her role as the sacrificial pawn.

*Case #2.* From the beginning of his life Norbert served as a self-object for his mother. He was designated as the child who would mirror her the way she wanted to be mirrored. She wanted to believe that she was a wise and good mother and wife who did everything for her husband and children and got little credit for it. She wanted to believe that she was a superior woman who had married beneath her. She was Irish, her husband was Italian. She liked the finer things--books, art, theater, music--while he was content to sit in front of the television set and watch football games, drink beer, and demand sex whenever he wanted it. She would "work her fingers to the bone," in order to see that the children had a cooked, nutritious meal every night, clean and ironed clothes, and were caught up on their homework. She was the martyr, her husband the slob. This was her vision of things.

Only her second-oldest son, Norbert, understood her the way she wanted to be understood. He stood by her completely. He was an almost exact mirror of her ego-ideal. He had to be. If he ever slipped and did not mirror her correctly-if he, for instance, questioned something, blurted out, "But Mother, maybe it's not necessary for you to cook three separate meals tonight to fit the schedules of everybody, especially since you have a headache and are feeling rundown," he was doomed. "Yes, it is necessary!" she snapped back. "If I don't do it, who will? Do you think your father would ever lift a finger around here? Don't tell me what to do! You sound just like you father when you talk like that. Just help me set the table or shut up and get out of my way!"

Devastated, he would strive even harder to be the perfect self object, resolving to keep his mouth shut. Even on her death bed--she died of cancer in middle-age--he continued to be the dutiful son, swallowing all his own hurt, rage, guilt, and jealousy, suppressing his real self in order to tell her once again that she had been the perfect mother and wife whose nobility had been tragically unappreciated. "Take care of things," she uttered as she died. "I will," he responded. Norbert's grandmother, like his mother, had been a martyr; his grandfather, like his father, was cold and distant. Hence his mother could not get what she needed from either of them and remained attached to them. Norbert's father, meanwhile, was reluctantly dependent on his own mother, visiting her once or twice a week until the day she died. Hence, from the start of their marriage, Norbert's parents were in conflict. They had not separated from their own families of origin. She had married a man much like her father and he a woman much like his mother. Both needed the other to be self objects, neither could do so. Their conflicts became displaced onto their children.

When her first child was born, she was disappointed to find that he was a boy. She had wanted a girl. Unconsciously, through identification with her mother's martyrdom and in reaction to her father's passive-aggression, she saw females as noble victims hopelessly at the mercy of male aggression. Thus she hated her son from the start, negatively transferring her cold father onto him and projectively identifying him (through identification with Mother) as a male aggressor who would add torment to her life. Naturally, her prediction came true; he became a noisy and aggressive child who would not mind her. Had she been able to hate him objectively (Winnicott, 1947), perhaps things might have turned out a bit better. Instead she denied her hate and did her duty, even going beyond duty in order to compensate for her disgust at her son's maleness. In fact, it appears she may have developed a reaction-formation, being overly nice, catering to his every demand. When he turned out to be a problem-when he turned out to hate her-she was terribly wounded. How could he hate her when she had been so nice to him? She would turn to her husband and exclaim, "I don't know what to do with him. You take over. Maybe you can understand him; you're both males." "The problem is, you've spoiled him," the father would say. "Sure, blame it on me," the mother would say. Eventually, they both decided that the problem was the son, thereby avoiding their conflict with one another and, of course, their own deeper feelings of rage. Instead of experiencing this rage themselves, their oldest son contained it and acted it out for them and they could then preoccupy themselves with him and his rage and forget their own. They saw him as a "bad seed." They could not figure out how he had gotten that way and why he persisted in his demonic behavior. Often she might bellow out during her evening prayers, "Why God, why me?"

It was into this environment that Norbert was born. Seeing that his older brother was a problem because of his rebellion against his parents, especially his mother, Norbert resolved early on to be the exact opposite of her brother, and to please his mother in every way. This meant that he must never assert himself at all, since even the mildest form of self-assertion seemed like rebellion.

His mother had seven children in all. About every year-and-a-half she had another child. Thus she had her third child, a girl, at a time when Norbert was amid the anal-rapprochement phase, and Norbert was enlisted as her helper. He noted how differently she treated this girl child, how much she valued her, as compared with her attitude toward himself and his older brother. Hence, be began devaluing his masculinity and forming a passive-feminine character. He helped his mother cook, clean, and when he was old enough, change diapers. When she complained about her sacrifices, he listened. When she showed off her knowledge of literature, painting, or music, he properly admired her. When she complained of her husband and her oldest son, he agreed with her, even though the message she was conveying was that masculinity was everything that was bad: it was menacing, indulgent, hateful, and vile. Somehow women put up with men, despite it all. Somehow she put up with his father at night, when he came to bed smelling of beer. But she was glad Norbert was not like that. She was glad Norbert was different than other men. Thank God for Norbert.

Norbert nodded and strived not to be a man, not to be anything really, but just to be his mother's reflection. If there was anything real about him, any edges that stuck out, she would have a target on which to direct her rage. By being her reflection, he could at least get a bit of approval now and then. Meanwhile, he was developing inferiority feelings about his masculinity and a compensatory attitude of superiority that would form the nucleus of his gender narcissism.

His father, meanwhile, was distant. He recalled that when he was four years old his father and older brother went to the World's Fair together. He wanted to go but his father told him he was too young. He felt excluded from the world of men. At the same time he learned how to manipulate his father as his mother did. He recalled that once, when his father came after him to spank him, he began to shriek hysterically (as he had seen his mother do), and his father laughed and said, "How can I spank you when you shriek like that?" His exclusion from the world of men and his narcissistic bond with his mother prevented his resolving either his castration or Oedipus complexes. As he grew older, he found himself admiring his father's chest, and wanting to touch his father while he was sleeping.

At the same time, his older brother picked on him mercilessly. Calling Norbert a "goody-two-shoes" and a "fairy" and a "queen" he would pounce on him, pin him to the ground, and force him to say "Uncle" or sometimes "Aunt" or sometimes "You're a wonderful person." These episodes were experienced as rapes. Hence, his relationship with his brother also reinforced the development of feelings of masculine inferiority and gender narcissism. Later in his treatment he would have nightmares of being attacked by a monster and of being unable to scream.

His castration and Oedipus complexes were severe; he was afraid of castration by everybody-his father, his older brother, and his mother. From adolescence on, his life was full of tension. His ego-ideal demanded that he always be in tune with others, as he had been with his mother, and if he was not completely in tune, anticipating every move, he would feel castrated. If he said one thing that somebody else laughed or frowned at, he would sink into a depression and castigate himself about it for days. There was not a moment in his life when he was not self-conscious.

In his early twenties he had a relationship with a woman. She was the one who took all the initiative in the relationship, and he went along with it. For a while he thought maybe he could be heterosexual, even though he was primarily attracted to men. In his relationship with his girlfriend he had to be the perfect self object for her, as he had been for his mother. Sexually, he had to please her and forget about himself. There could never be any negative thoughts or feelings between them. Everything had to be perfect. When it could no longer be that way--when he began having an almost constant undercurrent of negative thoughts about her and sexual impulses toward men, he broke off from her rather than share the negative feelings and thoughts or his homosexual yearnings.

His relationships with men were not much better. He was either super critical of himself or of the men he met. They had to be just right. They had to have a certain kind of chin, certain kind of eyes, certain kind of brows, certain kind of lips, certain kind of muscles on their chest, arms and legs, and most especially a certain kind of buttocks. He lusted after a "hunk" who represented to him his ideal of masculinity. This ideal was much like his father as a younger man, about whom he continued to dream. By bonding with such a man, he might dwell in the vitality of his masculinity and become alive and more manly himself. By being taken anally by such a man he might assuage his Oedipal guilt and be initiated into the world of men.

His gender narcissism manifested itself in a number of ways. First there was his preoccupation with his masculinity, which centered on his body and the bodies of his sexual objects. He revered the male body, saw it as infinitely more attractive, more magical, more powerful, than the female body. He revered the male genital. At the same time, he was constantly worrying about his hair thinning, about his skin blemishing, about his posture, about his tan, and particularly about his genitals and their functioning. This dichotomy represented his ambivalence-at one pole the masculine grandiosity, at the other the feelings of inadequacy.

His gender narcissism was also manifested-through identification with his mother and her disparaging of masculinity-in an idealization of the kind of man of which she approved: the feminine, sensitive man who was interested in the arts, supported women and women's causes, and would never ever assert himself with (i.e., oppress) a woman. He became a feminist male, more zealous about feminism than many women, in order to prove what a sensitive, moral man he was. This narcissism, which defended against his feelings of masculine inferiority and his rage at his mother, kept him in a state of constant tension and self-consciousness and prevented him from resolving that tension and forming a genuine relationship with himself (his true self) or with anybody else.

## Concluding Remarks

My aim has been to extend the concept of narcissism as developed by Freud and others. I do not believe there is much that is new here; rather it represents a reiteration of classical theories of male and female sexual development with an emphasis on the gender narcissism that is formed during such development. As such, it constitutes a new angle from which to view sexual development and the use of a new label, gender narcissism, for the particular kind of narcissism that Freud and others have previously described and I have tried to elaborate. I must add that I do not distinguish, as others have done (Kohut, 1971), between normal and pathological narcissism. What Kohut calls normal narcissism I call healthy self-esteem. Therefore I distinguish between self-esteem (health positive regard for one's self) and narcissism (an obsession with self).

Male and female narcissism manifest themselves in an idealization of gender, gender identity, and gender sexual characteristics and a disparagement of the opposite sex. These factors lead to an inability to form genuine emotional bonds with members of the opposite sex or with members of one's own sex. The bond that is formed is of a narcissistic kind-that is, an alliance designed to feed gender narcissistic needs (affirm one's masculinity or femininity) but leaves deeper emotional needs unmet. Since they are primarily geared to obtain narcissistic needs, the relationships of gender narcissists tend to be shallow and to deny reality.

Gender narcissism, being closely related to castration and Oedipus complexes, also interferes with sexual expression. For male narcissists, fear of castration, Oedipal guilt, and feelings of inferiority about gender combine to make sexual activity a self-conscious, compulsive experience. A similar compulsive self-consciousness inflicts female narcissists, for whom penis envy, Oedipal conflicts (about separating from mother and getting too close to father), and feelings of inferiority about gender combine as a disturbing force.

Classical theories about the etiology of gender narcissism have been borne out by this study. Close-binding, emotionally incestuous, or hostile-controlling mothers and passive, passive-aggressive, hostile, or absent fathers seem to predominate in the backgrounds of gender-narcissistic patients. Sometimes siblings also contribute to the problem. This does not mean however, that gender narcissism cannot be generated through another circumstance, such as when a father is close-binding with a daughter and a mother is absent. In contrast, the control group of random cases showed more of a separation from Mother, more of a bond with Father, and fewer complaints about sexuality.

Gender narcissism is resistant to psychodynamic therapy due to the intractability of gender grandiosity and to strong identificational bonds with idealized mothers. The anal-rapprochement stage seems to be a critical stage for the formation of sexual identity; hence, severe cases of gender narcissism cannot be reversed without great difficulty.

It seems evident, moreover, that gender narcissism not only contributes to individual sexual psychopathology, but also, because of the politicizing of feelings, to social pathology. Female narcissists with masculinity complexes are often militant feminists, as are male narcissists with femininity complexes. Both are also militant about homosexual rights. Indeed, militant feminism and militant homosexual rights have been closely linked; I dare say there is not a militant feminist who does not champion homosexual rights, nor a militant homosexual who does not actively support feminism. This may be seen as a societal manifestation of gender narcissism--a mass transference alliance of Mother and her idealizing sons and daughters against the Father on the cultural level.

I am well aware that much of my writing, including this last statement, is controversial. I am reminded of Freud's comment in a footnote to one his descriptions of female sexuality (1925), in which he observed that female psychoanalysts and male psychoanalysts with feminist sympathies would probably contend that his notions about female sexuality stemmed from his own masculinity complex. Like

Freud, I know that what I have written is going to be disturbing to some and will be viewed as an expression of my own sexism, my own homophobia, my own bigotry. However, not withstanding any complexes I may have, I maintain that the observations I have made here are still valid. I present them not out of maliciousness, but because our society, and Western society in general, has become inundated with social problems that I believe are to some extent connected with gender narcissism. Unless we are willing admit and confront a problem, we cannot solve it. The strife caused by militant feminism--with its attack on family values and disruption of conventional heterosexual relations--is the chief social pathology brought about by societal gender narcissism. In our culture, gender narcissism and other forms of cultural narcissism may be epidemic, and their mass rage may constitute our biggest agent of oppression.

*References:*

Adler, A. (1929). *Problems in Neurosis,* Ed. by P. Mairet. New York: Harper & Row, 1964.

Freud, S. (1909). Analysis of a phobia in a five-year-old boy. *Standard Edition, 10,* pp. 3 -152.

-- (1914). On narcissism: an introduction. *Standard Edition, 14,* pp. 67-104.

-- (1916). Introductory lectures on psycho-analysis. *Standard Edition, 15,* pp. 3-485.

-- (1918). The taboo of virginity. *Standard Edition, H,* pp. 192-108.

-- (1920). The psychogenesis of a case of female homosexuality. *Standard Edition, 17,* pp. 146-174.

-- (1922). Some Neurotic Mechanisms In Jealousy, Paranoia and Homosexuality. *Standard Edition, 18,* pp. 221-233.

-- (1925). Some Psychical Consequences of the Anatomical Distinction Between the Sexes. *Standard Edition, 19,* pp. 243-260.

-- (1931) Female Sexuality. *Standard Edition, 21,* pp. 223-246.

Gilligan, C. (1982). *In a Different Voice: Psychological Theory And Women's Development.* Cambridge: Harvard Press.

Horney, K. (1950). *Neurosis and Human Growth.* New York: Norton.

Kernberg, 0. (1975). *Borderline Conditions and Pathological Narcissism.* Northvale, NJ: Jason Aronson.

Kohut, H. (197 1). *Analysis of the Self.* New York: International Universities Press.

Mahler, M. S., Pine, F., and Bergman, A. (1975). *The Psychological Birth of the Human Infant: Symbiosis and Individuation.* London: Maresfield Library.

McDougall, J. (1984). Eve's Reflection: On the Narcissistic and Homosexual Components of Female Sexuality. Paper presented at symposium, *The Many Phases of Eve: Beyond Psychoanalytic and Feminist Stereotypes,* Los Angeles, Feb. 25.

Money, J., and Ehrhardt, A. A. (1972). *Man and Woman, Boy and Girl.* Baltimore: Johns Hopkins University Press.

Piaget, J. (1923). *The Language and Thought of the Child.* Cleveland and New York: World Publishing Company.

Roiphe, H., and Galenson, E. (198 1). *Infantile Origins of Sexual Identity.* New York: International Universities Press.

Schoenewolf, G. (1989). *Sexual Animosity Between Men and Women.* Northvale, NJ: Jason Aronson.

-- (1991). *The Art of Hating.* Northvale, NJ: Jason Aronson.

Socarides, C. W. (1979). A Unitary Theory of Sexual Perversions. In *On Sexuality,* Ed. by T. B. Karasu and C. W. Socarides. New York: International Universities Press.

Stoller, R. J. (1968). *Sex and Gender.* New York: Pantheon. Tyson, P. (19 8 6). Male Gender Identity: Early Developmental Roots. *Psychoanalytic Review, 73,* p. 4.

Winnicott, D. W. (1947). Hate In the Countertransference. In *Through Pediatrics to Psycho-Analysis, pp.* 194-203. New York: Basic Books.

--(1964). *Boundary and Space: An Introduction to the Work of D. W. Winnicott.* Edited by M. Davis and D. Wallbridge. London: H. Karnak.

# 4

# The Persistence of the Belief that Madness is Hereditary

For more than a century geneticists and social scientists have been trying to prove that mental illness is hereditary. Today most professionals and lay people believe that the hereditary nature of schizophrenia has been proven by accumulated evidence. However, a review of that evidence shows that such proof is far from conclusive. It is suggested, therefore, that the stubborn insistence on the genetic theory is itself the problem. A universal tendency to sweep under the rug the dark side of humanity leads to biased research.

## Introduction

Recently news of a research project was leaked to all the major news services and television networks. The media quickly jumped to conclusions, blaring out headlines like, "New Genetic Link to Homosexuality Found." Actually, a researcher in California, David Hamer, had discovered a possible link, but had not yet published his results; nor, of course, had anybody else replicated it. Later one of his assistants confessed to fraudulent methods and he was investigated by a government agency (Socarides, 1995). Yet, the popular media had announced this research as though it were a fact. This is an example of a human tendency with a long history—that of always wanting to attribute its problems to agencies outside of its control—the stars, inner demons, bad luck, the genes, etc. It is perhaps most prominent in our attitude toward mental illness.

Schizophrenia is the most salient case in point. Today most mental health professionals, as well as most lay people, believe that madness is inherited, transmitted through genes. It is more than a belief; it is a strong contention that is held up almost as if it were a law, one that seems to defy any attempt to deal logically with it. Advocates of the genetic theory of schizophrenia most often cite twin studies as ultimate proof that schizophrenia is a thing of nature rather than nurture, and once having cited their evidence they invariably turn a deaf ear to any further discourse, as though one would have to be crazy (schizophrenic?) to dispute such an obvious fact. Their behavior is reminiscent of some religious fundamentalists. Try to argue logically with a Christian that Jesus could not really have been the son of God, and he will just shake his head and smile sympathetically at you. Try to argue logically with a schizophrenia-is-hereditary devotee and you will get a similar reaction.

Yet, a review of the research that purports to prove that schizophrenia is inherited or biochemical shows that such research is far from conclusive. Has the research been refuted? Has other research indicated other possible causes? If so, how can we explain this persistence in the genetic theory of schizophrenia and mental illness?

**Genetic Transmission**

Theories asserting that schizophrenia is inherited can be divided into two groups; those which focus on genetic transmission, and those based on the assumption of a neurophysiological dysfunction or biochemical imbalance. Sometimes the two overlap.

Researchers have been trying to find a genetic basis for

schizophrenia since Charles Darwin (1859) emphasized the importance of heredity in the production of personality differences. The most often cited evidence for the genetic transmission of schizophrenia centers on twin studies. Early researchers would often come up with high concordance rates for monozygotic twins (up to 86 percent), while totally disavowing the influence of the environment. Recent researchers began speaking of an inherited predisposition to schizophrenia which interacted with environmental influence. Kolb (1977), summarizing concordance studies completed through the mid 1970s, found that concordance rates for monozygotic twins varied greatly from study to study, ranging anywhere from 14 to 86 percent, while those from dizygotic twins ranged from 0 to 22 percent. Geneticists claim that these concordance rates, found in many different societies at many different periods of time, demonstrating that twins separated from their mother at birth and raised in different environments can frequently both develop schizophrenia, show a definite genetic link. This genetic assumption is still maintained (Atkinson and Coia, 1995), and, in fact, recently a whole issue of *Nature* was devoted to it (Editor, 2010).

Lidz (1965) and Shean (1978), among others, have pointed out that monozygotic twins may have constitutional factors that predispose them to schizophrenia—they come from the same ovum and develop a unique identificational bond which results in a similar pattern of disturbed behavior throughout their lives. When one gets a cold, the other does, even if they are in different locales. In effect, twin studies may be interpreted as proving only that twins, due to their unique constitutions, are more susceptible to developing schizophrenia than nontwins. Hence, the data about monozygotic twins does not necessarily apply to the general population, nor does it even conclusively prove that twins have a genetic predisposition to schizophrenia. Other factors may be involved. For example, how traumatic is it for any infant to be separated from its mother at birth? And what about congenital factors? Does a schizophregenic mother transmit a schizophrenic tension state or biochemistry to her unborn child? In addition, studies have been conducted that failed to replicate this concordance.

One of the most stark studies ever done involved the Genain

quadruplets. Several standard American textbooks on abnormal psychology carry, in their chapters on schizophrenia, a photo of the four identical smiling Genain women. They became famous in psychiatric circles because all four of them were diagnosed as schizophrenic. The name "Genain" is a pseudonym chosen by researchers, and comes from the Greek "dreadful gene." Rosenthal (1963) provides a summary of the various researches that were done over the years. Genetic researchers calculated the probability of all four quadruplets become schizophrenic as one and a half million to one; hence they concluded that there was "compelling evidence" for a genetic base for schizophrenia. However, such researchers ignored the abusive and bizarre behavior of both parents. From the case history we learn that both parents came from dysfunctional families. Mrs. Genain only married Mr. Genain when he threatened to kill her if she did not. After they were married they became virtual recluses.

Upon giving birth to the quadruplets, the Genain parents charged visitors 25 cents to see their daughters, but soon Mr. Genain became obsessively concerned about their safety, erected a fence, locked all the doors, and patrolled the yard with a gun. When the girls went to school, he did not allow them to mix with other children. The parents were so obsessed about masturbation that they had a surgeon remove the clitorises of two girls. Afterwards, the two were tied to their beds for a month, and they wet their beds twice a day and refused to eat. Only once were the girls ever allowed to go to a party, and then Mr. Genain stormed in halfway through and took them away from it. He allowed them to sing in a church, but made them quit when he found out the choir was taking a recreation break. The girls grew up extremely repressed and passive (see Johnstone, 1996). However, all these family factors have been discounted by geneticists.

In addition to twin studies, researchers have used family risk studies to prove a genetic link to schizophrenia. Zerbin-Rudin (1972) studied the available literature and estimated risk figures of 9-16 percent for children of schizophrenic parents, 8-14 percent for siblings, 1-4 percent for nieces and nephews, and 3-5 percent for parents. Meanwhile, the incidence of schizophrenia among the genera l population was estimated at 0.8 percent (Shields, 1967). Researchers assert that this evidence shows a clear blood relationship in the incidence of schizophrenia. Proponents of this theory also cite statistics showing that the incidence of schizophrenia is about the same in differing cultures. Critics argue that these researchers are biased, in that they are setting out to prove a genetic cause and are aware of the diagnosis of the index case from the outset. Second, they note that such statistics can just as easily be interpreted as evidence of a transmission of schizophrenic styles of child-rearing.

Adoption statistics are another area of study. These compare the incidence of schizophrenia in adopted children and their biological families. Kety and colleagues (1974) surveyed over 5,000 adults who had been adopted in early life. They found a 13.9 percent concordance rate between schizophrenic children and their biological families, while only 2.7 percent of adoptive relatives were schizophrenic.

Such studies are flawed, Shean asserts, for several reasons. First, prenatal and early childhood environmental factors have not been accounted for. Not all adoptive children are taken from their mothers at birth; some remain with their mothers for weeks, months, even years. Second, most adoptive families know about the schizophrenic mother, hence, they have negative expectations toward the child that may influence their rearing attitude. This research is therefore far from conclusive.

Genetic research in general has been plagued by problems of diagnostic unreliability. Schizophrenia is not an easily or absolutely identifiable characteristic, hence diagnostic ambiguities result in considerable variability among populations of schizophrenic patients. Tienari (1968) observed that different concordance rates (6-36 percent) could be obtained form the same subject population by applying different diagnostic criteria. Shean also notes that genetics is a very complex science, observing that "the number of genetically different sperm or ova that a single human can produce is...eight million" (1978, p. 103). It is difficult, if not impossible, to track down a recessive gene that might transmit a vaguely defined abnormal pattern of behavior such as schizophrenia. Coles (1982) points out three critical distinctions that must be made when considering genetic theories of etiology: between single gene and polygenic inheritance; between a genetically determined disorder and a genetically determined predisposition; and between inheritance and mutation. All of these factors are sources of endless debate and lead to the inconclusiveness of any research. In addition, after years of looking for the gene that causes schizophrenia, no gene has been found (Harrison and Owen, 2003).

## Biochemical Theories

Biochemical theories assume that schizophrenia is caused by aberrant enzymatic or metabolic processes related to the neurotransmitters. Genetic and biochemical theories often seem to overlap, but biochemical defects do not necessarily stem from genetic sources. According to Frohman and Gottlieb (1973) biochemical studies have indicated inappropriate levels of plasma protein, indole animes and catecholamines, abnormal antibodies, disturbed hemolytic plasma factors, deviant carbohydrate metabolism, aberrant hormonal levels, abnormal levels of inorganic ions, and vitamin deficiencies.

Many investigators have claimed to prove that the dopaminergic synapses are involved in schizophrenic disorders (Shean, 1978). This theory comes from two sources. First, it was observed that amphetamines work on the brain's dopamine system to produce toxic amphetamine psychosis (the symptoms of which are similar to those of some forms of schizophrenia). Second, it was also observed that major tranquilizing drugs had what seemed like a curative effect on the topaminergic synapses (the symptoms of psychoses went away). From these observations and others, researchers began looking for biochemical causes of schizophrenia.

Others, such as Linus Pauling (1968) claim schizophrenia involves a vitamin deficiency, and prescribe large doses of niacin and vitamin C to cure it. However, Frohman and Gottlieb (1973) maintain that there is not enough data to show vitamins play any role in schizophrenia. Still others suggest a "transmethylation hypothesis" (Osmond and Smythies, 1952). Pointing out the similarities of mescaline-induced experiences and schizophrenia, and between the chemical structure of mescaline and epinephrine, they concluded that schizophrenics undergo a transmethylation which turns norepinephrine to epinephrine which in turn affects behavior.

Again, none of this biochemical research is conclusive. Kety (1969) asserts five reasons why: (1) there is no evidence that the heterogenous forms of schizophrenia have a common etiology, so findings from one sample may not be confirmed by another; (2) biochemical research is conducted on patients with a long history of hospitalization in overcrowded institutions of low hygienic standards; (3) the quality and variety of the diet of institutionalized schizophrenics is different to that of control groups; (4) prolonged emotional stress, indolence, and lack of stimulation or exercise may alter many metabolic and physiological functions; (5) Exposure to radical therapies such as convulsive therapies and antipsychotic drugs may effect metabolic functions, even after therapy ceases.

Because biochemical theories seem so simple and so easy to verify, many researchers have been quick to assume that biochemical research is therefore more valid than, say, psychoanalytic research. However, none has been substantiated. "The highly publicized claims for the discovery of bio hemi al etiological agents," Shean notes, "have not been confirmed when subjected to rigorous scientific testing by independent investigators" (1978, p. 126).

The genetic researchers continue undaunted. As soon as critics refuse one of their claims, they conduct new research whose intent is to answer the critics. It becomes evident they are not looking for the truth (which should be the goal of all research), but are looking for a way to finally answer all their critics and to prove, finally and definitely, the genetic basis of schizophrenia. Each new claim of a discovery or breakthrough in understanding a genetic of biochemical basis for schizophrenia is immediately publicized and accepted as validated before it has been subjected to rigorous testing. Often, when such claims are later refuted, the refutations are given no publicity whatsoever, and the general impression lingers that the original claim was correct.

## Environmental Research

Meanwhile little attention is paid by genetic researchers to the many detailed studies of the family environments of persons with schizophrenia. While giving lip service to these studies, the psychiatric establishment now states, as though it were a proven fact, that there is a genetic basis for schizophrenia and other mental diseases. Kolb, in Modern Clinical Psychiatry, citing the twin studies, asserts, "Over a half century of research into the genetics of schizophrenia has brought forward sufficient replicable evidence to leave little doubt of the existence of an inherited predisposition to the condition" (1977, p. 380). Kolb, like others, does not take note of Lidz's observation about the constitutional factor of twins, or the other variables, such as prenatal conditions; if he did, he would have to amend his assertion to read that there is sufficient replicable evidence to leave little doubt of the existence of a susceptibility to the condition among monozygotic twins. That, and only that, has been undoubtedly proved. It has yet to be proven whether that susceptibility is genetic or congenital.

Environmental studies are now seen as passé; even if they have not been refuted by the scientific establishment, they have been pushed aside by the steamroller of obsessive empiricism. Yet, in fact, they have never been disproved. Mahler (1968), Lidz and colleagues (1965), Bateson and colleagues (1981), Wynne and colleagues (1981), Laing and Esterson (1964) and Piontelli (1992), are among the most prominent examiners of environmental derivatives. Their findings remain as striking today as when they were first conducted, offering detailed observations of dysfunctional relationships.

Mahler concentrated primarily on observations of mothers and children at the Masters Children's Center in New York. While not denying the possibility of an organic basis for autism in some children (due to brain damage or some other birth defect) she demonstrated how important a mother's eye contact and other nonverbal behavior toward an infant can be. She noted many cases of childhood autism in which the mother's hostility toward the infant, due to a range of factors such as teen-aged pregnancy and postpartum depression, drove the child into a state of autistic withdrawal.

Lidz and colleagues conducted an extensive 12-year study of 17 schizophrenic families. These studies revealed characteristic patterns in the families of schizophrenics including (1) failure to form a nuclear family boundary because one or both parents remained primarily attached to family of origin; (2) marital schisms and lack of role reciprocity, or marital skews in which one partner yielded submissively to the domination and irrationality of the other; (3) failure to form a parental alliance and the blurring of generational boundaries between parents and children; (4)cognitive and communicational confusion, paranoid ideas, incestuous, and sex-role uncertainty; (5) failure to prepare children for separation from the family; (6) isolation of the family from the community; and (7) parental narcissism in which a parent failed to differentiate his/her own needs from the child. Lidz expanded on Fromm-Reichman's concept of the schizophrenic mother and added the concept of the schizophrenic father.

Bateson and colleagues coined the term, "double-bind," emphasizing how the schizophrenic mother puts the preschizophrenic into a double-bind. An example of this double-bind is the mother who verbally encourages her son to take initiative in school, yet when he attempts to leave home to visit a library, she entreats him not to leave her lest she become ill. Therefore, he is damned if he does and damned if he does not. He becomes confused, builds up anger that he cannot resolve, does not develop a mature ego, nor mature socialization skills. And, as the mother is unaware of putting the son in a double bind, the son can never bring this fact up to her without being shamed by her and made to feel stupid. He then further doubts his perception of things and withdraws from a direct relationship with her and from others.

Wynne and colleagues studied family transactions through the medium of conjoint family therapy and showed how "pseudo-mutuality"—that is, denial—in schizophrenic family systems tends to engender schizophrenic thought disorder. Laing and Esterson found much the same thing in their studies of eleven families of schizophrenics in England. For example, when Laing and Esterson interviewed a schizophrenic patient and her parents, they observed the parents making faces at one another when their daughter spoke, but when the interviewers pointed out that the parents were making facial expressions, they both completely denied it. When a child is treated mockingly by parents, and then encounters their denial when she mentions it, she can only become frustrated and enraged as well as doubting her perception of reality.

Piontelli's pioneering use of ultrasound to observe fetal behavior has verified the connection between prenatal environmental conditions and later personality development. These investigations began when she was analyzing an unusually restless 18-month-old toddler who was unable to sleep. Each day this toddler moved restlessly about Piontelli's office, as though looking for something, searching every corner, behind every curtain, around every chair. Now and then he would shake objects, as if trying to bring them to life. When she mentioned this to his parents, they burst into tears and recalled that the boy had been, in fact, a twin. His twin brothers had died two weeks before birth. "Jacob, therefore, had spent almost two weeks *in utero* with his dead and consequently unresponsive co-twin" (1991, p. 18).

This author has noted elsewhere that studies of multiple personalities offer additional proof that schizophrenia (or schizophrenia-like symptoms) are produced by environmental stress (Schoenewolf, 1991). In treating "Jennifer," it was noted that one of her seven personalities suffered from hallucinations, skewed thinking, paranoid projection, and motor disturbances. Her six other personalities might have been diagnosed as manic depressive, obsessive-compulsive, paranoid, impulsive-addictive, hysterical and schizoid. If seven different personalities, including one that is schizophrenic, can be produced in a single individual over the course of a childhood replete with harsh traumatic shocks (including sexual abuse before the age of three), the question of genetic susceptibility seem to become a secondary, if not moot, point.

Genetic researchers dismiss such studies as unscientific, unverifiable, and hence not to be taken seriously. Psychiatrists ask for more proof, as when Kolb (1977) commenting on Bateson's "double-bind," states, "What has not been done to verify its usefulness in this and other psychological states is to define and reconstruct the specific learning contexts of the various clinical expressions. This requires definition of a precise connection between the initial paradox and the resulting pathology" (p. 388).

If it is not empirical, it is not to be trusted—so the scientists seem to say. And yet, as psychoanalysts have pointed out, matters of human behavior do not always submit themselves to empirical testing. Scientists assume that social science survey and observational studies are biased, lack proper controls, and are plagued by too many variables. Yet empirical studies are just as often biased and unreliable, even though they are wrapped in the language and trappings of science.

**Human Narcissistic Disorder**

In the litany of a Church service certain phrases are repeated over and over, such as, "Jesus, the son of God," so that the accumulated effect is to make the believer come to accept that such a concept is beyond doubt. It is, in essence, a form of hypnosis. Much the same thing has happened with respect to genetic theories of schizophrenia and other diseases. They are repeated over and over, in textbooks, on television, on the internet, in newspapers and periodicals. Most people today, like Kolb, are convinced of an inherited predisposition to schizophrenia, despite the fact that there has not been any conclusive proof of it. In fact, incredibly, almost the entire psychiatric establishment and much of the mental health field has come to accept the genetic theory as a proven fact, when the only thing that has actually been proven is that monozygotic twins have a susceptibility to schizophrenia.

On the other hand, there is much evidence that schizophrenia is produced by the environment. It seems apparent that if an environment is schizophrenic, it will produce schizophrenia whether or not an infant is predisposed to schizophrenia. Can you imagine an infant confronted with the denial, projective identification, hostility, and double-binding behavior of an undiagnosed borderline or schizophrenic mother or father, looking up at the caretaker and saying, "Oh, no, you're not going to drive me crazy, because I'm not predisposed to schizophrenia!" Indeed, one can safely say, after considering all existing research, that while constitutional factors may play a part, as they do in all emotional disturbances, the environmental factor is by far the more crucial one. Having said that, do you suppose the media will immediately pick up on this assertion and lavish us with headlines like, "Psychoanalyst finds that disturbed environments cause schizophrenia"? Very unlikely. More likely the notion that families cause schizophrenia would be dismissed as dated, mother-bashing, parent-bashing, family bashing, and an insult to humanity.

To understand this stubborn refusal to look objectively at this question, I will introduce another concept. To get the deepest grasp of why there is this persistence in the belief in a hereditary wellspring of madness (as well as of other mental disorders), one must put aside the evidence and arguments and look instead at the process. Namely, there seems to be a phenomenon that has been visible throughout humankind's brief history. It has been given various names over the years, but for the purposes of this paper I will call it the Human Narcissistic Disorder (HND). In fact, let's give it a code number, so as to make it more palpable to the scientific establishment and so it will fit into the disorders of the DSM classification of mental disorders: HND 1000.01. Like individual narcissism, this cultural narcissism has at its core a grandiose denial ("Families are good and incapable of driving children mad") and an underlying rage ("...and don't try to tell me anything different!"). Grandiosity asserts that we are irrevocably good and defends against the reality of our the darker human side, which causes disturbances in our children. Any challenge to this defense results in a enraged attack on the person or group that makes the challenge.

Human Narcissistic Disorder has surfaced throughout history, whenever some new finding has proved to be a blow to the narcissistic grandiosity of humanity and that finding has been met with disbelief and scorn. The discoveries that the world is round, not flat; that the earth revolves around the sun; that our solar system is but one of many in the universe; that humans are evolved from lower animals; and that we in fact do not have free will but are genetically programmed and environmentally conditioned to believe and think the way we do—all these discoveries were met with rage and scorn (and still are by many people). Any discovery that bursts this bubble of humanity's grandiosity, of its sense of importance, righteousness, innocence, omnipotence, omniscience, or well-being, is resisted, sometimes mightily.

Humanity's resistance to the idea that the environment (parents, families) engenders schizophrenia is one of the latest aspect of HND. Basically, it is a desire to sweep unpleasantness under the rug, to deny "man's cruelty to man." From the beginning of recorded history children have been encouraged to hide their problems from others and often even from themselves, to keep their "family skeletons in the closet." Commandments of most religions exhort children to "honor your father and mother." Just as individuals are encouraged to repress painful thoughts and memories and remain unconscious of their links with present behavior, so also societies repress and remain unconscious of the cruelties of families.

Fromm (1990) was one of the first to consider whether an entire culture could be diagnosed as insane. Just as people can be schizophrenic, so can a society. Fromm talks about a society in which people escape into over-conformity and the danger of robotism in contemporary industrial society. In the present context, one might point to the conformity and robotism of people who persist in promoting the genetic view of schizophrenia and resist being aware of their psychological cruelty to others. A society comprised of families in which members are taught to deny, project, and displace anger (scapegoat a member of the family and putting the runt into a double bind), is a society in which genetic theories of the etiology of schizophrenia will abound. Indeed, such a society might not just prefer a genetic theory, it might insist on it, and would use public opinion as a force to shame and ridicule anybody who would dare to think otherwise (just as a parent will often shame and ridicule a child for daring to doubt the parent's love or good will).

Schizophrenia is humanity's darkest secret, one that we want desperately to keep out of sight because it reminds us of our own complicity in the matter. The unconscious desire to drive other people crazy, of which Searles (1959) has written, is a desire that hardly any of us wish to acknowledge, particularly those who are successful in doing so. This tendency to drive others crazy, primarily found in parent-child relationship but also prevalent in marital relationships, as depicted in the film, *Gaslight,* wherein a husband tries to drive his young wife crazy, may well be an inherent tendency, a survival mechanism. If a human is under stress, he or she will either sink under or try to push somebody else under in order to save himself or herself. Madness might be seen as a state of "being under," a withdrawal form active life and direct and meaningful communication in order to avoid the threat of being pushed under.

Searles (1959) found that the "effort to drive the other person crazy" was one factor regularly found in the cases he treated. "My clinical experience has indicated that the individual becomes schizophrenic partly by reason of a long-continued effort, a largely or wholly unconscious effort, on the part of some person or persons highly important in his upbringing, to drive him crazy" (p. 254). Searles saw this effort to drive another person crazy as a way of psychologically murdering the other without having to take responsibility for it, a way of externalizing one's own threatening craziness, and of regaining a sense of omnipotence and control over others. He believed this unconscious desire to drive another crazy extended to psychiatry, referring to "so many of us who show a persistent readiness to regard this or that kind of functional psychiatric illness, or this or that particular patient, as incurable—in the face of, by now, convincingly abundant clinical evidence to the contrary." According to Searles, this attitude may mask "an unconscious investment in keeping these particular patients fixed in their illnesses" (p.279). Searles' notion of people unconsciously wanting to drive other people crazy can be seen as yet another aspect of HND.

### Summary

The persistence in the belief that madness is hereditary is a relentless, obsessive drive to accumulate and prove theories that have never been validated by research. The stubbornness and often vehemence of the persistence may be indicative of a disorder. It has led to the treatment of schizophrenia with medications geared to maintaining the illness rather than curing it. It has led to centuries of biased research and skewed results. A tower of evidence proves nothing if that evidence has been misguided.

It would probably be much better for society if researchers spent their time looking into the causes of HND 1000.01. If we could find a cure for that, we could probably find a cure for everything else. Indeed, HND 1000.01 may be the "virus" that engenders schizophrenia. "The fault, dear Brutus, is not in our stars," Says Shakespeare's Julius Caesar, "But in ourselves, that we are underlings."

**References:**

Atkinson, J.M., and Coia, D.A. (1995). Families Coping with Schizophrenia, New York, Wiley.

Bateson, G., Jackson, D.D., Haley, J., and Weakland, J>H. (1981). *Toward a theory of schizophrenia. In Family Therapy, Major Contributions*, New York, International Universities Press.

Coles, E.M. (1982). *Clinical Psychopathology: An Introduction.* London, Routledge and Kegan Paul.

Darwin, C. (1859). *The Origin of the Species.* London, John Murray.

Editor (2010). Combating schizophrenia. *Nature, 468,* 133.

Frohman, C.E., and Gottlieb, J.S. (1973). The biochemistry of schizophrenia. In *American Handbook of Psychiatry*, edited by S. Arieti. New York, Basic Books.

Fromm, E. (1990), *The Sane Society*, New York, Holt Paperbacks.

Harrison, Paul J. and Owen, Michael J. (2003) Genes for

schizophrenia? Recent findings and their pathophysiological implications. In *The Lancet,* Vol 361, February 1, 2003.

Johnstone, L., (1996). The Gernain quadruplets. In *Changes: An International Journal of Psychology and Psychotherapy,* 14:43-49.

Kety, S.S. (1969). Biochemical hypothesis and studies. In The Schizophrenic Syndrome, edited by L. Bellak and L. Loeb. New York, Grune and Stratton.

Kety, S.S., Rosenthal, D., Wender, P., and Schulsinger, F. (1968). The types and prevalence of mental illness in the biological and adoptive families of adopted schizophrenics. In *The Transmission of Schizophrenia,* edited by D. Rosenthal and S. S. Kety, New York, Pergamon.

Kolb, L. C. (1977). *Modern Clinical Psychiatry,* 9th Edition. Philadelphia, W. B. Saunders.

Laing, R. D., and Esterson, A. (1964). *Sanity, Madness and the Family.* New York, Basic Books.

Lidz, T., Fleck, S., and Cornelison, A. R. (1965). *Schizophrenia and the Family.* New York, International Universities Press.

Mahler, M.S. (1968). *On Human Symbiosis and the Vicissitudes of Individuation.* New York, International Universities Press.

Osmond, H., and Smythies, J. (1951). Schizophrenia: A new approach. *Journal of Mental Science,* 98:309-315.

Pauling, L. (1968). Orthomolecular psychiatry. *Science* 160:265-271.

Piontelli, A. (1991). *From Fetus to Child: An Observational and*

*Psychoanalytic Study*. London, Tavistock.

Rosenthal, D. (1963). *The Genain Quadruplets*. New York, Basic Books.

Shean, G. (1978). *Schizophrenia: An Introduction to Research and Theory*. Cambridge, MA, Winthrop.

Schoenewolf, G. (1991). Jennifer and Her Selves. New York, Donald I. Fine.

Shields, J. (1967). The genetics of schizophrenia in historical context. In *Recent Developments in schizophrenia,* edited by A. Walk and A Coppen. British Journal of Psychology Special Publicaltion No. 1.

Socarides, C. (1995). How America went gay. *America,* November, 1995, pp. 20-22.

Tienari, P. (1968). Schizophrenia in monozygotic male twins. In *The Transmission of Schizophrenia,* edited by D. Rosenthal and S. Kety, New York, Pergamon.

Wynne, L.C., Ryckoff, I.M., Day, J., and Hirsch, S.I. (1981). Pseudomutuality in the family relations of schizophrenics. In *Family Therapy: Major Contributions*, New York, International Universities Press.

Zerbin-Rudin, E (1972). Genetic research and the theory of schizophrenia. *International Journal of Mental Health,* 3:46-72.

# 6

# Perverse Sexuality and Perverse Mothering

---

There have been numerous explanations of male sexual perversity over the years. Some have hinted at the mother's role in its development, others at the father's role. After a lifetime of research, this author concludes that male sexual perversity occurs in direct proportion to perverse mothering, a kind of mothering in which a boy's normal masculine pride and activity is demeaned and threatened, leading to a perverse response.

---

## The Meaning of Perversity

Social scientists have given various explanations for male perversity, as well as explanations of why perversity is more linked with males than females. In addition, they have changed the definitions of sexual disorders over the years--most notably by redefining homosexuality as a normal variant of sexuality. Having worked with a number of males over the years who suffered from a sexual disorder, as well as studying the literature, I have come to the conclusion that sexual perversity occurs in men in direct proportion to the perverse mothering they received as boys. I have likewise concluded that the preponderance of perversity among males is due to a cultural double standard with regard to male and female sexuality and the application of that double standard in childrearing

Perverse mothering is a kind of parenting in which a mother verbally or nonverbally disparages her son's masculinity and sexuality at a certain critical stage of development. A son's first intimate relationship is with his mother, and it is with his mother that he discovers his sexuality during the second and third year of his life. During this stage he discovers the difference between male and female anatomy; he explores masturbation; he learns to master his bathroom needs; and he acts out infantile sexual fantasies about his mother. During this stage the mother is constantly touching the boy. She changes his diapers and wipes his behind. She bathes him daily, including all his intimate parts. She witnesses how he is responding to her touch, how he is touching himself, how he is looking at her. The mother's response to the boy's developing sexuality is crucial to how it develops. If the boy touches himself and his penis becomes erect and he says, "Look, Mommy, what my peepee can do!" she can respond in a supportive or hostile manner. If she loves the boy and loves his masculinity, she will say, "That's very nice. You have a very nice penis," and she will mean what she says. In this case, the boy will develop normal self-esteem about his sexuality.

If the mother either directly or indirectly disparages his sexuality, and there is an ongoing relationship of this sort, the boy may develop some form of perverse sexuality. The mother may directly disparage the boy's sexuality by responding to the boy's masturbation with, "Don't touch yourself. That's dirty." Or she may support the boy's sexuality verbally but not nonverbally. If she sees the boy touching himself, and he expresses pride at what his penis can do, she may say, "That's nice." But with her eyes and her body language she may give a different message. Nonverbally she may give him the message that she doesn't want to hear about his sexuality. For example, if she says, "That's nice," and then looks away as if to quickly change the subject, she will be giving him a message that the subject of his sexuality is taboo. The boy will respond to her nonverbal cues more than to her verbal cues.

The boys sexual development starts in the second year of life but continues to develop throughout adolescence. In some cases it may lay dormant even throughout adolescence and continue to be suppressed in early adulthood. He may even get married and attempt to have a normal sexual relationship with his wife. But at some point his perverse sexuality will emerge and he will be compelled to activate it.

## Research on Perversity

Freud (1905) theorized that humans are born with unfocused sexual (libidinal) drives, deriving sexual pleasure from any part of the body. The objects and modes of sexual satisfaction are multifarious, directed at every object that might provide pleasure. Polymorphous perverse sexuality continues from infancy through about age five, progressing through three distinct developmental stages: the oral stage, anal stage and phallic stage. Only in subsequent developmental stages do children learn to constrain sexual drives to socially accepted norms, culminating in heterosexual behavior focused on the genitals and reproduction. Freud viewed homosexuality as the main form of sexual perversion, referring to it as "inversion," noting that homosexual sexuality was centered on the self due to a narcissistic fixation.

Elsewhere (1916) Freud attributed homosexuality to a close-binding mother and distant father. "In all our male homosexuals there was a very intensive erotic attachment to a feminine person, as a rule to the mother, which was manifest in the very first period of childhood and later entirely forgotten by the individual." He further wrote that homosexual boys also have a relationship with a "weak or distant father in those early years" (p. 58) which is also later forgotten.

Psychoanalytic literature attributes perversity particularly to males and has noted a particular family constellation that breeds perverse sexuality. Stoller (1968), who spent his life studying gender problems, found that in nearly every case of perversion there was a castrating mother and a weak or absent father. Mothers of transvestites, for example, were usually women who bore unconscious animosity toward men and strived to make their boys into little girls. "There is one consistent fact in the history of adult male transvestites," he writes. "This is the mothers' need to feminize their little boys. These mothers have an unusually strong envy of males which expresses itself in this rather subtle way" (p. 183). Fathers of transvestites, when they are around at all, are often passive co-conspirators and therefore unable to rescue the boy from the mother's psychological castration, and unable to model a healthy masculinity.

In general, all male perversions, according to Fenichel (1945) are the result of severe castration anxiety. When perverts reach the phallic stage and begin, as boys generally do, playing with their penises and exhibiting them with pride, a mother who has unconscious or conscious animosity toward males and toward male sexuality will shame or humiliate the boy to the point where he retreats from the normal heterosexual expression of his sexuality, back to some form of infantile sexuality. "The pervert, when disturbed in his genital sexuality by castration fear, regresses to that component of his infantile sexuality which once in childhood had given him a feeling of security or at least of reassurance against fear, and whose gratification was experienced with special intensity because of this denial of reassurance" (p. 327). The kind of denial Fenichel is referring to is the denial of the knowledge that his mother is penis-less. According to psychoanalytic research, upon discovering that some people do not have penises, boys feel guilty and afraid. Elsewhere, I have used the term phallic guilt (Schoenewolf 1989) to describe the feelings boys develop about having a penis when their mothers and other women do not; this phallic guilt and castration fear is heightened if the boy senses a sexual animosity in his mother about his penis, as Fenichel points out, causing him to regress back to infantile sexuality.

Fenichel believes that infants are natural perverts; or as Freud put it, polymorphously perverse. They can have sexual feelings in all parts of their bodies and can have them for a range of objects-- including males, females, dogs, cats, or inanimate things, and they can have perverse fantasies about all those objects and more. Klein (1932) thoroughly studied these fantasies by observing young children at play. These fantasies involved such things as feces and urine, and contain scenes of infantile notions of rape, sodomy, or murder. According to Fenichel, we all have the capacity to be perverts, since we have all gone through this initial polymorphous perverse stage. However, those of us with castrating mothers or passive fathers will become fixated at that stage and hence more prone to develop perverse forms of sexuality as adults.

Other psychoanalysts are more or less in agreement on this issue, although each stresses a different element of the family constellation. Gillespie (1956) saw perversions as a defense against competing with father for mother's love. He posited that in perversions there is a retreat from the phallic expression of sexuality and assertiveness, which causes the regression back to a preoedipal stage of development. In this preoedipal stage, sexual expression retains an oral or anal mode or becomes attached to a secondary object such as a shoe or a panty.

Socarides (1978, 1979), who, like Stoller, specialized in research on the perversions, developed a unitary theory of the perversions which adds to Stoller's conclusions. Like Stoller, he emphasizes the importance of the child's interaction with his parents. In specific, he focuses on the rapprochement subphase of development (from about 15 months until 3 years of age). In his view, mothers of perverts are generally over-attentive and close-binding, while the fathers are usually hostile and rejecting. He believes that the child's sexual orientation hinges on whether he is able to separate from his mother and form an adequate identification with his father. "At the center of all these conditions [perversions] lies the basic nuclear fear, that is, the fear of merging with, and the inability to separate from, the mother" (1979, p. 185). According to Scoarides, perverts have a fear of re-engulfment by mother, which harks back to the primitive fantasies that infant children have of being sucked back into their mother's wombs.

Khan (1978) emphasized the alienation that is at the core of all perversions. "The pervert puts an impersonal object between his desire and his accomplice: this object can be stereotype fantasy, a gadget or a pornographic image. All three alienate the pervert from himself, as, alas, from the object of his desire" (p. 9). He speculates that this alienation was also present in his relationship with his maternal figure during the earliest stages of boyhood.

Chasseguet-smirgel (1985), Kaplan (1993) and McDougall (1995) regard avoidance of realities represented by Oedipal dilemmas as the basis of immature sexualities. Men with a perverse sexuality are attempting to deceive themselves and others. They try to hide that their sexuality is superior to normal heterosexuality, and that this secret superior quality of their sexual pleasure and/or aims for pleasure constitutes their main personal fulfillment (rather than aggression and revenge). In fantasy they have reinvented the primal scene because the realities it represents --in particular that the difference between the sexes is a condition of sexual desire--were too painful to bear. They retreat to an infantile form of sexuality in which the symbolic sexual object is idealized.

Shengold (1992), who conceived of the term "soul murder" with respect to parenting that so neglects or abuses a child that it robs him of his or her very vitality, extends this concept to his view of perversions. He concentrates on the anal period and to the development of anal narcissism and the subsequent retreat to an anal-narcissistic form of sexual expression. The development of the anal-narcissistic defense symbolizes a return to the self-absorbed overvaluation of early childhood and "the uniqueness and glory of the limited, sensorily...and mythically charged contents of one's own garden of Eden" (p. 129). It consists of a "panoply of near-somatic body-ego defenses" that children develop during the anal stage that "act as a kind of emotional and sensory closable door that serves to control the largely murderous and cannibalistic primal affects derived from the destructive and from the perverse sexual drives of early life" (p. 24).

As previously noted, most social scientists attribute perversity mainly to males. It is generally believed that there are more male homosexuals than females, and that other forms of female deviation are rare. Stoller's (1968) explanation of why male perversity is apparently more common than female perversity centers on the fact that it is generally the mother who has the closest relationship with both children in infancy, and hence it is generally her attitude which has the greatest impact on how perverse a child becomes, and which perversion he adopts. In cases where the father is the main caretaker from birth on, a female pervert such as a transsexual is more likely to develop. He has reported a few such cases. However, the psychoanalytic definition of perversity may be too narrow, perhaps focusing on individual symptoms rather than on the larger societal picture.

If we look at this larger picture, we may see forms of female perversity that escapes public attention, protected by a double standard that views men more critically than women. In addition, more women than men are prone to an asexual existence and what H. S. Kaplan (1979) calls "inhibited sexual desire," a phenomenon that may be seen as a female equivalent of a perversion. In actuality, it appears there may be as many female perverts as male.

There is also an apparent double standard with regard to male and female homosexuality. Female homosexuality is generally more acceptable to society than male homosexuality. Indeed, certain lesbian celebrities seem to be particularly revered because they are lesbians. Females do not see their homosexuality as a problem to the same extent as males and may not be as likely to seek help; hence they do not become officially counted as homosexual. In addition, since, as Kaplan notes, females generally have less sexual desire than males, female homosexuality is often of the latent variety. This makes it even less visible. "Homosexuality in women," Freud (1920) asserted, "which is certainly no loss common than in men, although much less glaring, has not only been ignored by the law, but has also been neglected by psychoanalytic research" (p. 146).

One also finds a double standard regarding male and female exhibitionism. Male exhibitionism is considered a perversion because, in the eyes of society, it is seen as repulsive. In fact, it is illegal for a man to reveal his genitals in public. Meanwhile a certain amount of female exhibitionism is not only acceptable but has become a fashion trend during many periods of history and in many cultures. Even blatant female exhibitionism (when say a woman stands in her window naked or opens her coat to expose herself on the street) is not viewed as repulsive, but merely idiosyncratic and sexy.  Similarly, women who dress in men's clothes, who become excited by wearing men's jeans or men's underwear, are not called transvestic, for it has become socially acceptable for women to do so.  Yet it would appear that a large percentage of women have transvestic tendencies, more so than men, and are never thought of as perverts.  Men who wear women's clothes are unequivocally labeled as transvestites.

What I am pointing out here is that women are allowed much more leeway in how they express their sexuality and in how they behave and dress than are men, and this social double standard has an impact upon who is seen as perverted and who feels perverted.  It may also reinforce an individual's perverse tendencies by adding another level of the forbidden to fuel his desire.  In actuality, there is probably a correlation between perverse behaviors by females and by males, since the two sexes continually play off one another; hence perversity would be more or less equal in each sex.  For males, perversity usually involves a substitute form of sexual gratification, while for females it often entails some form of rejection of male sexuality.  In males, castration fear is the primary cause of the deviation, while for females penis envy lies at the root.

This correlation between the sexuality of males and females also has an effect on the formation of perversity in men, as I have previously pointed out.  Male sexual perversity is in direct proportion to perverse mothering; and perverse mothering is in direct proportion to male perversity.  The two go hand-in-hand. The following case history will demonstrate this thesis.

**Case History**

All the cases of this type involve the development of perverse sexuality in male children through perverse mothering. In each case I have handled, the mother treats the boy's developing sexuality and masculine aggression as if it is unacceptable, unsavory, and sometimes repulsive and even dangerous. Often there is a direct or implied feminizing of the boy. Moreover, the mothers in most of my cases are controlling to the point that they manage to discourage and suppress anything in the boy that smacks of masculinity, male sexuality, or sexual pride. This attitude tends to damage not only his sexuality, masculinity and self-assertion but also his self esteem as a male and as a person. At the same time it prohibits normal male expression of sexuality. Since the formation of sexual perversion occurs primarily at the ages of two and three, the mother is the primary agent of influence. At this age, as Bowlby (1979) points out, a child has formed a strong attachment to mother that precludes any attachment with other objects, such as the father. Bowlby used the term "imprinting" with regard to this attachment, referring to the name used with regard to the instinctual attachment of baby animals to their mothers. Later, toward the age of three, the father starts to have an influence, and then we may also use the term "perverse fathering" for those fathers who are distant, hostile, or in some other way reinforce the mother's parenting style and do not bond with the boy or model healthy male sexuality or assertiveness. The case below is typical of the ones I have encountered in my practice.

Mr. A came to me when he was twenty years old. He was brought in by his mother, who became alarmed when she caught him looking at an internet porn site. It was not just any porn site, but rather a porn site devoted "femdom"—a term referring to scenes of women dominating men, tying them up, torturing them, kicking them in the testicles with high-heeled shoes, stabbing their genitals with the heels of the shoes, and verbally putting down their genitals as they did so. Sometimes the scenes would end with the woman giving the man a begrudging hand job while continuing to verbally assault him for being a wimp. His mother wondered into his room while he was in the bathroom and saw enough to convince her that her son was disturbed. She and his father interrogated him until they got him to confess that he had engaged in watching such porn for several years. They insisted he see a therapist.

The son and mother came in together for the first session. The mother did most of the talking, telling what she had seen, how she felt about what she had seen, and what she wanted from the therapy (she wanted me to make him normal). She described at length how "shocked and concerned" she and her husband were about her son. She had a great deal of difficulty talking about the pornography she had seen. "One scene, well, I don't know how to say this...there was something...I don't know what it's called...." The scene apparently involved a strap-on dildo being used by a woman and inserted into a man's anus. This is what really appalled her. She was terrified that her son was homosexual. She expressed no curiosity about her son's feelings or how he had developed those feelings. She wanted to know if she could call me now and then to check in on progress. My first impression of her was of a very controlling person who also wanted to control the therapy and who, at the same time, had no idea at all of how controlling she was. The son was slight of build and smiled a lot. The mother was short, round, and firm, and she never smiled. She looked like her muscles were so tightly wrapped around her bones that if you bent an elbow too quickly a bone would snap.

Mr. A's mother called me every few weeks to get a report on his progress. Primarily she needed reassurance that he was not homosexual. She was also afraid that the kinky pornographic scenes she had witnessed meant her son was crazy. A few months later Mr. A's father called to make an appointment. He was a mild-mannered man who treated me with a great deal of respect. He seemed to have been sent in by his wife to get a sense of me. He expressed concern that his son was becoming aggressive, describing an incident in which Mr. A was driving and the father had offered guidance from the backseat and Mr. A had asked the father to stop being a backseat driver. "That seemed rude to me and also to my wife." Actually, I had been working with Mr. A to help him to become more assertive; I tried to explain this to the father, and he nodded as if he understood. But I don't think he really did.

From the second session on the son came alone. He was very shy and polite and called me "Sir." Like his mother, he had a very difficult time talking about sex. He didn't even want to use the word "sex." Nor could he say "homosexual" or "perverted". Instead he would haltingly speak of an attraction that made him uncomfortable or of a compulsion that made him wince. When I asked him how he felt about his mother bringing him to therapy, he said he felt fine about it. He thought he probably needed it. I asked if he felt hurt at all by her bringing him to therapy and he said no, he wasn't aware of any feelings like that. I asked him how he felt when his parents questioned him after his mother had seen the porn. He said he could understand *how they felt*. I asked him again how he felt. He didn't know. He was almost like an automaton, answering my questions but not volunteering anything. Upon some prodding, he began to tell me his story.

Mr. A was a junior in a private Eastern college. His parents were paying the tuition and he was expected to come home every weekend. His father was a stock broker and his mother a housewife. He was expected to talk to his mother every day on the phone, and sometimes his father as well. He had never had sex with either a woman or a man. He hardly ever masturbated because it made him feel guilty. His only close bonds were with his parents and his younger brother; he had no close friends. The family was very religious and he was contemplating becoming a priest. His brother and he were both adopted. He reported that his mother and father had tried to have a baby for several years and then they had given up and gone the adoption route. Mr. A could never remember his father and mother exchanging a sexual kiss, and as far back as he could remember they slept in separate rooms.

He could not remember any dreams or fantasies, so I told him to keep a journal. His first masturbation happened, he said, by accident. He was about fifteen and lying on his stomach on the floor of his room and he began to rub himself against the floor because it was a strange sensation, and suddenly he had an orgasm. He was horrified by the experience, faintly aware that it was sexual. He thought that it was very sinful to masturbate. He thought that it was sinful to think about having sex with a girl. He thought it was even more sinful to think about sex with men. The persona he showed to peers was that of an asexual guy, a clown, harmless, noncompetitive and a good listener. His two passions were religion and collecting movie musicals.

In the beginning he could remember almost nothing of his early childhood. Gradually bits and pieces came up. A memory popped up of his mother telling him it was sinful for him to touch himself, then another memory of his mother refusing to tell him the name for his penis, then another memory of wandering into the bathroom and seeing his mother naked and her muttering, "Get out!" An important detail of the last memory was that his mother was wearing red high-heeled shoes. There were no feelings connected with any of these memories. The angriest he ever remembered his mother becoming was when he didn't lift the lid before he urinated. He said she "flipped out like she was having an attack of rabies." Although he didn't recall anything about potty training, he did recall that his mother was "obsessed with germs" and that she would give him and his brother enemas once a month to "clean out" their systems. He recalled that the enemas weren't "unpleasant," and that, in fact, "in some strange way I looked forward to them." He also recalled that at some age, he couldn't remember exactly when, he had cried that he hated his mother. She immediately slapped him and told him that she would forgive him because the Devil had obviously gotten inside him. He recalled other things later on, such as his mother confiding in him about his father, whose temper she resented. "Don't be like your father. He's not a good model," she repeated over and over. As the pieces came up I was able to put together a picture of an austere childhood in which responsibility, obedience and diligence were primary. He was not encouraged to play, especially with neighboring children, whom her mother viewed critically. Sexual play and any talk of sexual subjects was strictly forbidden. He was not allowed to express real feelings, especially negative feelings, nor to disagree with either of his parents. Assertiveness was seen as aggressive. At the same time, he was repeatedly reminded of how lucky he was to have been adopted by them and what a happy family he had found.

This is one of those cases that seems to clearly demonstrate Liang's theory (1971) that the parents in a family are like hypnotists who, very early on, make strong, repetitive suggestions that determine what a child becomes. As Liang puts it, "The hypnotists (the parents) are already hypnotized (by their parents) and are carrying out their instructions, by bringing their children up to bring their children up...in such a way, which includes not realizing that one is carrying out instructions" (p. 71). Liang explains that this state is easily induced under hypnosis, when an individual is instructed, for example, to walk across the room and open the window upon waking from the trance. The hypnotist might also instruct the individual to remember nothing about the suggestions but to think of a good reason for opening the window. The individual wakes up, opens the window, and exclaims "It's warm in here." A parent may induce a particular form of behavior by suggestion, such as by telling a child again and again that sex is dirty or that the products of his penis (urine, semen) are dirty. The child (in our case, Mr. A) grows up to develop negative attitudes toward his penis without remembering why he feels that way.

After Mr. A had been in therapy for a few months I was able to do a diagnosis. He suffered from a mixture of disorders. He was confused about his sexual orientation, sometimes fantasizing about males, sometimes about females, but in either case in his fantasies he was always the subject of their cruelty and domination. Therefore I saw him as having a bisexual orientation with masochistic features. He also had a masochistic personality disorder, which led him to often get into situations where he was bullied, ridiculed and in other ways disparaged. He also had features of dependent personality, as his parents had thoroughly trained him to be dependent on them, and finally I detected an avoidance personality disorder--a tendency to want to avoid any conflict or any situation in which he might be rejected. This mixture of mental disorders caused him to be unable to cope with the day to day situations that came up in his life, to procrastinate about things (such as deciding on a college major), and to eschew college social activities, job interviews, and relationships in general. The mixture also led him to escape by watching movie musical every spare moment, sometimes all night long.

He also continued to watch BDSM porn (as it's called in the industry) and feel guilty about it. He was attracted to certain things in particular: dominant, sadistic women who wore high-heeled shoes, who stabbed a man's genitals with them, and wore strap-ons and anally penetrated the man. I had him talk about his sexuality, his fear of masturbation, his compulsion to watch porn, and his reluctance to seek out friendships. I tried to be a reasonable and compassionate alter ego, to show him how his own superego should be. About six months into therapy he was starting to feel a little stronger and he began a relationship with a fellow student at his college.

It was she who initiated the relationship. They had started out as friends and one day she suggested they go further, so for a few weeks they tried a sexual relationship. He told me that early on he had seen a pair of high-heeled shoes in her closet and fantasized about her stabbing him in the penis with them. She turned out to be a girl who was quite ego-centric. I encouraged him to verbalize his feelings to her and he did. Unfortunately, she was completely unable to hear his feelings and, indeed, felt victimized by him. When he told her he felt afraid of sex with her, she cut him off and responded, "What are you saying? What am I, some kind of monster? So it's my fault you can't get an erection?" She could only see things from her own perspective, and she expected him to relate to her on her terms. For a long time he never tried anything sexual with her other than kissing and petting she initiated, thinking it would be offensive to her. She took the lead in all matters. When they finally had sex one night, she ridiculed him again, as she had several times before, because he wasn't able to get an erection, and because he was so "wimpy in bed." She tried to get him erect for a long time, then sighed and demanded that he go down on her and satisfy her. "It's the least you can do." Although he felt hurt by her behavior, he also felt excited. He said, "Something about it felt almost familiar, comforting." For many days after that he had fantasies of her using a strap-on dildo on him. This thought excited him more than anything.

However, he felt so guilty and conflicted about the relationship that he couldn't bear to go on with it and broke off soon afterwards. On the one hand he had his strong feelings of sexual attraction to this fetish. On the other hand he had equally strong feelings of guilt related to his religious sentiments and his lifelong training that sex was sinful and dirty, especially the kind of sex that stirred him most.

His treatment ended abruptly before the year was out. His mother expressed concern about his progress during her telephone conversations with me and indicated that her insurance would be running out. One day I received an email from Mr. A thanking me for my service and promising that he would contact me again if he needed my help.

### Discussion

Mr. A's masochistic fantasies of torture and anal penetration, his fetish for high-heeled shoes, and his attraction to a woman who was controlling and sadistic, all correlated with his mother's treatment of him as a young child. From the pieces of memory that had come up and what I knew of his mother from her visit to my office and her telephone calls, I surmised that his mother had been quite controlling to the point of being obsessively controlling. She herself obviously suffered from mental disorders, most likely obsessive-compulsive disorder and possibly also histrionic disorder. In a quiet way she seemed to tyrannize the family. She not only assaulted Mr. A's sexuality and masculinity, making him feel that both were disgusting (i.e., the fit of temper she had when he did not lift the lid before he urinated), she also discouraged any signs of initiative that would separate him from her. She trained him to talk everything over with her, including even the minutest details of his eating or bathroom habits, and was made to feel that he couldn't judge anything or decide anything on his own.

The memory of Mr. A's wondering into the bathroom and

seeing his mother naked, wearing red high-heeled shoes is also relevant, not only to his fetish about high-heeled shoes, but also to his attraction to phallic women. It would appear that his fetish was directly linked to this memory, which was heightened by being forbidden when his mother shouted at him, "Get out!" As the old adage goes, if you forbid a child to do something, he will want to do it all the more.The monthly enemas were linked in his mind with sexual penetration and hence tie in with his desire to be penetrated by a woman. When his mother slapped him for saying he hated her and told him he had "The Devil" in him, this not only reinforced his feeling that his masculinity was evil, but that his feelings were bad. Eventually he learned that he could not set his own boundaries, he could not have his own thoughts, particularly sexual thoughts, he could not have any sexual thoughts about her or about any female, he could not have any real feelings (but rather had to act "as if"), and he had to allow his mother to frame how he saw himself. His mother was apparently completely unaware that the had any mental disorders, and was convinced that she and only she knew what was right and wrong in the family and in the world. Neither Mr. A nor anybody else could ever contradict her. Little wonder then that as an adult he was attracted to a woman who had high-heeled shoes in her closet and who was as sadistic and self-centered as his mother.

Krafft-Ebing (1886), who was the first psychologist to extensively study perverse behavior, made a distinction between what he called 'physiological fetishism', or a preference for certain particular physical characteristics in persons of the opposite sex, and what he defined as 'pathological, erotic fetishism'. This was not merely directed to particular portions of the body, but extended to inanimate objects, usually articles of female apparel, or towards particular materials such as furs or velvet. But there was no hard and fast dividing line. The fetishist of the body part was stimulated by something which would normally arouse the sexual instinct, but his sexual interests were restricted to that particular part. There were also fetishists who were attracted to some bodily part without wanting to have sex, and those interested in particular kinds of bodies--for example, those exhibiting some kind of deformity. Krafft-Ebing also suggests degrees of attraction, from states in which intercourse was more pleasurable if the object were present, to states in which sex was less pleasurable if the object were absent, to states in which the man experienced impotence if the object were absent.

Krafft-Ebing attributed the development of fetishism to some event whereby erotic feelings became associated with some particular body part or object; this is still today usually considered to play a significant part in its etiology. While invoking environmental circumstances, he also suggested that individuals who formed these bizarre associations were predisposed to psychopathic states and excessive sexual desire, in keeping with his theories about the role of degenerate heredity and neuropathy in the etiology of sexual disorders. I differ with Kraftt-Ebing on this score, because I do not think heredity plays any role in perversions.

Freud's (1927) interpretation of the fetish is that the object represents a symbolic phallus, and it operates as either a protection against the fetishist's fear of castration, or a denial of the penis-less state of the woman. By focusing indirectly at an object instead of at the woman, the fetishist distances himself from the castration threat. It seems also to be the case that the fetish operates as a defense against the fear of castration (impotence) if it is employed in a coital situation: it may do this by acting as a reliable stimulus to arousal and erection, or possibly more magically by its association with sexual arousal.

Greenson (1966) described a case in which he was able to observe the formation of a fetish as it happened. Lance, who was five and a half, was fond of walking around in his mother's high-heeled shoes, and had actually done so since before he was one year old, when he had started to walk. At the time he had put on his mother's shoes and his older sister and his mother thought it was cute, so they did not discourage him (and in fact, through their approving laughter encouraged him). As Greenson noted, "Later on he was able to run up and down stairs in these shoes, to climb trees in them, ride his bicycle, etc. He gradually put on other items of clothing: blouse, stockings, purse, hats, etc., until he began to insist on dressing like a girl" (p. 252-253). Greenson relates that Lance's father was on very bad terms with his mother and was hardly present at all in the household. Hence Lance's personality was influenced by his older sister and his mother. Of his mother, Greenson said, "The tactile and visual overexposure to her body served to confuse his gender identity (p. 264).

A more recent writer on the subject, Bancroft (1989), brings in behavioral experiments that demonstrate that the male erectile response is capable of being conditioned to react to unusual stimuli. In these experiments, male subjects were conditioned to respond to various inanimate objects that were paired with females. Hence classical conditioning was linked to the development of fetishes. The reason why the conditioned response to particular stimuli results in the formation of a fetish more often in the male may be, Bancroft suggests, because of the obviousness of penile erection. This sets up a visual and sensory link between the object of the stimulus and sexual arousal. Women may be less likely to identify pleasurable feelings invoked by certain objects or textures as specifically sexual in nature (experimental evidence demonstrating women's physiological signs of arousal, even though they denied erotic response, to sexually stimulating visual materials tends to corroborate this possibility.

Mr. A's perversity, like the cases of Krafft-Ebing and

Greenson, involves a child whose perverse behavior was reinforced by situations in his childhoods. Numerous writers have made the connection between the development of perversity and perverse parenting, but none have come out and declared that perversity in a male child is in direct proportion to perverse mothering--and later perverse fathering. Such as the theory that I am proposing here, based not only on my work with Mr. A and others, but also on my reading over the literature. First of all Mr. A's retreat from, and avoidance of sex, was directly related to his mother's censorship of sex and her own avoidance of it. His attraction to masochistic relationships with women who had a sadistic and derogatory attitude ward his masculinity and sexuality seemed to be directly related to his mother often cruel and derogatory attitude. As for his fetish (the high heeled shoes), it seemed to have been reinforced by his vision of his mother's shoes during the bathroom scene, and the forbidding remark that accompanied this vision--"Get out!" This angry exclamation apparently aroused excitement, curiosity and libidinal involvement. In addition, the mother's unawareness of her feelings also matched up with the boy's unawareness of his feelings.

There are some humans whose identity and sense of self is very fragile. In such people, the discrepancy between what is true and what they want to believe is so large that they will do anything to avoid the truth. They construct an elaborate myth, or lie, about who they are, why they do what they do, what they believe. This, in act, is the narcissistic mode of being, and that narcissism is especially prominent in cases of gender narcissism. Mr. A's mother was of this sort. She was like the Queen in the children's story, "Snow White," who had to have a mirror that told her she was the fairest of the land. Her husband and children had to mirror her exactly. If they didn't, she would fly into a rage. Hence she went about her perverse mothering unabated.

## Concluding Remarks

Sexual perversity arises when the relationship between the sexes goes awry. I believe there is a correlation between perversity in males and perversity in females. Each affects the other. Perverse mothering results in male perversity. Male perversity, in turn, elicits female perversity in many complex ways, from girlhood to womanhood. Female perversity, in turn, provokes male perversity, particularly within the mother-son relationship. Female perversity is most evident in styles of mothering. Male perversity is most apparent in perverse sexual activities. Perverse mothering reinforces perverse sexual development in boys, while perverse fathering models behavior fueled by castration fear and perverse ideology. This chain can be traced back for generations.

I anticipate that some will object to the term "perverse mothering," because it will be seen as insulting to mothers. However, if my theory is correct: that perverse mothering leads to the development of male perversity, and visa versa, then it would seem more important for us to cure this syndrome and this form of sexual disorder than to spare the feelings of the persons who engender it. It is also insulting to an alcoholic to tell him he has a drinking problem or, as AA would put it, a disease. Yet it must be done if the alcoholic is to cure himself. We seem to have become a society that would rather enable than cure; that is, enable parents with mental disorders to think they are normal (and thus spare their feelings) than to cure them (which means telling them the truth) so that they can have the proper attitude toward her children.

The notion that perversions are simply a matter of choice and should be accepted is also fashionable today. I saw a news report about a mother who wrote a book about her son, "The Princess boy," about a boy who liked dressing in girl's clothes. This mother was embraced as a heroine of human rights. The truth is that a perversion is not a simple matter of choice concerning clothing. Mr. A's problem was more than a fetish about high-heeled shoes; it was an overall disturbance that affected all aspects of his life. Those who have studied perversions have observed the alienation, deficiency of self-esteem, and fear of self-assertion that are generally associated with perversions. Perverse behavior and perverse mothering is growing in the West and so are social problems. When we look at any kind of behavior, we need to look at the big picture. What is the effect on society?

*References:*

Bancroft, J. (1989). *Human Sexuality and Its Problems.* New York: W. W. Norton.

Bowlby, J. (1979). *The Making and Breaking of Affectional Bonds.* London: Tavistock.

Chasseguet-Smirgel (1985). *Creativity and Perversion.* London: Free Association Books.

Fenichel, D. (1945). *The Psychoanalytic Theory of Neuroses.* New York: Norton.

Freud, S. (1905*). Three Essays on the Theory of Sexuality.* Standard Edition: 7.

-- (1916). Freud, S. (1916). *Leonardo Da Vinci and a Memory of His Childhood.* Standard Edition, 11:57-137.

-- (1920). The psychogenesis of a case of female sexuality. Standard Edition: 18:146-174.

-- (1927). Fetishism. Standard Edition, 21: 147-157.

Gillespie, W. H. (1956). The general theory of sexual perversions. *International Journal of Psycho-Analysis*, 37:396-403.

Greenson, R. (1966). The Technique and Practice of Psychoanalysis, Vol. 1. New York: International Universities Press.

Kahn, M. M. R. (1979). *Alienation in the Perversions*. New York: International Universities Press.

Kaplan, L, J. (1993). *Female Perversions*. London: Penguin.

Kaplan, H. S. (1979). *Disorders of Sexual Desire*. New York: Simon & Schuster.

Krafft-Ebing, R. V. (1886). *Psychopathia Sexualis*. London: Bloat Books, 1999

Liang, J. D. (1971). *The Politics of the Family*. London: Tavistock.

McDougall, J. (1995). *The Many Faces of Eros*. London: Free Association Books.

Schoenewolf, G. (1989). Sexual Animosity between Men and Women. Northvale, NJ: Jason Aronson.

Shengold, L. (1992). *Halo in the Sky: Observations on Halo and Defense*. New Haven, CT: Yale university Press.

Socarides, C. W. (1978). *Homosexuality*. Northvale, NJ: Jason Aronson.

-- (1979). A unitary theory of sexual perversions. In *On*

*Sexuality*, ed. T. B. Karasu and C W. Socarides, pp. 161-188. New York: International Universities Press.

Stoller, R. J. (1968). Sex and Gender. *The Development of Masculinity and Femininity*. London: H. Karnac, 1984.

# 7

# The Psychology of Hate

This entry from the *Encyclopedia of Human* Behavior defines hate as a state of arousal or excitation in humans in which anger, negative judgments and impulses of destruction predominate. This state is produced by a combination of biological and environmental factors. There are various pathological states of hate, and manifestations of hate are numerous, ranging from subtle indirect expressions to outright violence and war. However, not all hate is bad; some hate is destructive while other hate can be constructive.

## The Biological Roots of Hate

Hate itself is not innate; however, the emotion of anger and the impulse toward aggression are part of the human constitution. And since hate is generally associated with anger and aggression, we can therefore say that it is indirectly innate.

An innate aggressive drive has been observed throughout the animal kingdom. Countless investigations have proven that fighting behavior in animals is genetically programmed and they have uncovered innate, species-specific patterns of fighting. For example, cichlids (a species of fish), even when they have been isolated from parents at birth, begin to fight with rivals by beating them with their tails and pushing or pulling them with their mouths; marine iguanas reared in isolation fight by butting their heads together; lava lizards lash one another with their tails; fighting cocks kick at one another with their claws; and roe buck attack with their antlers. All of this fighting happens spontaneously at a certain point in development.

An innate aggressive drive has also been observed in human beings and has primarily been linked to the "struggle for survival" (Charles Darwin's term) or to a territorial instinct. Aggression in human history is associated with the hunting and gathering of primitive men, with the territorial separation of—and strife between—individuals, groups and nations, and to the formation of social hierarchies or ranking orders. One can also see manifestations of this drive in the rough play of young boys and in the athletic competition of adults. Indeed, all humans show the unmistakable tendency to keep their distance from strangers due to a fear of their aggression.

Eibl-Eibesfeldt (1974), an ethologist, has noted that the disposition for aggression can be found in all human societies throughout the world. Threat displays by means of ornament, weaponry, feathers, masks, skins, boots, and phallic exposure as well as facial expressions of threat and rage are universal. People from around the world stomp their feet and clench their fists when they are angry. Also widespread throughout the world is the glorification of aggression through heroic sagas, coats of arms, and medals. Indeed, the history of humankind is the history of conflict and war.

Biologically, aggression is associated with a "fight or flight" response that arouses the sympathetic nervous system and the endocrine system. This is a coordinated operation that goes into effect when an individual feels stress. The stressor excites the hypothalamus (firing brain cells) to produce a substance that stimulates the pituitary and adrenal glands to discharge corticoids (such as adrenalin) into the blood. This in turn elicits thymus shrinkage and releases sugar; and at the same time it also arouses the sympathetic nervous system, which contracts muscles and blood vessels. If an individual is in a state of arousal over a period of time, that can further affect the body's operation and chemistry. In addition, sudden increases of sexual hormones such as testosterone and estrogen can also arouse aggression.

Experimental psychologists have demonstrated a rage reaction by attaching electrodes to the hypothalamus. Subjects have been induced to states of extreme anger and have been impelled to perform acts of violence. Such experiments have also shown that while subjects are in such a state of induced rage, their cognitive abilities change; anger leads to negative judgments (hate) and the desire to eliminate the source of the anger (the stressor) by destroying it. The drive-reduction theory in psychology—stating that human motivation stems from the need to reduce imbalances in homeostasis—describes this phenomenon.

There is some variation in the amount of innate aggression in each individual at birth. Thomas and Chess (1968) discovered that some babies are easy to care for, some are cranky and difficult to care for, and some are slow to warm up. Their research proved that humans are not blank slates when born but come already equipped with temperamental differences. It is not clear, however, whether this variation in infant aggressiveness is due to genetics or to environmental conditions during pregnancy. Research has shown, for example, that mothers who are depressed (a state of anger and hate turned inwards) during pregnancy give birth to hyperactive infants. On the other hand, not all cranky babies have depressed mothers.

The neural correlates of hate have been investigated with an MRI procedure (Zeki and Romaya, 2008). In this experiment, people had their brains scanned while viewing pictures of people they hated. The results showed increased activity in the medial frontal gyrus, right putamen, bilaterally in the premotor cortex, in the frontal pole, and bilaterally in the medial insula of the human brain. Zeki and Romaya concluded that there is a distinct pattern of brain activity that occurs when people are experiencing hatred. The link between brain activity and hate does not in and of itself implicate a genetic cause (brain activity can also be affected by the environment), but it does point to biology.

Hate, then, is the cognitive component of the "fight or flight" arousal state and as all other genetic aspects of emotion. This state of aggressive arousal differs from other states of excitement such as anxiety or nervous anticipation, although these too involve the sympathetic nervous system. The biological roots of aggression eventually stimulate negative thought patterns in the brain. We hate that which frightens, frustrates, or unsettles us. This hate (and the state of arousal that underlies it) can be temporary or long term, and it can be conscious or unconscious. In some cases people can be in a state of chronic tension and not know it, and they can feel hate and not be aware of it.

### The Environmental Roots of Hate

While there is undoubtedly an innate aggressive drive in humans, that drive cannot become aroused in and of itself. Aggression and hate depend on an interplay of innate and environmental factors. The mixture of latent (biological) and environmental factors may differ from individual to individual.

There are numerous theories about what kinds of environmental factors lead to aggression and hate. One theory focuses on the stressful changes in the environment that require adjustment: getting a divorce, getting fired, getting married, having a child, losing a loved one—these all bring about stress and are sometimes accompanied by aggression and hate. Another theory centers on frustration, holding that aggression and hate are linked to frustration of some kind (unrequited love, envy, unfulfilled ambitions, etc.). Another posits that aggression and hate are connected with threats to survival, as when a rival threatens to take one's job or the government takes away one's food stamps. Another theory holds that hate may be transmitted through various psychological means such as identification (as when a child identifies with a parent) or indoctrination (as when an individual or group is "brain-washed" into adapting a negative attitude toward another individual or group.

Studies of infants show a relationship between bonding and aggression. There is a period of life in which bonding with a loving caretaker is essential for survival. In one study, 91 infants in a foundling home during a war were separated from their mothers after the age of 3 months and fed by a succession of busy nurses.  Thirty-four of the infants died by the second year, and a pattern was observed.  Upon first being separated from their mothers, infants would typically cry and cling angrily to whatever nurse was feeding them (aggression turned outward); then they would go through a phase of anaclitic depression, lying sullenly in their cribs (aggression turned inward); then motor retardation would set in; and finally they would develop marasmus (somatizing their aggression into problems with eating).  These studies show that bonding is critical during this early phase of development, and that aggression and destruction erupt as a defense against the loss of this bonding (Spitz, 1965).

Hence, the seeds of the environmental contribution to the formation of aggression and hate are laid in earliest childhood and are transmitted in the milieu of the family.  Our first experience of love stems from this earliest bonding with our maternal caretaker, a bonding that, when successful, evokes feelings of gratitude, security, fulfillment, and contentment (Klein, 1957).  Our first experience of hate also stems from this period.  If this first relationship is deficient, we feel cut off, frustrated, threatened, and enraged.  We want to destroy this deficient caretaker (bite the breast that feeds us) or, if that is not possible, to destroy ourselves.  In other words, when our survival is threatened, the biological "fight or flight" response kicks in, our system is aroused, and we become enraged and hateful.  This first relationship is not only the prototype and precursor of what is to come, it may also create fixations or "faults" that establish a tendency toward hating.  Like underground faults that lead to future earthquakes, human development fixations may lead to future emotional disturbances, aggression, and hate.

As we develop other environmental factors also help to shape our capacities for loving and hating.  Other figures—the father, siblings, grandparents, aunts, and uncles—begin to exert an influence in how we love and hate.  We form identificational bonds with those we admire and those we fear and tend to incorporate their ways of loving and hating.  If our parenting is punitive or abusive (and thereby hateful), we may grow up to be punitive and abusive to others (or to submit to abuse and/or abuse ourselves). If the parenting is permissive (a disguised form of hate under which a parent unconsciously withholds proper guidance), we may grow up to be self-indulgent and bratty (hatefully inconsiderate and demanding), but permissive to our own children and those who ally with us. If our family values are religious and distrustful of those who are not religious, we may grow up to adopt these values. We may feel that anybody who is not of our faith represents a threat to our security and hence is to be hated (i.e., to be pitied and rescued). If our family values are ideological and distrustful of anybody who does not share our ideology, we may grow up to adopt this ideology. We may then feel that anybody who is not of our ideological or political persuasion represents a threat to our security and hence is to be hated (i.e., ridiculed and dismissed).

Envy and jealousy are often closely related to hate. When we feel envious or jealous, our "fight or flight" response is also aroused and we feel resentment (a form of hate) toward those we envy and experience their existence as an insult and threat to our own. However, the extent to which envy and jealousy prevail in each individual's psychodynamics depends upon upbringing. A tendency toward feeling envy or jealousy may result from childhood spoiling and pampering, from an identification with a parent who has this tendency, or from early childhood fixations that result in inferiority or castration complexes. The latter cause individuals to feel that they, their bodies, their sexual organs, and their lots in life, are inferior, disadvantaged, or threatened.

Later, in adulthood, both personal and larger social and cultural factors can influence our hatred. If we already have fixations from early childhood, any situations in our adult lives that repeat the events of those fixations will upset us, arouse us, and induce a hate reaction. If we have lost our mother at two years of age, any loss later on may bring about a breakdown into depression (self-hate). If we have felt severely deprived, any deprivation will be severely upsetting; if we have felt extremely indulged and pampered, any failure of our later environment to duplicate this indulgence and pampering will arouse rage, etc.

In addition, those who have had deficient bonding (or socialization) in early childhood and who have developed fixations or tendencies toward negative thinking and hating will be the most influenced by aversive social or cultural factors. They will be the first to join movements that give them a justification for hating some designated enemy. They will be the first to rail against another nation that has temporarily been designated as a country's enemy. They will be the first to discriminate against others or other groups (while accusing the other group of discriminating against them). They will be the first to join any angry mob.

Psychological tests show that how we perceive things is greatly influenced by our personality. For example, the Rorschach Inkblot Test may be given to several individuals and each will see different things in the ink blots. In a section from one of these blots, some individuals may see two angels with wings, while others may see two boys urinating, and still others may see two scuba divers roasting fish over a fire. What we see in these blots depends on our personality make-up (i.e., whether we are obsessive-compulsive, histrionic, paranoid, psychotic, or the like). In other words, our early childhood conditioning influences how we perceive the world; we may perceive some event as being threatening (and respond with anger and hatred), while another person may perceive the same event differently. Threats and hate are often in the eye of the beholder.

Numerous social and cultural factors may arouse aggression and hate. Times of war and economic depression are two of the most dramatic examples of this. During such times, wide-scale anger, fear, depression, and sometimes hysteria run high, and each individual in a society feels affected by such emotions and these can lead to attitudes of blame and hate for that which is designated as the cause of this misfortune (the enemy country, the government, Republicans, etc.). Social or cultural changes may also arouse aggression and hatred. For example, an anthropologist studied how an abrupt change in the system and values of a primitive village resulted in an increase in community stress and aggression. Before the change, the community as a whole cultivated and distributed food more or less in a communistic fashion. When it was decreed that all individuals would henceforth be responsible for their own subsistence, there was an aggressive scramble to acquire the uncultivated wet valleys and a subsequent increase in animosity and criminality. People became hostile to one another, feared one another, envied one another, and became ruthless in dealing with one another. Something like this occurred in Russia when the Communist government toppled in 1991. Poverty and overcrowding can also arouse aggression and hate, as can a lack of meaningful job opportunities. The range of social factors is myriad.

Authority figures can arouse and shape hatred. Stanley Milgram's famous experiment at Yale University (Milgram, 1974) provided a scientific understanding of this phenomenon. In his study he told his subjects—men and women from all walks of life—that they were participating in an experiment to test the effects of punishment on learning. Each subject was asked to take the role of teacher and to deliver electric shocks to a "student" who was actually a paid actor. The student was strapped into a chair in a separate room and received apparent electric shocks. The teacher was instructed to ask the student questions, and was told by the experimenter to administer various doses of electricity by using knobs on a fake electric generator. The knobs were labeled from 15 to 450 volts. The teachers were instructed to give increasingly stronger shocks, and the students would pretend to receive the shocks and cry out and moan in agony and beg the teachers to stop. If a teacher seemed doubtful about administering the shocks, the experimenter, standing beside the teacher, would say in a firm, authoritative voice, "You must go on." The experimenter would reassure the teacher that no harm was being done. Although some subjects showed signs of great conflict, 65% of them continued to deliver what they thought were 450 volts of electricity to a screaming human being. Underneath label of "450 volts" was a disclaimer: "Warning: Severe shock."

This experiment showed that to some degree or another people are willing to administer electric shock (act out hate) if an authority figure gives permission to do so. There are several explanations for this. Throughout the history of humankind we have shown a need to believe in something greater than ourselves and to obey it—whether it is a king or a president or a Pope; whether it is a God or many gods or a sacred book underneath some religion or mythology; or whether it is an idea or philosophy or political movement. This higher authority absolves us of responsibility. We particularly look for ways in which we can act out hate without feeling responsible or guilty about it. Hence, to the degree that we have not fully separated from our parents and fully matured, we will need such surrogate authorities to believe in and take responsibility for our decisions. In addition, to the extent we have developed fixations and faults, we will have pent-up rage and potential hatred, and we will look for an excuse (an authority figure's permission) to vent it.

The state of hating, then, is the culmination of a complex process involving the interplay of the innate human aggressive drive, early childhood conditioning, and later personal and societal environmental forces. Sometimes hatred erupts for a short time and is a temporary response to a specific event; while in other cases hatred is chronic and becomes an ingrained trait resulting from deeply traumatic or ongoing aversive events.

### Manifestations of Hate

Manifestations of hate range from the obvious and simple to the subtle and complex. Obvious and simple forms include direct verbal expressions such as, "I hate you!" or "You stupid idiot!" as well as acts of violence such as murder, rape, or war. More subtle and complex manifestations comprise a multitude of manipulations, ploys, stings, attitudes, and acts through which hate is indirectly or covertly expressed. These include, to name just a few examples, forgetting an appointment, pretending to like people whom one hates and thereby "killing them with kindness," having an affair with a married man or woman, steeling memo pads or paperclips from the company for which one works, or telling a child to "stop crying or I'll give you something to really cry about."

Generally, one can say that those people who have attained emotional health, established genuine bonds with others, and feel connected to their vocation, will manifest the least hate. People will manifest more hate if they have not matured emotionally, have not established genuine bonds with others, and do not feel connected to a vocation. The latter will feel less secure and hence their aggressive response and hatred will be more easily aroused, either toward others or toward themselves. They will act out in various ways in order to try to compensate for their feelings of insecurity, alienation, and rage—such acting out being the result of their hate. The more aggression they bring into the world, the more disturbed will be their relation to the world.

Hate can be manifested in different types of psychopathology, either indirectly or directly. A passive-aggressive personality acts out anger in very indirect ways. Instead of telling you he hates you, he will forget your dinner appointment and then apologize profusely. An obsessive-compulsive personality expresses hate by over-controlling people and refusing real intimacy. A masochistic personality will provoke others into being hateful so that he/she can feel (hatefully) victimized and superior. A paranoid personality denies his own anger and projects that others are out to get him. (In doing so he unwittingly causes others, through projective identification, to want to get him.) A histrionic personality expresses hate through sexual teasing and fits. A depressive personality hates the world and also hates himself. His hate may be somatized has insomnia, or various pains and aches. A schizophrenic personality expresses hate through various grandiose delusions (through which he triumphs on enemies).

As noted above, hate can be expressed in three basic ways: it can be expressed in a direct, verbal way, it can be acted out, and it can be somatized. Direct verbal expressions of hate include any verbal statement of hate including curses, insults, threats, death wishes, and the like. The acting out of hate includes any action that is rude, hostile, rejecting, excluding, manipulative, deceitful, defiant, shaming, ridiculing, contemptuous, threatening, violent, and the like. Somatizing hate has to do with the "bottling up" of aggression so that it takes a toll on one's own body, as when one develops heart disease due to a stressful, hate-inducing life experience. Somatizing also includes using illness to manipulate others, as when an individual develops a hysterical paralysis out of resentment at not being cared for—such paralysis forcing others to care for the individual.

According to Freud, most of our hateful, aggressive impulses remain unconscious. What we are conscious of is the most surface reason for our hate. Thus we may tell a friend we hate a certain person because he is always trying to get attention. What we remain unconscious of is that, on the deepest level, we hate that person because we are jealous of him for getting attention that we wish we could get. We may not wish to acknowledge that we hate our brother, for there is a strong social taboo against such hatred; so instead we may show great kindness to this brother and even convince ourselves that we love him, but at the same time we may constantly forget his birthday, neglect to write to him, flirt with his wife, and in other ways act out unconscious hate. We chop down tropical forests and drive gasoline-fueled automobiles to advance our immediate goals while at the same time passively killing our planet and remaining collectively unconscious of our own mass death wish.

The most destructive manifestations of hate occur in families. "Power does not corrupt men," Bernard Shaw said; "fools, however, if they get into positions of power, corrupt power." To be a parent is to be in a position of absolute power over another human being, and unfortunately, many parents harbor unconscious aggression and hate that gets taken out on their children. Indeed, no occupation or even government gives its leader as much power as a parent has over a child, and that power is held practically sacred and shielded from the public eye. In a sense, each of us, as children are slaves to our parents. Some slave owners are loving, some are not.

The root cause of much environmental hate is the dysfunctional family, with its hotbed of unresolved unconscious anger. Parental expressions of hate can begin even before birth. Much recent research has focused on how traumas to the unborn fetus can affect later personality development. Mothers can express passive hate during pregnancy if they smoke, drink or take drugs, if they are careless with their diet, or if they behave recklessly. Fathers can express hate by abusing the mother during pregnancy causing stress, which in turn affects the growing fetus. Once the child is born parents can express hate in the obvious ways such as beatings, sexual molestation, scapegoating, degradation, or neglect, or more subtle kinds of emotional abuse, such as when a parent constantly compares one child unfavorably with his older brother or with his friends and makes him feel inferior. Rene Spitz, observing 203 mother and infant dyads in an institution, wrote of the indirect and unconscious ways caretakers can express hate during the first year of life. For example, he described caretakers who related to their infants with "primary anxious over-permissiveness" and others who acted out "hostility in the guise of anxiety." In each of these cases, the caretakers were compensating for unconscious feelings of resentment toward the child (usually an unwanted child) through an exaggerated anxiety and over-concern with the child's welfare. He noted a high degree of eczema in the infants of such caretakers. It is a general principle in psychoanalysis that an obsessive over-concern with somebody's welfare masks an unconscious wish for their harm.

The family can be a cycle of hate and, generation after generation, a breeding ground of psychopathological hate. A caretaker can suffer from depression, particularly postpartum depression, resulting in her complete rejection of her infant during the weeks right after birth. Research has shown that maternal deprivation during the earliest stage of infancy can lead to severe disturbances, creating fixations that program an individual to later have a tendency to withdraw from contact with others and develop various psychopathologic traits such as depression, sociopathic personality, or schizophrenia.

An obsessive-compulsive caretaker may be obsessed with neatness and order to an extent that he or she will not allow any of the children to ever enjoy their existence and may, in turn, engender an obsessive-compulsive personality in the children. A caretaker may be a self-defeating martyr type, continually bemoaning his or her life, so that the children get not real love or attention but feel somehow responsible for victimizing the caretaker. This can affect their self-esteem and functioning later on, and they may later replicate this behavior with their own children. One parent may be abusive to the children while another may be passive-aggressive, silently or weakly allowing the abuse to go on. Children of abusive parents often grow up to abuse their own children.

On a broader spectrum, cultural forms of hate, such as racism and sexism or religious discrimination, have existed throughout history. History books are full of stories of mass discrimination, crusades, and exterminations of one group by another group. For example, in Nazi Germany 6 million Jews were rounded up, tortured, and exterminated in death camps. The Nazis decided that the Jews were evil exploiters of Germany, poisoning the purity of the German people, and therefore had to be eradicated. This gross expression of prejudice and cruelty by one people against another may be explained by focusing on the cultural milieu of Europe at the time. After Germany lost World War I, it was forced to sign a "humiliating" treaty with other European countries. Thereafter Germany became the scapegoat and laughing-stock of Europe. Germans were left thoroughly demoralized and sank into a psychological and economic depression. In the midst of a depression, people look for someone on whom to take out their anger. Along came Hitler, an authority figure who gave them permission to blame it on the Jews.

Milgram's study, mentioned previously, was spurred by the Nazi phenomenon.

During the course of history, some prejudices were approved while certain others were condemned. Hence, the Nazis approved prejudice against Jews, Christians at one point in history sanctified prejudice against people who held different religious beliefs, conducting inquisitions and witch hunts against heathens. In China, during the 1970s, the notorious "Gang of Four" formed the Red Guards and sent them out to rid the country of people who were politically and culturally incorrect; they roamed the countryside imprisoning and killing innocent people, burning houses, destroying monuments, and generally terrorizing everyone. In America, during the McCarthy hearings of the late 1940s, there was a mass persecution of communists (or anybody who looked as if he or she might have communist leanings). Later, McCarthy and his followers were condemned. Social movements often start out with idealistic goals of reforming some social problem, and they just as often end up as hotbeds of hatred that lead to mass hysteria.

Mass hysteria is a gradual or sudden eruption of collective

pent-up aggression and hate. If, say, many individuals have innate aggression which has unconscious sources, such individuals may later collectively be pushed into mass hysteria by current events. When a movement comes along that provides them with an opportunity to vent that pent-up hate toward an approved target group, they will be quickly and eagerly do so. The movement (Milgram's authority) gives them permission to do whatever they will. This collective hate may eventually get out of hand, as it did in Nazi Germany, the Crusades, and the Chinese Cultural Revolution.

Prejudice is a knife that cuts both ways. There are instances of real prejudice (unfounded hatred of an individual or group) and there are other instances in which charges of prejudice are a manipulation the aim of which is to discredit an opponent, to avoid taking responsibility for one's own hate, and to gain special privilege (due to being a victim of prejudice). A cause, religion, or movement becomes an extension of one's identity, mirroring one's ideal self, while that part of the self one wishes to disown—that is, the aggressive or hateful self—is projected onto the "out" group. We and our group are "in," good, righteous, and without ulterior motives. The "out" group is bad, morally repugnant, and imbued with evil motives. The more disturbed individuals are, the more they are prone to splitting others into stereotypes of good and bad, rather than seeing people as complex human beings. In our times, many liberals demonize conservatives this way, and many conservatives devalue liberals this way. Wilfred Gaylin (2004) notes that "Whereas the hater must demonize the object of its hatred, the prejudiced individual is more likely to dehumanize the object."

Acts of interpersonal violence as well as mass violence in wars are the most extreme manifestations of hate. When people are aroused to an extent that they kill each other, it is always due to fears that their own lives are in jeopardy. Jealous lovers kill because they feel that they themselves have been psychologically murdered by their lover's real or imagined infidelity. Wars are in part innate battles over territoriality (part of the human genetic endowment) and in part due to aversive environmental conditions. Narcissism (in the form of patriotism) often plays a role. German pride was hurt by the loss of World War I and by their economic depression. To "save face" Germany started World War II. Japan, wishing to expand its territory and enhance its narcissistic megalomania, joined in. Other nations felt threatened by them and like dominoes, one by one, were drawn into the war as each of their aggressive drive was stoked.

### Constructive and Destructive Hate

Not all hate is destructive. In general, the more mature an individual or country is, the more it can be aware of its hateful feelings and express them in a constructive way—that is, in a way that resolves conflict rather than feeding it. Hence, most direct verbal expressions of hate are constructive, while most acting out or somatizing of hate is destructive. There is a popular misconception that "love cures all." If by love one means, "Let's all be nice to each other and suppress our aggression and hate," then such sentiments, no matter how lofty, are misleading. They fail to appreciate fully the nature of aggression and hate; it cannot be willed away through calls for unity. The antidote to destructive hate is constructive hate, not guilty pseudo-love.

Donald Winnicott (1949), a British psychoanalyst, tells a story that illustrates this point. He once had an orphan boy live with him and his wife. This boy, who was about 9, was quite unsocialized and would have binges in which he would menace Winnicott and his wife and destroy their furniture. Winnicott noted that each of these incidents would arouse intense feelings of hate. The boy, he interpreted, had a need to induce others into hating him in order to feel worthwhile. To help the boy develop, Winnicott believed he had to let him know that he did indeed hate him. "If the patient seeks objective or justified hate, he must be able to reach it, else he cannot feel he can reach objective love," he writes. Therefore, each time the boy went on a binge of aggression, Winnicott would take him outside and set him down on the front porch, rain or sleet or snow. There was a special bell the boy could ring and he knew that if he rang it he would be readmitted into the house and nothing would be said about his fit. Each time Winnicott put him outside, he told the boy, "I hate you for what you just did." It was easy for Winnicott to say that, because it was true. Moreover, he believed it was not only necessary for the boy's development, but also necessary for himself. For had he not constructively expressed his hate, he could not have continued to live with the boy "without losing my temper and without every now and again murdering him."

In other words, constructive expressions of hate involve mature ego control of the aggressive drive and hate; they consist of expression it in such a way as to counter destructive expressions of hate. Couples who use constructive hate can resolve their arguments, while couples who fight in destructive way end up having the same arguments over and over. Nations who counter the destructive hate of other nations with constructive hate will be more likely to resolve disputes, while nations who counter destructive hate with more destructive hate will end up in war. Constructive hate is usually conscious, while destructive hate has unconscious roots. If we act out hate in an unconscious way, there is little change of resolution. If we insult somebody and when they respond with anger we retort, "I didn't do anything, you're over-reacting," or "Well, you started it," we are denying own aggression, hence preventing resolution. Similarly, all refusals to engage in constructive dialogue represent destructive hate.

Freud thought that civilization itself was a cause of discontent and therefore a breeding ground of aggression and hate. Manifestations of destructive hate do seem to be spiraling as civilization becomes more crowded and technological (and thereby alienating). We now have the power to push buttons and kill millions without actually experiencing what we are doing (another illustration of Milgram's experiments). Technology has made our lives easier and spoiled us to a point where we have become addicted to ease and cannot do without it, even though it is destroying our planet and ourselves. Like caged animals, we have become imprisoned by our own civilizations, and have developed more and more disturbances and illnesses.

The solution to interpersonal, as well as world, problems lies in a deeper understanding of hate, and in particular, in a deeper understanding of the differences between constructive and destructive hate. At the deepest level, every expression of hate is a defense against a real or imagined threat, a compensation for feelings of inferiority or powerlessness, and a plea for attention. Understanding how destructive hate comes about and what it really means is to react to it in an appropriate way, not with a guilt-ridden sentimental cry for unity, nor with a punitive cry for revenge, but with an honest expression of one's feelings--that is, through the expression of constructive hate. Love is relating genuinely to another human and to the world. Constructive hate is love.

*References:*

Eibl-Eibesfeldt, E. (1974). *Love and Hate, The Natural History of Behavior Patterns*. Shocken, New York.

Freud, S. (1930). *Civilization and It's Discontent.* Hogarth, London.

Gaylin, Wilfred (2004). *Hatred: The Psychological Descent into Violence.* Public Affairs Books, Washington, D.C.

Klein, Melanie (1957). *Envy and Gratitude*. Hogarth Press, London.

Milgram, S. (1974). *Obedience to Authority*. Harper and Row, New York.

Schoenewolf, G. (1989). *Sexual Animosity between Men and Women*. Jason Aronson, Northvale, NJ.

-- (1991). *The Art of Hating.* Jason Aronson, Northvale, NJ.

Spitz, R. (1965). *The First Year of Life*. International Universities Press, New York.

Winnicott, D. W. (1949), "Hate in the Countertransference. In

Basic Books, New York.

Thomas, Alexander, Chess, Stella, and Birch, Herbert C. (1968). *Temperament and Behavior Disorders in Children.* New York, New York University Press

Zeki S, Romaya JP (2008). "Neural Correlates of Hate." PLoS ONE 3(10): e3556. doi:10.1371/journal.pone.0003556

# Part 2 - Practice

# 8

# Psychological Factors in Cancer

---

Recent research has shown a link between childhood abuse and adult cancer. This does not mean that cancer is necessarily caused by environmental stress, but stress does seem to be a factor in the etiology of some forms of cancer. For example, symptoms of depression and anxiety are linked to patients with cancer of the pancreas. The following case about a man who developed testicular cancer illustrates one instance in which childhood trauma seems to be a factor in the later development of cancer.

---

**Introduction**

A while back I analyzed a young man who had developed cancer in one of his testicles—the right one, to be exact. In reconstructing his history, we were able to trace the etiology of the cancer, at least in part, to psychological factors. Since this case is one of the most clear and striking examples of a possible psychological etiology of cancer that I have encountered either directly or in the literature, I have decided to put the case on record.

Peter (the pseudonym for the patient) began treatment when he was in his early twenties. He was a tall, muscular man with a nervous constitution. The symptoms he presented were insomnia, impotence and anxiety, with occasional bouts of agoraphobia. He was functioning poorly on both social and professional levels, unable to assert himself in either area due to a strong fear of castration. He defended against this fear through repression, reaction formation, denial and avoidance: he was a great procrastinator. He presented a mixed bag of often conflicting personality features, including masochism, passivity, hysteria and obsessive-compulsion.

Even though he was a large man—around six feet and eight inches tall, with a broad chest and broad shoulders—who towered almost a foot above me, he was quite submissive toward me from the beginning, as though he feared I might at any moment give him a good thrashing. Seemingly in constant terror, he would sit up in his chair and keep me under surveillance at all times with his large brown eyes. I had the impression that if I made any sudden move or said anything that might be construed as threatening he would be out of the door in a second.

Our initial dialogues were not notably fruitful. "I don't know," came out of his mouth again and again. This was his favorite phrase, often the first and last thing he would utter during a session.

"What don't you know?" I asked him on one occasion.

"I don't know."

"You don't know what you don't know?"

"Yes, I don't know."

"Try saying, 'I don't want to know.'"

"I don't want to know."

"How does that feel? Does that feel right?"

"I don't know."

"You don't know if you don't want to know?"

"Right, I don't know."

We would go around and around like that. For a month or two it was difficult to get straight answers from him, and only bits and pieces of his history fell through the cracks of his character armor. It became evident that he felt he needed to be very defensive with me to the point where he ended up negating both himself and me, preventing anything meaningful from happening during the sessions.   Little by little I managed to find out that he had recently had an operation to remove his right testicle.  It had become malignant soon after he had left college and moved to New York—puffed up with a tumor that had doubled the size of the gland itself.  Fortunately, the left testicle was not impaired and—oddly—he did not present any concerns about losing it.

I also found out that he had undergone this operation in secret.  He had never told his family or his friends about the cancer or the surgery, due to feelings of shame and fear.  In particular, he feared that his father would be enraged at him.  He was terrified of his father and protective of both parents, whom he still saw regularly on weekends at their home in Queens, New York.  As far as he was concerned, his parents had done the best they could.  "I don't want to blame my parents," he said, repeating one of the most common statements of patients at the beginning of therapy.

"Is that why you didn't tell them about the operation?" I asked nonchalantly.

"I don't know."

"You don't know why you didn't tell them?"

"Yes, I don't know."

Eventually we were able to work through the "I-don't-know" and "I-don't-want-to-blame-my-parents" resistances and began to piece together the details of his history.  As we did, we began to understand the psychological meaning of his cancer.

### The History

The major trauma of Peter's childhood centered around bed-wetting.  He had wet his bed from the ages of three to eight—by which time he was in the second year of elementary school.  This was a dark age for him, enshrouded in childhood amnesia, and he did not at first clearly recall it.  He knew the bed-wetting had happened because his mother talked about it and it had become a part of the family history.

But he was only able to reconstruct a detailed memory of it through dream analysis. Upon recalling the period, he began to let go of some of his debilitating repression.

During most of his childhood years he had suffered from night terrors, in which he would wake up with a start, his heart beating wildly, and scream out, "No! No! No!" at the top of his lungs as he broke into a cold sweat. He would never be able to recall the content of these terrors, despite the fact that he would be semiconscious when he had them. During his adult years he continued to have recurring nightmares covering the same theme and was again able to recall very little of their content.

Slowly, during the course of therapy, he began to remember and bring forward fragments of these nightmares to the treatment. He would dream about being attacked on the street by strange men; about thieves coming into his apartment and stealing his clothing or his computer; about walking in the woods and stepping in a steel trap and being stalked by a bear; about being trampled by a herd of Buffalo. All these fragments had fierce men or animals in them and he would always note a certain look in the eyes of the attackers. The looks said that they had something on him, they knew his dirty secret, and they knew he was going to have to pay for his "crimes" in a way that meant losing his manhood.

After about a year, he brought in his first dream in which his father appeared. His father was standing in the background as two men attacked him. In this dream his father was but a silhouette and it took a while before the patient recognized him. He brought in another dream in which his father was more clearly recognizable; he was on the phone talking to his mother while a rabid dog with foaming mouth tore off his right arm. He brought in still another in which his father watched as a gang of black teenagers cornered him in an alley and kicked him in the testicles. This last dream proved the turning point in the reconstruction. The image of being kicked in the testicles by black men reawakened the fantasies that were attached to the original traumatic period.

"You know, I used to have fantasies all the time of being kicked in the balls," he said. "In fact, now that I think of it, I used to have fantasies that black men were kicking me in the balls. I also had fantasies of my father kicking me."

"Why black men?" I wondered.

"I don't know."

"What color is your father's skin?"

"Hmmmmm. I never thought of that. His skin is dark. I take after my mother. My skin and her skin is lighter than my father's. She's Irish. My father's got half Columbian and half Indian blood."

From that session on he began to remember his early childhood more and more clearly. Basically, he had gotten caught up in a crossfire. His father, he said, was a "Spartan": his mother an "Athenian." His father was a macho man whose manners were crude and temper on the edge. His mother was a meek woman who attempted to appease her husband by indulging him in every way. Clinically, the father was obsessive-compulsive with sadistic features. He was obsessed with order and discipline. The mother was oral-impulsive with masochistic and passive-aggressive features. She utilized a martyr attitude to guilt-trip her husband and indirectly act out her anger. When Peter was born, he was drawn into the center of their conflicting characters and became the focus of their war of ideology. She indulged the boy and was critical of what she called the "physical abuse" by her husband. He was strict and punitive with the boy and critical of what he called the "spoiling" by the mother.

During the toilet-training stage the mother's tendency was to go easy on Peter. If he didn't want to go to the potty, that was all right. Let him enjoy being a child as long as he could. After all, he would be called upon to meet life's many responsibilities soon enough. The father, on the other hand, would insist that the boy sit on the potty as long as it took for him to make a deposit of his valuable feces. Hence, the boy was caught between the indulgent, emotionally incestuous day world of his mother and the harsh, threatening, jealous, disciplinarian night world of his father. Consequently, the boy clung to his mother and dreaded the father's homecoming each night, and his toilet training became flawed.

I use that word "flawed" deliberately to denote that a fixation developed at that stage. Just as the flaws underneath the earth's crust which developed in its early formation portend future quakes, so also the flaw in Peter's toilet training (his early formation) would lead to a future breakdown of his socialization. In specific, this pregenital fixation predisposed Peter to the bed-wetting that began to occur during at around the age of three. The bed-wetting was, at the same time, a symptom that was directly related to, and induced by, the war of ideology (liberal vs. conservative ideas) between his parents. He became the conduit through which that war was funneled.

When the bed-wetting began his mother was indulgent toward the habit and his father was antagonistic. It soon became a family ritual that pitted the mother and son against the father, and one that was symbolic of the oedipal nature of the mother-son and father-son relationship. The mother's indulgence of the bed-wetting had an erotic undertone; each time it occurred, she would whisk the boy out of his bed and gently bath him, taking care to clean his private parts, speaking to him softly and conspiratorially so as not to wake the father. "Quiet, let's not wake the old bear," she would say. She would then put a clean sheet on his bed and hold his hand until he went back to sleep. Little wonder then that the habit, being thus reinforced, not only continued but intensified.

However, in time the father found out about the nighttime clandestine activities. Once he did, he insisted on taking over the handling of the bed-wetting. "It's your fault he pisses in his bed, because of your spoiling," he said to the mother. "I'll cure him of the habit, *pronto!*" He began to stay up nights and wait just outside the boy's room at the time when he usually soaked his bed. Peering around the doorway, he would wait until he saw or heard a movement (such as Peter's hand moving toward his genitals) or began to smell urine. Then he would pounce on the boy, throw back the covers, and yell at him. "Stop it! Stop it right now! Stop it, I said!" The boy would awaken with a start, his father's huge body on top of him, his father's dark eyes glaring at him, and begin to shiver and sob. His mother would rush in and scream at the father. His father would scream at the mother. She would clean him under the father's scrutiny and he would say, "That's right, pamper his little pecker so he'll turn out to be a fairy."

This ritual continued from the age of three to eight. For the first two years the struggle between the son and father, and between the mother and father, grew more intense. The son's bed-wetting came to be an insult to the father's pride, or, to put it more clinically, it was experienced as a narcissistic injury, as something shameful and unmanly that reflected on his own manhood. Moreover, to a fellow who grew up in the macho culture of South America, the son's closeness with his mother smacked of male treason. Finally, the son's continued enuresis was perceived as an act of deliberate defiance of the father's authority; this too was a threat to his male pride.

Narcissism was also involved in the mother-son relationship; the son became a self-object to the mother. Her indulgence had strings attached—or perhaps we should say it had an umbilical cord attached; he was expected to mirror her as she wanted to be mirrored—as the loving, warm, long-suffering wife, who did not harbor a shred of ill-will, who did not get the credit she deserved and had to put up with the abusive treatment of her brute of a husband. The son was expected to mirror her by being her ally against the father and playing the role of the long-suffering son beside the long-suffering wife.

With regard to the act of wetting itself, Peter recalled with fondness the euphoric sensation of urinating, the gentle warmth as the urine trickled between his legs and surrounded his crotch and backside, and the sweet smell of the urine hovering about the nighttime air. Later, of course, when the urine had cooled and become sticky and the smell had turned bitter, he would experience discomfort. Then would come the terror of his father's wrath, mixed with the anticipation of his mother's loving touch. In fact, the enuresis had the unconscious meaning of an ejaculation (this came out in his associations), and since it was an act that allied him with his mother against his father, it also meant intercourse with her and murder of him.

The fact that it had this unconscious meaning made the boy all the more fearful of the father's Oedipal rage. The talion principle (projecting that his father wanted to murder him) was ever-present in his relationship with his father, and it was predominant in shaping his character. The father, for his part, seemed to be the very epitome of the jealous oedipal father. He made it his mission to pry the boy loose from his close bonding with his mother.

As the second year passed, father and son became locked in a mighty battle of the bed. The father stepped up his terrorist attack on the son, growling now as he threw on the lights at the slightest sign of enuresis, jumping on the bed, pulling the boy's pants down and yelling, "Ah ha! What did I tell you? What did I tell you?" He would glare at the son, smiling maniacally, grinning as if he knew everything about the boy, everything about his dirty secret (his incestuous love for his mother). "Didn't I tell you not to do that? Didn't I? You don't listen, do you? I guess I'll have to teach you a lesson." Sometimes he would shake the boy until Peter thought that his head was going to rattle off of his shoulders. Sometimes he would turn the boy around and spank him. During these times, Peter would fear that his father was going to hit his genitals and injure them, so he would hold onto them with both hands. On one occasion he recalled his father saying something like, "You'd better hold on to your balls, because if you keep pissing in your bed I may just rip 'em off! How'd you like that? How'd you like it if I ripped 'em off? Then you'd just have a little nub of a dick and no balls! Ha, ha, ha, ha!"

The more the father terrorized him, the more the habit became stubbornly entrenched. In fact, the habit now took on a compulsive quality. Peter recalled that despite his mounting fears of his father and his craving to stop the habit and thereby avoid his father's attacks, he could do nothing about it. He would go to bed determined not to do it, but do it all the same and at about the same time. Nor did he experience the pleasurable sensations that had once been linked with the wetting. The more the father attacked the habit, the more the habit became reflexive, like some awful hiccoughs of the groin that would not be calmed, despite its incurring the mad dog of the night.

Eventually the mother and son won this battle. The father, seeing that the habit was getting worse rather than better, finally threw up his hands in disgust and told his wife, "You can have him. You caused the problem. You deal with it. He's no son of mine anymore." The son was an oedipal conqueror, but he had a heavy price to pay. From then on, the father was hostile and distant to the boy, treating him as one might treat the worst kind of traitor.  Without the father's active resistance to it, the habit lost part of its purpose; it continued for a few more years and then fizzled out.  It stopped not because of anything the father or mother had done, but because Peter began to be shamed by his peers at school.  The main cause of this shaming was that some little friends of his found out about the habit when he slept over and his bed was soaked in the morning.  His two mates teased him for months at school, telling everyone else about it.

By the end of the second grade the bed-wetting had stopped completely.  Just as the habit stopped, he began to have the night terrors.  The night terrors came almost every night during the latency period.  While the bed-wetting itself appeared to be a compulsive, ritualistic enactment of his incestuous cravings for his mother and oedipal struggle with his father, the drama associated with the bed-wetting seemed designed to master the flood of anxiety produced by the years of trauma, as well as to gain sympathy from his mother and appease his father.  That drama and connected trauma led to the night terrors.  Whereas during the earlier time he had awakened with a wet bed, now he awakened with a wet body, sweating profusely, and screaming.  Almost every night he would wake up screaming and his mother would come to his bed to calm him.  He didn't remember what he was screaming about, but his mother told him later he often had a begging tone: "No, no, please don't!"  It was not until the dawning of adolescence that he began to have the fantasies of his father kicking his testicles that were to plague him throughout his teen years and early twenties.

He had these fantasies almost daily, sometimes after an interaction with his father, sometimes after interactions with teachers or boys at school.  He imagined his father storming into his bedroom, throwing him onto the floor, and kicking at his crotch with his pointed Italian shoes.  Or he would be taking a shower and imagine that his father might break into the bathroom and tear away the shower curtain, push him down into the tub, and stand over him, kicking and laughing.  Or he would be coming home at night and would imagine that his father was lurking in the bushes around the house and would jump him before he got to the porch, tackling him and kicking him hard between the legs.  These fantasies were interspersed with those of black men kicking him.

Along with these fantasies, he began to become aware of a constant tension in his testicles, especially the right one. We speculated that because of his daily fantasies of being kicked in the testicles, he had unconsciously began to tense up this part of his body in anticipation of such an assault. After years of this kind of chronic tension in his right testicle, he became aware of a soreness there. Eventually he became aware that the size of his right testicle seemed larger than that of his left testicle. By his early twenties, his right testicle had grown to about twice the size of the left one, and it had an odd shape. By then, it felt sore all of the time.

He had put off going to see a physician, afraid of what he might find out. When he finally did, the cancer had invaded his testicle to a point where it could no longer be saved. The years of chronic tension had taken their toll.

### Related Research

Cancer has not generally been considered to be a psychosomatic disease, although there have been scattered speculations about the psychological component of cancer over the years. Kolb (1977) notes that symptoms of depression, anxiety, and a premonition of serious illness are among the most frequent presenting complaints of patients with cancer of the pancreas. Such patients tend to suppress their rage responses and have often suffered a significant loss in their object relations in the preceding months. Monroe (1972) and Coles (1977) assume a psychological component to all diseases, including cancer. "All physical disorders may, in some degree, be precipitated by nonbiological, nonphysical factors" (Coles, p. 204). Among psychoanalysts, Reich (1933, 1948) made the most extensive study of cancer. He calls it a "living putrefaction of the tissue" that is associated with an individual's unconscious damming up of energy through muscular contraction, or what he calls "biopathic shrinking." Baker (1957) elaborated on Reich's work, noting that cancer is the last stage in an ongoing process of organ deterioration, and it is most prevalent in "the most armored places"—that is, in the sexual regions of males and females, where tensions of unconscious sexual conflicts become localized and somatized.

A recent study by researchers at the University of Toronto showed that physical abuse in childhood was linked with the development of cancer in later life. The findings were based on a 2005 Canadian Community Health Survey focusing on the provinces of Manitoba and Saskatchewan and showed a 49% link between childhood abuse and adult cancer. Of the 13,092 respondents, 7.4 per cent stated that they had been physically abused as children by someone close to them, and 5.7 per cent said they had later been diagnosed with cancer. The odds ratio diminished only slightly to 47 per cent when the numbers were adjusted to take in unhealthy behaviors such as drinking or smoking. Fuller-Thomson said there might be many reasons for this link. She speculated that chronic stress a child abuse victim would be under might elevate levels of cortisol (the stress hormone). The chronic release of cortisol is known to weaken the immune system, which would then interfere with the immune system's ability to detect and get rid of cancer cells.

The gist of these theories is that an individual suffering from chronic stress in any organ will eventually develop cancer in that organ. Such long-term stress causes biochemical changes that hamper the body's metabolism. Chronic sufferers of ulcers of the stomach or colon, for example, are prone to developing cancer in these organs. This has been medically documented: what has not been well-enough documented is the psychological aspects of this development. (It is perhaps ironic that the psychoanalyst who provided the deepest exploration of the psychology of cancer was himself a victim of it; Reich died of cancer soon after being imprisoned during the 1950s for obstruction of justice.)

While he did not explore the connection between psychology and cancer, Alexander (1950) nevertheless provided an explanation of the psychological etiology of many ailments as well as the personality conflicts of those prone to them. Among them was the ulcer patient. He sees ulcer-prone individuals as oral characters whose sympathetic nervous systems are always switched on and whose stomachs are continuously producing acid in anticipation of taking in food. He traces this phenomenon back to fixations during the oral phase of development, when the child's oral needs are in some way deprived or over-stimulated. Hence, as an adult, the ulcer patient has an inadequate stimulus barrier and constantly needs soothing. Reflexively, he readies his stomach to take in food (an act of self-soothing) in order to calm the stress. However, by constantly flooding the stomach with acids, an ulcer develops. Over a period of years, if not treated, the ulcer may become cancerous.

It should be noted that recent medical research by Marshall and Warren (1983), for which they won the 2005 Nobel Prize, has dismissed the notion that ulcers are not caused by stress, and instead points to a stomach infection with the bacterium *Helicobacter pylori*. This bacterium is said to be the culprit in nearly 80% of stomach ulcers and in more than 90% of ulcers in the duodenum, the first portion of the small intestine. However, since their research was done it was discovered that a great number of people have this bacteria in their stomach but do not develop ulcers. So, even though a bacteria may be involved, this does not dismiss stress as an accompanying factor, as stress will weaken the immune system's ability to deal with the bacteria.

Following the same line of reasoning, a woman might develop breast or ovarian cancer or a man prostate cancer (three of the most prevalent forms of malignancy) in a similar way: through chronic stress in those particular organs. As is now commonly known, not all women who have the gene related to breast cancer develop breast cancer; stress would seem to be the crucial factor. One of my patients developed a tumor in her breast about a year after having an abortion, during which time she had felt an ongoing tension in her breasts. She expressed a great deal of resentment about the abortion, related to the frustrated desire to nurse and nurture a baby. This strong desire harked back to the apparent frustration of her infantile oral needs by a mother whose husband (the patient's father), abandoned her when the patient was still an infant. This event caused the mother to lapse into depression and abandon her infant daughter, thereby seemingly fixating her daughter at this stage of orality.

Hess (1955) studied a case of breast cancer that developed after a patient lost her father to cancer. He interpreted that the patient's cancer stemmed partly from guilt feelings about his death, an over-identification with him, and a wish to avoid her depressive pain. A young male patient of mine developed prostatitis in his twenties and early signs of cancer; fortunately he was able to work through a lot of his formerly repressed thoughts and feelings in therapy and the prostatitis eventually subsided. He had experienced constant tension in his prostate glands since his early adolescence, and revealed a history of conflicts about his homosexual impulses.

Faller (1993), studying 120 lung cancer patients found that certain causal attributions of the disease appeared to be a result of a specific way of coping. Using an interview and questionnaire, the study focused on the patient's emotional state and coping mode before and during the onset of cancer. Faller found a connection between emotional distress and the specific coping mechanisms of these patients which were of a deficient nature. However, he was not sure whether subjective causal attributions were determinants or epiphenomena of coping with the disease.

### Conclusion

To understand the specifics of one case of cancer is perhaps to highlight something about all cases. Peter's case, while perhaps not typical, is not atypical. It began with a pregenital fixation, produced by inadequate object relations, which in turn seemed to lead to the development of strong oedipal and castration complexes. His oedipal guilt and incestuous fantasies about his mother and his terror of his father aroused both complexes. The same object relations that produced them also prevented either complex from ever being resolved. To overcompensate for these complexes (or flaws), he had to chronically tense up (Reich's "biopathic shrinking") a part of his body—namely, the right testicle. Why the right testicle? I would speculate that "right" had for Peter an unconscious symbolic connection with "male" and "father," while left had a similar connection with "female" and "mother." In addition, our patient was from a Catholic background and therefore one can speculate that his familiarity with a litany which states that Jesus (God's son) sat at the right side of his Father, may have had an impact on his development as well. Hence, his right testicle belonged to his father, his left to his mother.

The chronic tension in his right testicle ebbed and waned according to the events of his life. Generally, any interactions with his father, even the most perfunctory exchange of glances, would bring about a rise of tension. Interactions with other male authority figures, and with other males in general, would likewise produce more tension. At the same time, relationships with the opposite sex were also threatening, for they signified a reactivation of incestuous thoughts toward his mother and the associated castration fears.

The development of the malignant tumor came after he had graduated from college and was on his own in the city. Perhaps it had been developing all along, or perhaps there was something about being on his own that contributed to the process. Sometimes freedom itself can be threatening to one who has been enmeshed in the throes of a dysfunctional family system. Selye (1971) observed that the conversion of chronic stress into organic ailments often occurs not while the object producing the stress is present, but after the stressor is removed and the body no longer has to immunize (defend) itself against it. At this point the body runs out of resources and becomes exhausted. Without anything to defend against, reaching the stage of exhaustion, the body relaxes and becomes susceptible to illness.

It would seem from this case history and others that at times cancer may have a psychological component which precedes or coincides with the biological. At other times, as when a toxic chemical invades the body, the cancer may have primarily a physical origin. Soldiers who are exposed to chemical warfare come to mind. In addition, there is a relationship between chronic stress, the immune system, and biochemical changes in the body. Due to humankind's general resistance to looking at psychological trends, about which I have commented elsewhere (1991, 1997), the psychology of cancer has remained largely ignored and uncharted. A recent text on psychosomatic disorders, for example, does not even mention cancer (Wilson and Mintz, 1989). If just a fraction of the funds spent on cancer research were devoted to psychological components of cancer, we might make more headway in curing this disease.

*References:*

Alexander, F. (1950). *Psychosomatic Medicine.* N.Y., Norton.

Baker, E. F. (1967). *Man in the Trap.* New York, MacMillan.

Coles, E.M. (1981). Clinical *Psychopathology: An Introduction.* London, Routledge & Kegan Paul.

Faller, H. (1993). Subjective theories of illness: determinants of epiphenomena of coping; a comparative study of methods of studying lung cancer patients. *Zeitschrift fur psychosomatische Medizin und Psychoanalyse,* 39:356-374.

Fuller-Thomson, E., Brennenstuhl, S. (2009), Making a link between childhood physical abuse and cancer: results from a regional representative survey. *Cancer* 115 (14): 3341–50.

Garrido Pereira, C.A. (1994). Unity without equality; pathway of consent. *Revisita Brasileira de Psicanalise,* 28:51-60.

Goldberg, J. (1995). Psychoanalyzing the body. *Modern Psychoanalysis,* 20:91-102.

Hess, N. (1955). Cancer as a defense against depressive pain. *Psychoanalytic Psychotherapy,* 9:175-184.

Kohut, H. (1971). *The Analysis of the Self.* New York, *International Universities Press.*

Kolb, L.G. (1977). *Modern Clinical Psychiatry,* 9th Edition.

Philadelphia, W. B. Saunders.

Marshall BJ, Warren JR. *Unidentified curved bacillus on gastric epithelium in active chronic gastritis.* Lancet 1983;1(8336):1273-1275

Monroe, A. (1972). Psychosomatic medicine I: the psychosomatic approach. *The Practitioner,* 208:162-168.

Nair, L., Deb, S. and Mandal, J. (1993). A study on repression-sensitization. Personality characteristics and early childhood experience of male cancer patients. *Journal of Personality and Clinical Studies,* 9:87-94.

Reich, W. (1933). *Character Analysis.* New York, Touchtone.

-- (1948). *The Cancer Biopathy.* New York, Touchstone, 1978.

Schoenewolf, G. (1991). *The Art of Hating.* Northvale, NJ, Jason Aronson.

-- (1997). The persistence in the belief that madness is hereditary. *Journal of Contemporary Psychotherapy,* 26:379-390.

Smadja, C. (1995). Approach to psychosomatic research: results of a study conducted with women suffering from breast cancer. *Revisita de Psicoanalisis,* special issue 4, 207-219.

Selya, H. (1974). *Stress Without Distress.* Toronto, McClellen and Stewart.

Wilson, C.P., and Mintz, I. L. (1989). *Psychosomatic Symptoms.* Northvale, NJ: Jason Aronson.

# 9

# Schizophrenia in a Dysfunctional Family

---

The focus of this paper is on a case history that describes, in detail, the dysfunctional family factors, including paranoid personality disorder, alcoholism, hysteria and masochism, which led one man to being diagnosed as schizophrenic. I suggest that similarly intensive family studies are necessary before we settle on genetic theories of madness.

---

In recent years many if not most mental health professionals seem to be leaning towards a genetic etiology of schizophrenia. They cite research with twins and other studies which, while not conclusive, seem to make a strong case for that conclusion. At the same time, most people acknowledge that the environment also plays a role.

The pendulum has swung from nature to nurture and back to nature during the last century. Until the time of Freud and psychoanalysis, physicians had attributed madness mostly to genetics—or to other causes having nothing to do with the environment, such as demonic possession or the influence of the stars. In the middle of the twentieth century, bolstered by psychoanalytic studies by Laing and Esterson (1964), Lidz et al. (1965) and Mahler (1968), professional literature from all fields began emphasizing the family and its effect on schizophrenia. Lidz wrote of "schizophregenic mothers" and "schizopregenic fathers" who through twisted and abusive treatment drove children to schizophrenic withdrawal. Today psychiatry in general, and even many psychoanalysts, are again emphasizing genetic explanations.

In considering the fact that throughout most of history doctors have sought a hereditary explanation for mental illness and only for a few decades has nurture been given etiological relevance by social scientists, I see a parallel to what happens to individuals and families in therapy. Most patients do not want to look at their past, and do so reluctantly. They do not want to look objectively at their family dynamics and, in fact, charge therapists with trying to make trouble by focusing too much attention on such matters. Laing (1971), noting this censorship and amnesia connected with the family and early childhood, theorized that parents hypnotize children to hypnotize their children to hypnotize their children.

> Hypnosis may be an experimental model of a naturally occurring phenomenon in many families. In the family situation, however, the hypnotists (the parents) are already hypnotized (by their parents) and are carrying out their instructions, by bringing their children up to bring their children up...in such a way, which includes not realizing that one is carrying out instructions (p. 71).

The tendency of human beings in general—and of psychiatry in particular—may stem from a collective childhood amnesia of the kind to which Laing refers. As children all of us are conditioned to honor our fathers and mothers by religions and by family value systems. We are told and shown numerous ways not to express thoughts and feelings directly but to disguise them, so we learn to deny, displace, and externalize. We are told repeatedly in numerous verbal and non-verbal ways (induction) that we and our families are part of the same team—it is us against the world. We are told again and again by our parents that they are doing the best they can, and they become upset when we

170

question them. Hence, we learn that to scrutinize or criticize the family is tantamount to treason.

Family studies are needed to counter this resistance to looking at our families with an objective eye. Even though there have already been numerous family studies, I have had the opportunity, through my family practice, to observe one particular family for a number of years and to analyze the main environmental forces that led to the formation of a schizophrenic character. Indeed, the environmental forces in this case seem unusually compelling.

**The Family History**

Regarding lineage, there was only one outbreak of schizophrenia in the immediate ancestry of this family. An uncle, the mother's brother, had suffered a breakdown following the death of his wife. There was some alcoholism scattered about, and one suicide by the paternal grandfather, who was in his 70s at the time and depressed by ill health and economic worries. On the positive side the family also had shown strains of musical talent: a great uncle had become a famous conductor and composer.

The nuclear family in this case was comprised of a father, mother, and four sons. It was the fourth and last son who was diagnosed as schizophrenic.

The father and mother had married when he was 19 and she was 20. They had been high school educated. Shortly after the father's father had committed suicide, the mother became pregnant. The father reluctantly married her and they moved into the family house. The first son, whom I will call Son A, was born about six months after their marriage.

The father had a modicum of musical talent and played trumpet in local dance orchestras. At one time he even had his own band, but he did not get along with people and the band fell apart. After a few years he was not playing the trumpet anymore and blamed his blighted ambitions on his wife. His drinking problem increased through the years, and so did hers, and their fighting grew more and more vicious.

A second son, Son B, was born a year and a half after the first;

A third, Son C, came four years after the second; and a fourth, Son D, came five years later. With each successive son, the father's alcoholism increased. He would stay out at bars until late at night, then come home and yell at and sometimes beat his wife. She would exacerbate conditions by sexually demeaning him in front of the sons, lacerating him with a sarcastic tongue, turning her sons against him. Often he would threaten to kill her, and on several occasions he actually took out his hunting rifle and pointed it at her. Far from being a nurturing environment, this family milieu was more a prison of terror for the sons.

Each successive son received poorer parenting. The first son, Son A, had adequate parenting. Both parents made him a narcissistic selfobject. He would be the musician that the father could not be, and the good and loyal perfect son who would make his mother proud. From the time he could hold a trumpet, the father sat with him and taught him everything he knew about music. When he was still a boy the father took him along to dance jobs and had him join the band. The mother held Son A up as the model for all the other sons to follow. He went on to become an honor student and won a music scholarship to college.

When she became pregnant with Son B the mother wished for a girl. His birth, and that of each successive son was a disappointment in that respect. In addition, Son B was not as talented or as attractive as Son A. The mother used to openly compare the two, and would say to friends, "Yeah, Son B just doesn't have the brains or talent that Son A has, but he tries hard." Son A, noting the parent's preference for him, unmercifully teased son B, and the parents allowed it, viewing such teasing as harmless childhood play. Son A could defeat Son B at just about any game, and then would tease and gloat about it, causing Son B to accumulate jealousy and resentment of the older brother and to develop inferior feelings. In addition, Son B could not do anything about this jealousy or resentment, could not express it in the family—since Son A was the apple of his mother's eye and the peach of his father's, and for both parents he was the model of all that was good and noble. If Son B said anything about the older brother, his mother would disqualify it. "Don't be silly. Son A is just playing with you. He doesn't mean anything." Such responses caused Son B to doubt his own perception and always to yield to his older brother's perceptions (and later, in transference, to the perceptions of other authority figures). He developed a reaction-formation toward this older brother and began to idealize him as his mother did.

The third son made the family dynamics more complex. Once again, this son had not been planned, and once again the mother, and also the father, hoped for a girl child. However, the third son was an exceptionally attractive, intelligent and talented child, and the mother took to him, as did the oldest brother, allying with him against Son B.

When Son C was four, Son B eight and Son A ten, they sang together in a talent show. This was a significant event in all their lives. It was during the course of rehearsing for this show that the family discovered that Son C was a musical prodigy. One day as they practiced the son they were to sing in the contest, "My Bonnie Lies Over the Ocean," Son A was trying with no success to teach Son B to sing the second harmony. (The plan was for Son A to sing the melody, Son B the second harmony, and Son C the base.) Suddenly Son C said, "I can sing the harmony." He proceeded to do so flawlessly. Son A was amazed by this and so were the father and mother. Son C became the celebrity of the family and the three sons went on to win the talent show. Meanwhile, Son B was mortified by his failure to sing the harmony and smitten with jealousy and hatred of this younger usurper, this precocious four-year-old who had out done him.

From that time on, especially after Son D was born, Son B began teasing and physically picking on Son C. In fact, a hierarchy had formed: the father abused the mother, and Son A, following his father's example, was abusive to Son B. Son B in turn began to abuse Son C and son C developed a negative attitude to Son D. At the same time, Son A was the "chosen one" of both parents, and for the time being, Son C was also given special treatment by both parents (as a narcissistic extension of themselves—the musical genius who would make the family proud).

Such was the stage upon which Son D entered the family, some five years after the birth of Son C.

### The Pathogenic Family Environment

Son D was born at a time when the family had reached its apex of dysfunctionalism.  During her pregnancy the mother had a violent fight with the father.  He socked her in the eye and she threw a sugar bowl at him that made a gash across his forehead, requiring several stitches.  She grabbed her three sons and ran off to her parents' house, where she remained for several weeks.  She contemplated divorce, but in those days divorce was still a difficult thing, and she did not know how she would survive with three, and soon four, sons.  After a while, the father perhaps typically of alcoholics, became penitent and sent her flowery letters begging her to come home, promising he would be good.  She went back.  Within a week he had gotten drunk again and shoved her onto the floor and called her a "stupid whore."

And then came the new baby.  Even before he was born, he was assaulted indirectly, for each time the father socked or shoved the mother it created havoc in the form of emotional and physical upheaval inside the womb.  Glover, et al. (2002) in a study of 7,144 mothers and babies in England, found that women who reported experiencing high levels of anxiety during pregnancy were twice as likely as non-stressed women to have children with behavioral difficulties, depression and anxiety.  Dingfelder (2004) cites research by van Os that found a link between prenatal stress and schizophrenia.  After his birth, Son D found himself in a family milieu where he was at most an afterthought and at worst another nail in his father's coffin and a burden in his mother's arms.

The following is a schematic account of the negative forces each family member directed at the new child.

#### The Father

The father was an alcoholic who drank beer from the time his job finished until late in the night.  He also seemed to have paranoid personality disorder: he was obsessed with the idea that his wife had caused all his misery by forcing him to marry her and then by getting pregnant three more times and saddling him with domestic responsibility.  From prenatal times onward, Son D was assaulted by this father.  The father's attitude toward the new child was hostile and negating. He acted as if the new baby did not exist. He stayed out almost every night at bars and blamed the mother for being so stupid as to get pregnant again. This new child was seen as trapping him forever in family slavery, destroying once and for all his dreams of fame as a musician. He had by now given up on his trumpet completely and supported the family working at a blue collar job for low wages. Son D was the final blow to his ambitions.

The father acted out his frustration by degrading and terrorizing the mother and indirectly the family and by neglecting Son D. Almost every night he would come home drunk and lay into her for making him marry her. "How could I marry a stupid whore like you?" Often in the early mornings he would wake her for sex and she would cry out, "Help me, he's going to kill me!" and one of the older boys would be called upon to intervene. Threats of death were constant. This atmosphere of terror was omnipresent, and must have been felt by Son D from the moment he was brought home from the hospital: the father himself was the chief source of insecurity and fear.

### The Mother

The mother, frustrated that Son D was not a girl, nevertheless proceeded to treat him as if he were a girl. She dressed him in dresses until he was three or four, and curled his blond hair. Thus she created in him a gender confusion. However, although he received a lot of attention from her, that attention was influenced by her own drunkenness and by her malevolent relationship with her husband. Often she would be yelling in the boy's ear (at the father) as she held him, or rocking him roughly, or ignoring his cries completely as she tangled with the father. The baby was, understandably, an anxious one who did not sleep well, and the mother did not have the patience to deal with him, since she felt her own life was, as she kept repeating, "a hell on earth." Hence the baby received much of the mother's displaced anger.

Nor did she have the patience to deal with the antagonism among her three older boys. (She kept ignoring any signs of discord and idealizing them, as her "three fine sons," even when they were hammering each other.) All she could say to them was, "Now why don't you all just get along." They were somehow to learn magically to get
175

along, while the mother and father were threatening to kill each other. She was a histrionic with masochistic features who could not set her own boundaries with her husband or with friends, much less help her sons learn to set boundaries with respect to each other's and their own feelings.

In particular, she did not deal effectively with the jealousy that Son C felt for Son D. Not only did she have no patience for Son D, she had no patience for Son C either, shaming Son C when he expressed jealousy of the new arrival who had suddenly displaced him in her favor. She made Son C feel worse rather than reassuring him, so that Son C began acting out by wetting his bed (emulating the new baby) and attacking the new baby with a vengeance. Finally, she was a woman who loved to take care of babies but had no idea of how to nurture growing boys. Hence, she "babied" this last son long beyond the appropriate time. Even when he was a teenager, for example, she still used a "baby-talk" tone with him and treated him as if he were some child-man, never quite taking his thoughts and feelings seriously, as she did with the eldest son. This kept him dependent on her and precluded his emotional separation from her and the development of independent self-respect.

### Son A

The oldest brother was not interested in the new baby. He was the "prince" of the family and basked in his princedom—his mother's and father's idealization and the special privileges it bestowed on him. This youngest sibling, in his mind, did not matter. He could see that he did not matter to either of his parents, so he did not matter to him. He was interested in son C because he had allied himself with him—they were the two musical geniuses of the family—against son B, who was his chief rival. Moreover, he had noticed that as soon as the mother mentioned that she was pregnant with a fourth child, Son B made it known that he would ally himself with Son D. It was to be a factionalized family, two against two. At any rate, Son A was 11 years older than the youngest child, and was soon to be a teenager and involved in his own world far removed from the youngest child. The youngest was of no use to him, hence his attitude toward Son D was one of neglect (rejection).

### Son B

Son B was joyous when Son D arrived on the scene. He had long felt at odds with everybody, the ugly duckling of the family. His father and mother both favored his older brother, and his mother and older brother both teased, demeaned and bullied him. Son A, for example, would enjoy beating Son B at every game and then would tease Son B when Son B got angry about this. The Mother would always join with Son A and bemoan, "God just didn't give you the intelligence he gave your older brother." In addition, Son A had also allied with Son C against Son B, and his father and mother had, in turn, given special treatment to Son C because of his musical talent. With Son D's birth, he anticipated having at long last an ally against this stacked deck. Even before Son D was born, Son B kept whispering to Son C, "Now you won't be getting all the attention anymore. How will it feel, not getting all the attention?" and "He's going to be twice as talented and twice as smart as you. He'll be better than you in every way." The stage was set for Son B to make Son D a narcissistic extension of himself, just as the parents had made Sons A and C into narcissistic extensions and Son A had made Son C into one. Hence, Son D would be expected to be a genius by Son B before he was even born.

As Son B grew up and began to speak, Son B took Son D under his wing and drilled into him that he was a superior person, better at music and better at school and better at everything than Son C. He would also invariably take Son D's side if Son D got into a fight with Son C (which was often). This kept Son D dependent on Son B and kept him from developing his own personality naturally. Son D from birth onward had to live up to Son B's impossible expectations for him.

### Son C

Son C hated Son D and did to him what was being done to him by Son B and by the rest of the family. While he had been the youngest member of the family, Son C had enjoyed a kind of celebrity not only because he was the baby but also because of his musical ability.

He was a celebrity and along with that celebrity there was a period of grace. During this period he had a protected status. However, as soon as Son D was born, he became the forgotten boy; the father and mother were preoccupied with each other and the mother with the new baby. When his mother no longer treated him as special and the family forgot and then ignored his musical talent, Son C became needy; his mother responded by displacing her anger at the father onto Son C, yelling, "I don't need two babies!" The older brother, who had been his ally, was preoccupied with his junior high and high school activities (being an honor student, etc.). And Son B was suddenly allowed to unleash all his pent-up jealousy and rage at Son C, who no longer enjoyed his protected status.

Son B's teasing and physical abuse of Son C knew no bounds; he was constantly degrading and hitting him, and continually demeaning his musical talent, of which he felt so jealous. This harassment was so unrelenting and traumatic to Son C that when he became an adult he chose not to develop his talent but went into another field entirely.

Meanwhile, Son C began dishing it out to Son D. While Son B was treating the new baby like a god, cooing over him and worshipping him and welcoming him as his own personal avenging angel whose genius would far outstrip Son C's, at the same time Son C was telling Son D that he was a stupid jerk who would never amount to anything. An intense rivalry ensued between the two youngest sons. Son C harassed Son D at every step, teasing him, making him cry, ridiculing him, shaming him, and generally abusing him.

On one occasion, he refused to let Son D play with him and some neighborhood kids, humiliating him in front of the others, calling him "too young and stupid to play with older kids," exhorting him to "go away and stop bothering them." Later he lacerated the younger brother for embarrassing him in front of his friends, and emulated his father's attitude toward the mother. "Why do you always have to follow me around? You're the cause of all my problems. I wish you had never been born." Sometimes the mother managed to come out of her depression long enough to intercede on Son D's behalf, but sooner or later Son C would have his way with Son D and punish him for existing.

In short, the buck always stopped with Son D. He bore the brunt of everybody's rage.

## The Seeds of Schizophrenia

As I wrote the foregoing section, I wondered if it would all sound confusing to the reader. If so, imagine how confusing the situation must have been to Son D. It is easy for a grown-up parent to drive a small, defenseless, impressionable infant or small child crazy. After all, an infant is a totally vulnerable and complete slave; no one has more power than a parent over an infant. Hence, we all know what it is like to be slaves; but some slave owners are better than others.

In the case under consideration, slave owners (parents) were quite disturbed, and the seeds of madness were laid in the first few vulnerable years of Son D's life. To begin with, he could not have felt entirely safe and restful in the womb. Then, upon being brought into this dysfunctional family milieu with its swirling currents of jealous, despairing and murderous rage, he must have experienced very early emotional trauma. A number of psychoanalysts (Freud, 1911; Winnicott, 1965; Mahler, 1968; Pao, 1979; Searles, 1979; Kernberg, 1980, Frosch, 1983; Seinfeld, 1990) have theorized that people diagnosed with schizophrenia have major fixations in the symbiotic phase, the earliest phase of development. During this phase it is assumed that the infant experiences itself and the mother as one and the same organism. If the infant during this stage does not become adequately bonded with the mother, or cannot successfully separate from her (but remains emotionally and symbiotically connected with her) a healthy ego will not be formed, with all its attendant and necessary functions such as frustration toleration, reality testing and self-soothing. Nor will healthy self-esteem develop.

It seems likely that this kind of fixation may have been the case with Son D. During the first months of his life his mother and father had reached the most destructive point in their marriage. They had separated and contemplated divorce shortly before his birth, and the mother had moved back into the house only a month before having her fourth child.

It is not unusual for mothers to feel some degree of postpartum depression following birth, but for a mother in the throes of marital discord, a battered woman who had no network to turn to for help in the small town where she lived, and who was scorned by her father and her own older sisters, the postpartum depression would probably have been much deeper.

Let us look at it from the perspective of Son D. He opens his eyes to see his mother. She picks him up and she is smiling. Then she is frowning and yelling. Then she is rocking him too fast and he is crying. She whispers and sings to him, but she is not really looking at him and sometimes she is even glaring at him, and she is always yelling. He can feel her stomach and her breasts shuddering against him when she yells, and he is scared. When she rocks him it does not comfort him because he can feel her shaking like some human earthquake. Sometimes he can hear her voice shrieking in another room, and other strange voices, and he does not understand that he does not feel safe.

She dresses him in girl's clothes, curls his hair and says, "You're the daughter I always wanted!" At the age when he discovers he has a penis and his mother does not, he asks, "What is that?" She replies, "It's nothing." "Am I a boy?" "No, you're the daughter I always wanted. I'm just kidding. You're a boy." He does not know what he is, and the mother gives him confusing messages.

These confusing signals are compounded by the conflicting forces of other members of the family. His father frightens him and he shrinks from this menacing man and clings to the mother. His oldest brother disregards him as though he did not exist. And his two immediately older brothers use him for a human tug o' war game. One is treating him like a god, the other like a devil. Son D had no healthy relations; no male figure to model himself on and learn healthy coping methods from, and no female figure with whom to form a healthy attachment.

The sibling relationships in this family were crucial to the formation of Son D's psychopathology. If Son D had had a sibling to turn to who could have given him a sane and accepting response, he might have survived. Unfortunately everywhere he turned he got another twisted response. It is true that Son B took Son D under his wing and treated him like royalty, but his response to Son D was neither sane nor accepting. Son B could not accept Son D as he was, for he had grandiose expectations for him. He expected Son D to be more talented than Son C so that Son C would be forced to experience the same humiliation he had felt. The trouble was, Son D turned out to have only a fair ear for music. Year after year Son B touted Son D's musical prowess, and year after year that prowess failed to develop and Son D became a disappointment in Son B's eyes. When he proved not to be musically inclined, Son D tried to live up to Son B's intellectual expectations for him. Now Son B told Son D over and over that he would be smarter than Son C and smarter than everybody—the true genius of the family. Unfortunately, Son D also had only average intelligence. Yet, just as he had pushed himself to please his older brother who so believed in him by trying and trying to excel at music, so now he desperately pushed himself to prove his intelligence, burying himself in vocabulary books, poetry, and generally posing as the genius. But ultimately, these grandiose expectations only served to add to Son D's frustration. Is there anything more agonizing than being constantly expected to do something that you do not have the wherewithal to do?

Meanwhile, Son C attempted in every way he could to make Son D's life one of complete misery, and often he succeeded. Son C was with Son D more than any of the others, and he had ample time to undermine, tease, beat up, and deceive, scorn, and befuddle the younger brother. For example, when Son D learned to belch and could even belch out the letters of the alphabet, Son C used this achievement (of which he was jealous) to undermine and tease the younger brother. He would ask Son D to belch out the alphabet. The latter would have to swallow a lot of air to belch that much. After he had swallowed a lot of air, Son C would rush up and push in his stomach, thus jamming up the potential belch. Son D would scream and frantically begin swallowing more air to try to start a new belch. Son C would again press in his stomach at the last minute, then laugh at the younger brother's misery. A few days later Son C would beg Son D to belch the alphabet again, promising he would not press in his stomach. Of course he would press it again and laugh even more loudly.

Not only did this youngest son have nobody to turn to for a sane response, he had nobody on whom to dump his frustration. Each of the other sons had a younger brother as an object for displaced rage. The abuse trickled down from parent to oldest son to next oldest to next oldest. For Son D, there was nobody else. He had to take everything that everybody dished out and "eat it"—or, to put it psychoanalytically, internalize it. Obviously, his internalized object relations began to mirror those of his external world—they became a miasma of confusion, grandiosity, jealousy and rage.

Shengold (1979) has written extensively about this kind of psychological murder that so often happens unwittingly to children, describing it as a process in which "the victim is robbed of his identity and of the ability to maintain authentic feelings. Soul murder remains effective if the capacity to think and to know has been sufficiently interfered with—by way of brainwashing' (Shengold, 1979, p. 557). Day by day Son D was told to think what others wanted him to think and be what others wanted him to be. He was told to be a girl, to be a musical genius, to outsmart his brothers. He was also told he was a jerk, and that he should shut up and go away and die. Not only was he being brainwashed, but he was also being brainwashed by three separate prison guards—his mother and his two older brothers—all of whom had conflicting messages for him to learn and follow.

The seeds of schizophrenia had been set by the time he entered elementary school. The actual onset of madness would not occur until he left home, but the fixations were there and the resulting conflicts in her personality (like underground faults in the formation of land) and would cause an eruption when the time was right. He appeared normal, though rather eccentric, during his adolescence. He played in the high school band, as had all his brothers, and made fairly good grades (though he did not distinguish himself as had the oldest brother). The only abnormality was that he seldom dated. But nobody really noticed, because it was felt he was too brainy to be interested in girls.

The one family event that may have exacerbated his condition during his high school days was the divorce of the parents. They had separated several times during the years, usually after the mother had called the police and the father had been held in jail overnight. Finally, when Son D was in his second year of high school, they did get a divorce. This left Son D at home alone with the mother (all the other sons were in college or in the army by then). During these years he began making more and more demands on her financially and otherwise, and several times he came home drunk after a night out with friends. Their relationship became increasingly problematic, and the mother complained to the oldest son, "I don't know what to do about Son D. Sometimes he scares me." Her denial of her own aggression and her treating him as if he was some kind of bad seed probably further confused him and hastened his withdrawal.

It was after he left home and went to college that he began to self-destruct. Very early on he got into trouble over taking and selling drugs and was put on probation by his college. By the end of his Freshman year he had dropped out of school entirely. He then disappeared for a few months and nobody knew where he was. Then his mother received a letter from him saying he had decided to disown the family. He had changed his name legally, and included a copy of the legal paper indicating that his name had been changed to one that alluded to a pure heart. After this letter, nobody heard from him for a year. Yet, nobody felt any remorse or guilt about his break from the family.

The family went into shock. Nobody could understand why he would want to cut himself off from the family and change his name. For the most part they could not fathom that he might be angry at them, or that he might have had to run away from their twisting messages, jealousies, and rages in order to try to salvage his lost self. The family was in complete denial about their complicity in the matter, and suggested that he had inherited their uncle's madness. The oldest brother seemed to speak for all when he remarked, "He's just trying to get attention."

It was not bad genes or attention seeking, but faulty ego formation and arrested emotional development that did him in. Unfortunately, Son D had never been able to develop a strong enough ego to stand independently, nor the emotional maturity to bond with others outside the family, and so his attempt to find himself failed. A year later they received word about him from the warden of a prison. He had held up a cab driver at gunpoint in another state and was serving time. During his time in prison his behavior became so bizarre that he was transferred to a mental hospital, where he was diagnosed as suffering from paranoid schizophrenia.

### The Clinical Picture

When he came to the hospital he had regressed to a childlike, dependent state of being. Symptoms of his oral fixations abounded. He chain-smoked cigarettes. If he could get his hands on any alcohol or marijuana he would drink or smoke it down as fast as he could. He slept very little and spent his days agitatedly pacing his room or sitting in a chair rocking back and forth, his eyes darting around.

Generally, he appeared to be meek toward the staff in the hospital, while at the same time continually trying to get them to give him more cigarettes, more medication, more books, etc. However, this appearance of meekness was merely a cover, and occasionally his narcissistic rage would spurt out in the form of an insulting remark or a barbed question that seemed to come out of left field during the course of some otherwise trivial conversation.

He was no longer very much in touch with reality. He had a delusional system in which he saw himself as a misunderstood genius, a poet, a man of vision whom nobody could understand because nobody else was on his level. Due to this superiority, he felt entitled. In his mind, when he had held up the cab driver at gunpoint, he was simply acting out his entitlement. Superior people such as himself did not have to live according to common rules. He saw himself as a superior man like Raskolnikov or a romantic philosopher like Nietzsche, or a poet like Rilke, and idiot savant whose poetry and philosophy would some day be discovered—when the world was advanced enough to discover it.

In actuality his poetry—and the sketches with which he decorated it—constituted a kind of confused rambling and doodling. Spiral notebooks were scrawled with handwriting that turned this way and that without consistency, and with words crossed out and put back in and crossed out again. The poems were filled with the long words he had so studiously learned during his adolescence when he pored over vocabulary books to please his older brother, and often seemed, in a crude way, to be an imitation of the poems of nineteenth century romantics.

> I feel a coldness inside me,
> A malevolent coldness inside me,
> A maleficent chilliness inside me,
> A splendiferous cold of yore inside me.
> And I wonder, what would Nietzsche think
> The great Nietzsche if he were sitting here
> In my room, looking at my bottle of beer.
> Without any fear,
> Drinking with an insipid leer
> Until he got good and drunk and began to jeer?

Other poems were intended to be visionary and Biblical, permeated with prophesies of

> Death will come inexorably
> Invidiously
> And then a hundred and one trillion skulls
> Will explode all over the highways and byways
> But it's okay with me
> They do not know, but they think they know,
> They do not go, but they think they go.
> I look at them from my inviolate perch.
> And watch the skulls splatter into a trillion pieces—
> Brother, can you spare a dime?

The poems, like dreams, could be interpreted as symbolic expressions of his delusional system (the oneness with Nietzsche, etc.) his depression (the malevolent coldness), his paranoid rage against the world (exploding skulls), and his feeling that only he on his "inviolate perch" would be spared the inevitable doom, while his brothers would not be. In fact, he had projected the rage that he had internalized from his family, onto the world, seeing the world as an evil thing that would try to destroy him but would eventually, in a triumphant reversal, destroy itself.

This rage had not simply taken possession of him from nowhere. It had come from the dysfunctional family. He had become the carrier of the family's psychopathology, had been emotionally contaminated by their collective acted-out animosity. All his smoking, drinking, pacing, twitching, rocking and the rambling tone of his speech and poetry, were symptoms of this rage and his attempts to keep it under control.

He had regressed back to the point of his fixations. Emotionally he was a child, a child of about two years old. He was a dependent toddler, dependent now on the hospital where once he had been dependent on his mother and his older brother—Son B. Both the mother and older brother had cultivated his dependency, always doing for him and thinking for him instead of letting him do and think for himself. The older brother, Son B, continued to nurture that dependency, as well as the grandiose delusional system, during the ensuing years, allowing Son D to live as an outpatient in his apartment, again doing for him, still waiting for and urging him to prove his genius. Son D reciprocated Son B's kindness by exploiting him financially and getting into trouble (exposing himself from a window of Son B's apartment to a teen-aged girl across the way). Soon he was sent back to the hospital.

There were also, in his poems and in his behavior, indications of a homosexual conflict, but this homosexual inclination did not fit into his grandiose view of himself and had to be repressed. This latent homosexuality echoes Freud's theory about paranoia. "On the basis of clinical evidence," he wrote, "we can suppose that paranoiac are endowed with a fixation at the stage of narcissism, and we can assert that the amount of regression characteristic of paranoia is indicated by the length of the step back from sublimated homosexuality to narcissism" (Freud, 1911, p 67). In Son D's case, his latent homosexuality revolved not only around the negative oedipal complex (stemming from his intense attachment to his mother and the fear of a hostile father), but also around his relationship with his hostile older brother, Son C. Indeed, once when he was ten and Son C was 15, the younger brother had, on his own initiative, walked over and fondled the older brother's genitals while the latter was lying on his bed, and some of his later fantasies contained homosexual allusions to Son C. In instances such as this, homosexuality represents a need to appease a hostile and dominant male figure by offering himself sexually. Ironically, this need had to be repressed for it would have been totally unacceptable to Son B, who had become Son D's alter ego—or more correctly ego (since Son D never managed to develop his own ego). To avoid awareness of this homosexual conflict, he had retreated—true to Freud's theory—back to an earlier pregenital kind of narcissism.

Unfortunately, none of the state hospitals to which Son D was sent had adequate programs of psychotherapy. They were mainly facilities for dispensing psychiatric medication. Son D was put on tranquilizers and given only perfunctory counseling, which focused primarily on the practicalities of his present life. There was little attempt to go back to his early childhood and help him unravel the pathogenic upbringing that had so early on derailed him. At any rate, by the time he had come to the hospital, he was in such a state of regression and so paranoid that it would have taken many years of extensive psychotherapy to reach him.

He is now nearing the age of 50. He lives on Social Security Disability allowance in a cheap rooming house. He spends his money as soon as he gets it on cheap wine and an occasional prostitute, to whom he reads his poetry. He makes no attempt to get in touch with his family any more, and they make no attempt to contact him.

### A Predisposition?

The theory of hereditary schizophrenia has not been proven. Twin studies, even though there have been a great number of them over many years that have been replicated, do not prove that schizophrenia is hereditary in non-twins. They prove only that twins may have a certain predisposition to schizophrenia, due to the nature of being a twin and all it entails, and that only about 40% of identical twins are both schizophrenic. Other studies that point to a chemical imbalance or changes in the hypothalamus are not conclusive evidence of genetics since such imbalances or brain changes can also be caused by stress. At the same time environmental studies of families, of the link between prenatal stress and later psychopathology, and those that show there is a greater proportional incidence of schizophrenia in the ghetto than in wealthy neighborhoods (Shean, 1978), provide evidence of an environmental explanation. Finally, evidence that schizophrenia runs in families is, at best, a confounding variable; since we don't know if it's genetics or generation upon generation of bad parenting that causes this phenomenon.

But even if there is a supposed genetic predisposition to schizophrenia, the environment cannot be dismissed as a factor. Unless families are perfectly healthy, there will always be some psychopathology to deal with. And unless we understand and deal with family dysfunction, as well as the societal factors that impinge on it, we will continue to be a breeding ground for mental illness.

*References:*

Dingfelder, S. F. (2004). Programmed for psychopathology. Psychological Monitor, Vol. 34, Number 2.

Freud, S. (1911). Psycho-analytic notes on an autobiographical account of a case of paranoia (dementia paranoids). *Standard Edition*, 12, 3-84. London, Hogarth Press.

Glover, V. (2002), Prenatal stress and psychopathology. *Journal of the American Academy of Child and Adolescent Psychology*, Vol. 14, No. 12.

Frosch, J. (1983). *The Psychotic Process*. New York, International Universities Press.

Kernberg, O. (1980). *Internal World and External Reality*. Northvale, NJ, Jason Aronson.

Laing, R. D. and Esterson, A. (1964). *Sanity, Madness and the Family*. New York, Basic Books.

Laing, R. D. (1971). *The Politics of the Family*. Harmondsworth, Penguin.

Lidz, T., Fleck, S. and Cornelison, A. R. (1965). *Schizophrenia and the Family*. New York, International Universities Press.

Mahler, M.S. (1968). *On Human Symbiosis and the Vicissitudes of Individuation*. New York, International Universities Press.

Pao, P. (1979). Schizophrenic Disorders: *Theory and Treatment from a Psychodynamic Point of View*. New York, International Universities Press.

Searles, H. (1979). *Countertransference and Related Subjects*. New York, International Universities Press.

Shean, G. (1978). *Schizophrenia: An Introduction to Research and Theory*. Cambridge, MA, Winthrop Publishers.

Shengold, L. L. (1979). Child abuse and deprivation: soul murder. *Journal of the American Psychoanalytic Association*, 17, 533-60.

Winnicott, D. W. (1965). The *Family and Individual Development*. London, Tavistock.

# 10

# Dealing with Character, Sex, and Race in Psychotherapy

This paper looks at the complexity of issues that required analyzing when a black female patient entered treatment with a white male psychoanalyst. Before the father or mother transferences could be dealt with and traced to their sources in childhood traumas, the cultural transference had to be resolved. In particular, the therapist had to confront the patient's ambivalent feelings about him as white and male, as well as understand and resolve his own cultural countertransference.

At a certain point during her first session I noticed a muted, almost deadened quality in her movements. "What are you feeling?" I asked.

"What feelings? I have no feelings," she quickly replied.

"Of course you have feelings."

"If I do, I don't know about them."

"You never feel happy or sad?"

"No."

"You never feel angry?"

"No."

"Scared?"

"No. I'm telling you, I don't have any feelings."

"How long have you not had any feelings?"

"As long as I can remember."

Audrey sat before me with a wry, confident smile. To me, and to the world in general, she certainly appeared to have feelings. At that moment her wry smile and her direct gaze seemed to indicate a degree of anger and bitterness. However, the rest of her—the matter-of-fact voice, the blank eyes, the limp body and arms, the legs that were dangling from the chair, the conservative black dress that was draped over her like a blanket—all suggested resignation. I sensed a well of feelings locked inside her, but she had dissociated from them. Hence, even though physically she was an attractive woman, because of this dissociation and its allied contraction of energy, my first impression was of a plain and repressed personality.

I gazed at her, sorting out what she had told me so far. She was in her late thirties and came from an educated African-American family. She had called me after she had tried working briefly with several other therapists, including a black therapist and a woman therapist, none of whom she felt had been able to understand her. She did not know if any therapist could, especially a white male—but she was determined to give it one more try.

"If you don't know what you're feeling," I asked, "how can you know what you are?"

"I don't," she replied, again in her matter-of-fact manner, as though discussing the weather. "I don't know who I am on a personal level. I only know who I am symbolically."

"And who are you symbolically?"

"I'm a black woman. I'm a black woman who has spent her life fighting racism. I'm a symbol, you see. A symbol of the black struggle. I don't have a personality separate from that symbolism."

"But as a symbol you have feelings?"

She flashed the wry smile again. "Only anger at racism. That's it.  That's all I'm allowed to be angry at."

"Allowed?  By whom?"

"My father."

"You're only allowed to be angry if your father permits it?"

"That's right."

"And he allows you to be angry about racism?"

"You got it."

"Are you aware of any anger at me, being that I'm a white therapist?"

"In that I have a generalized anger at whites, not to mention men, I could work up some anger at you on that symbolic level. On that symbolic level, I also have anger at blacks for their black racism toward whites.  But not on a personal level.  On a personal level I have no feelings.  I pretend to have feelings.  In my daily life I smile at people and show gobs of sympathy and love and understanding.  I play the role of the virtuous, caring woman.  My brother calls me Saint Audrey.  He says I have a saint complex, whatever that means.    I play the role magnificently and people tell me their problems and look up to me.  But inside I know I'm faking.  I have no real feelings.  It's all an act.  Inside there's nothing but a void."

### From the Literature

Audrey's case, perhaps more than any other that I have dealt with, confronted me with the overlapping tasks of resolving resistances stemming from issues of character, sex, and race.   Such cases have become more frequent in recent years and they require their own method of working through, a method that necessitates the distinguishing of character from sex and sex from race, as well as differentiating the transference relationship from the real relationship.

Upon first meeting her, Audrey seemed to fit the description of what Deutsch termed the *as if* personality type.   In the early part of the twentieth century in Vienna, she met with a number of such personalities, young women who had dissociated or depersonalized to a point where they had no sense of any kind of identity, who went through life hiding behind a façade. "The individual's whole relationship to life has something about it which is lacking in genuineness and yet outwardly runs along 'as if' it were complete" (Deutsch, 1942, p. 263). Perhaps such young women were more prevalent during the Victorian era, when societal sexual repression was so all-encompassing. Deutsch saw these personalities as schizoid types, on the border of schizophrenia. Today they would probably be called borderlines.

However, the research on borderlines has advanced considerably since Deutsch's day. The "as if" personality might be seen as one variation of borderlines in which splitting and loss of a cohesive self is a most prominent feature. Now it is generally recognized that borderlines represent a mixed bag of characterological trends, encompassing sadomasochism, bipolar features, paranoia, narcissism, hysteria, and impulsivity, among other things. There are some features common to most borderlines: They tend toward splitting, they tend toward primitive idealization and devaluation, often in rapid succession, and they suffer from, as Kernberg puts it, an excess of aggression. Building on Klein's (1932) work on projective identification, on Jung's (1927) and Winnicott's (1953) concepts of the real and false selves, on Jacobson's (1964) work on borderline depression, and on Balint's (1968) depiction of "basic fault" personalities, Kernberg explains that excessive aggression is warded off through splitting and the associated defenses of primitive idealization, omnipotence, devaluation, denial, and projective identification. By splitting themselves from their negative self and object representations, borderlines are able to protect their positive (false) self and object representations, but as a result they do not establish a strong ego nor a cohesive self. Neutralization of aggression never takes place, as the integration of positive and negative self and object representations cannot occur when splitting predominates.

Audrey's character type matches Kernberg's (Kernberg, Selzer, Koenigsberg, Carr, and Appelbaum, 1989) precise description of the borderline personality organization based on three structural criteria: identity diffusion, primitive defensive operations, and deficient ego and superego functioning. Kernberg writes of the subjective experience of chronic emptiness, contradictory self-perceptions and perceptions of others, which lead to a lack of personality integration. Audrey often reported a chronic emptiness (representing a dissociation from her feelings and the inability to make a genuine emotional connection with other people), and she demonstrated a lack of personality integration and contradictory perceptions of self and others. She appeared to be a borderline with both typical borderline features and an "as if" quality. She was, in a sense, an amalgamation of a Kernbergian borderline and a Deutschian "as if" personality.

Kernberg considered Deutsch's "as if" personality to be a preliminary description of the borderline (1975, p. 7). I would say, rather, that it is instead a variety of borderline. Although I found the identity defusion of which Kernberg speaks, as well as certain primitive defensive operations such as splitting and projective identification, in the transference, I also found a rather predominant emphasis on the sense of not being a real person or, as she put it, "not having any feelings," which contrasts with the Kernbergian model, as does her obsessive-compulsive substructure which differs from the usual impulsive one. However, it later turned out that she did have feelings but was not in touch with them.

She seemed to have a manic-depressive core to her personality—an excess of aggression that got channeled into a bipolar mood cycle. That is, the aggression was externalized during manic episodes, or it was taken out on herself during depressions. She related a pattern of working obsessively at some job or another, climbing the ladder, and then suddenly one day not being able to get out of bed to go to her job. She would invariably get fired, then lie in her bed for days and feel nothing until she managed to flip back into the manic mode. Her claim to have no feelings had its source in her superego (her father's voice) which demanded that she be a saint and thereby censored almost all her real feelings. Hence, she was completely unaware of her aggression, her mania, or its meaning. She projectively identified other personalities as being aggressive to towards her, while she, "Saint Audrey," had to endure it.

Audrey's personality development had been arrested somewhere back in her early childhood, and as an adult she did not know who she was. She had a finely honed façade, but her façade was unreal, not centered in her feelings, and hence it was fragile. She did not possess a mature ego or a cohesive self. She suffered from identity diffusion and low self-esteem stemming from the sense of a void inside her (where her feelings should have been). Her ego could not adequately perform ordinary tasks such as reality testing, affect toleration, or delayed gratification. For example, she could not tell whether I really cared about her or whether I was just out to exploit and dominate her (like her father). Her splitting precluded her being able to achieve real intimacy with any individual, and bound her destructively to her father. If people believed her false self and had negative feelings toward her, she resented them.

She had spent her adult years in a virtual exile from herself and from others. She had had only the briefest kinds of relationships with men in which she would give herself to them and then not see them again. She related to them as a saint, as Saint Audrey, listening to them, controlling them, keeping them at a distance, thereby maintaining, in her words, "a sense of superiority." Relationships with women were nonexistent—competitive urges toward them sabotaged all attempts by women to relate to her. Intellectually gifted, she would excel at jobs for a year or two then be unable to continue, unable to carry on the charade (her "as if" self) or suppress the accumulation of negative feelings any longer. The one secondary gratification that sustained her was her narcissistic belief in her own innate superiority—an intellectual and moral superiority—and she clung to this belief as a child clings to a security blanket. This secret delusion compensated for her exile: she was alone, she told herself, because she was too good for the world, too good for Blacks, too good for Whites, and hence no one could understand her, including her string of therapists.

However, understanding and resolving Audrey's characterological resistances was only one aspect of a complicated case. She also presented what I have referred to elsewhere (Schoenewolf, 1993) as cultural resistances and what Grey (1993) terms the *enactment of social imperatives*. Such resistances, in contrast to characterological resistances that are related to the transference, have their main source in cultural influences. She had resistances related to my being a

"Caucasoid" (as she once jokingly called me) and a male. While these resistances had connections to childhood developmental factors, they seemed also to be attached to two current cultural movements—embodying radical African-American and feminist beliefs—which had been incorporated by her superego. I was a white, and whites, according to current radical black ideology, cannot possibly understand blacks. I was a male, and males, according to current radical feminist ideology, cannot possibly understand females. The former resistance stemmed in part from her identification with her father—a black radical minister—as well as from a black cultural milieu in which whites are viewed as oppressors and exploiters. This is not to say prejudice and discrimination doesn't exist, but rather that this particular patient saw discrimination everywhere, even when somebody was trying to help her. The latter resistance apparently had its origin primarily in the radical feminist culture that currently permeates all aspects of our society, which views males as oppressors, exploiters, and sexual abusers. In addition, since her ego ideal (formed mostly through her relationship with her father) identified herself as a martyr and a victim, she was all the more susceptible to the radical feminist notion of woman-as-victim and the radical black notion of black-as-victim, along with the narcissistic grandiosity of moral superiority inherent in these stances.

These resistances posed considerable obstacles—on top of those presented by her characterological resistances. In addition, from her contradictory statements about race and gender I gathered that her identity diffusion prevented her from identifying herself as a black or a white or even as a woman. She did not feel comfortable with either blacks or whites, nor at home with either her masculine or feminine side. This added additional confusion to her resistances, which required a gradual and painstaking sorting out and working through.

My work with her consisted not just of treating an "as if" or borderline personality, but also in conducting cross-cultural therapy. This entailed having to find a way to strengthen Audrey's reality-testing function to the extent that she could distinguish between the discrimination against blacks and women that does exist, and the discrimination she imagined when she was in a depressive state, and which she then projected onto and identified as belonging to me. It also entailed sorting out my own countertransference to determine if I indeed harbored discriminatory feelings or whether they had been projected onto me.

## The Reconstruction

Audrey was a middle child, caught between two half-brothers. The older brother was the offspring of her father and his first wife, who died during labor. The younger brother was the child of her father's third wife, her stepmother. Her father was African American with dark skin. Her biological mother was Native American with lighter skin. Audrey resembled her mother in both shape and skin color, while her brothers had the darker skin of their father. She grew up in the South.

She did not see much of her father during her first three years. He developed an illness and was in and out of the hospital, and for a time it appeared he might die. During that period she recalled being close to her mother. Her earliest memory was about an incident of urinary incontinence. She wet her pants while at nursery school at the age of 4, and felt horrified by it. But her mother was "very kind" and told her "Those things happen." I tentatively interpreted the centrality of this memory as indicative of a trauma that may have led to the development of an obsessive-compulsive trend in her personality; she had to be perfect, neat, lest she "shamed" herself. The memory of her mother's kindness may be a screen memory masking her own guilt—perhaps oedipal guilt about having later succeeded in getting rid of her mother and having her father all to herself.

Sometimes around the same year her father came home from the hospital and began a long convalescence. At first he seemed like a stranger and Audrey was afraid of him. One night she heard her mother and father quarreling. She wobbled sleepily into their bedroom to find her mother aiming a pistol at her father—the pistol her father kept in a drawer beside the bed. As Audrey stood in the doorway, the gun went off, wounding her father in the shoulder. While the father was in the hospital being treated for this wound, her mother explained why she had shot her father. They were having an argument about which school to send Audrey to the following year. Her father, who was a minister active in civil rights causes, wanted to send her to an all-white school in order to force the school to integrate. Her mother was absolutely against it, saying she did not want her daughter to be used this way. Their feelings about this issue were quite strong, and her father was stubborn about his right, as the father, to decide the matter.

Her mother was convicted of assault but did not serve any time in prison. As a compromise solution, she agreed to a divorce and to giving up custody of her child. She also agreed not to see Audrey again. Hence, at the age of 5 Audrey was separated from her mother and did not see her again until she was 21 years of age. She recalled going to the train station with her mother on the day the mother packed her things and left. As her mother was about to board the train, she ran up to her, leaving her father and brother standing behind, and clung to her, crying.

"Please don't leave me," she begged. "Please, please, please don't leave me, Mommy! Please! Let me go with you! Why can't I go with you?" She did not want to stay with her father, who was still a stranger to her.

"You have to stay. The court said so. I can't do anything about it. But I'll always be thinking of you, and I'll always love you."

As she returned to the house with her father and older brother, she felt terrified, knowing that her father had seen her beg her mother to take her away. From then on she believed she had to be extra careful to please her father, lest he exact revenge on her for being "a traitor." This may have reinforced her obsessive-compulsive features.

Even before her mother had gone away, during the time things were being decided in court, it had been her task to care for him during his convalescence. This care included bathing him. Until she had shot him, his wife had done this bathing, but afterwards he did not want her to touch him and enlisted Audrey to take over this chore. She recalled seeing her father's penis and wanting to touch it (he washed that part of himself), and had many erotic, Oedipal fantasies about being her father's wife and having his children. Later, in treatment, she brought in a dream that alluded to this period.

In the dream, she was masturbating a horse or some kind of four-legged animal. It had a dog's penis, but the animal was bigger than a dog. When I asked for her associations to this dream, she recalled bathing her father and seeing his penis. I interpreted her confusion about what kind of animal she was masturbating to the confused feelings she must have had about bathing her father—a mixture of resentment about being taken away from her mother, erotic excitement at winning her father and being privy to such intimacy with him, guilt about crossing the incest taboo, and perhaps a fear and envy of this appendage, which she and her mother did not possess, and which left them both helpless under its power. In addition, the horse and dog perhaps symbolized her feeling that her father was an "animal" whose aggression she feared.

Soon afterward, her father remarried. His third wife was light-skinned like her mother but much younger. From the time the stepmother appeared, any semblance of intimacy with her father ceased completely. Indeed, her stepmother quickly intervened and would often not allow Audrey to even talk with her father, asserting that, "He's busy, don't bother him." Her relationship with her stepmother was quite strained. The stepmother was competitive and jealous of her, and enjoyed flaunting her sexual relationship with her father by kissing him and sitting on his lap in front of the children, acting like a child herself.

It was at this time that her father began sending her to all-white schools. Each fall they would move to a new town and he would make pronouncements in each district about the evils of segregation, and he would defiantly being his older son and daughter to each new school, usually accompanied by Federal marshals. Audrey remembered the isolation  of being the only black student in each school, but also the sense of moral superiority of having all of these white students hate her and feeling pity for them. She recalled moving from town to town, never being able to make any friends, black or white, never being able to make any lasting attachments other than those to his own immediate family.

"That must have been when I developed my Saint Audrey persona," she remarked, upon recalling this period. "My father would always preach that my brother and I should only have love and pity for the white students. We weren't supposed to have any hatred for anybody. We were supposed to be above it all. However, we could see that this was a case of 'Do as I say, not as I do,' for it was quite evident that he had tons of anger toward whites. So while on a verbal level we were told not to have anger at whites, his own behavior told us that in actuality it was allowable."

What was definitely not allowed was to have any anger—nor any complaint whatsoever—about her father or her stepmother. Her father had a temper the intensity and unpredictability of which was terrifying. His way of whipping her, for example, was to have her lie on her bed, place a pillow over her head, and sit on her so she could not move or scream. "You are very very bad," he would assert, and give her one hundred whacks. If he heard a scream, he would yell, "Swallow it!" This way of punishment, with its combination of physical abuse and negative indoctrination, termed by Miller (1983) as "poisonous pedagogy," insures, according to her research, that a child will become severely repressed and will be prone to defenses such as splitting and dissociation, since the child has been told she is very bad if she even thinks anything bad about her father.

The refusal of the father to listen to anything other than positive statements toward him caused her to feel more and more alienated and disturbed. As she became more disturbed, she developed a reputation as the family oddball. Her brothers teased her about being oversensitive. Her stepmother saw her as a threat and condescended to her. She was the only girl, the daughter of a woman who her father never talked about, the child with lighter skin. She perceived a double standard in the way her brothers were treated and the way she was treated by her father and by her paternal grandmother, who would visit frequently. Grandmother doted on the father and Audrey's brothers but was contemptuous toward her. There was apparently a generational pattern in the family of showing extreme favoritism toward sons and contempt toward daughters. But she could say nothing about any of this, nor did she trust her perceptions about it. Indeed, she appeared to introject the family's perspective, demeaning herself and idealizing her family.

A dream she brought to therapy during the initial stages

shows this introjection and idealization. She was on a boat with her family. Suddenly they disappeared. The boat moved along a river, and on the bank she saw statues of Greek gods, all toppled over. She realized her family was still there but asleep. She woke them and asked, "Did you see that?" "No," they answered. "We didn't see anything." She told them to look back, but they could not see the statues. The dream seems to indicate her idealization (her family as Greek gods), as well as her anger in the form of a wish for them to disappear (as they did in the beginning of the dream), or at least to be knocked down off their pedestals. The fact that she can see something that they can't see perhaps denotes her need to repress and hide her aggression—her wish to get rid of them—from her family, as well as representing her family's continual misunderstanding of her. It may also show her alienation from them (she is the oddball in the dream, as in real life)—that is, her introjection of their attitude toward her. Finally, viewed from a gender or racial perspective, the toppled statues might also suggest her wish to topple white male oppression.

Her false self, erected upon the fragile foundation of the narcissistic delusion of superiority and control, was shattered one day when she was 35 years old. She had met a man whom she thought was different from the rest, whom she believed was on her level. He was a black man with "education and class." He was a businessman with an air of confidence and determination, and that attracted her to him. They saw each other for a few months and he seemed to understand her like nobody else had ever understood her. He understood her the way she wanted to be understood (which I silently interpreted as his mirroring her grandiosity). She opened up to him, even felt sexual pleasure, and entertained thoughts of marrying him. Then, on that pivotal day, she received a bank statement indicating that her $30,000 in savings, which she had been planning to use for law school, had been withdrawn. The man had disappeared and she was never able to find him. She had lost him, her money, and any semblance of well-being. She sank into a lengthy depression.

She reported that upon hearing of this incident, her father, stepmother and two brothers abandoned her. When she wrote them, they did not answer. When she called them, they were brief and perfunctory.

"They were embarrassed by my problem rather than sympathetic," she recalled. "They saw me as an embarrassment to the family." At about that time, she had a recurring dream in which she found her family dead—her father, stepmother, and two brothers. She did not know how they had died, but she buried them in a pit in the ground. Somehow she could see through the dirt, as if she had X-ray vision, and saw the rats eating their bodies. She was unable to make sense of this dream; for in her waking life she continued to view things from her family's perspective (they were ideal) and did not harbor any anger at them; if they deserted her now, she decided, they probably had a good reason. I saw the dream as denoting not only her rage at her family, but also the rage that was taken out on her self (in the "pit" of her stomach), the result of this ultimate betrayal by the family she had still hoped would someday acknowledge her worth.

Upon being evicted from her apartment a year after this incident, her younger brother finally took pity on her and invited her to move in with him. For a year she slept on a couch in his living room, unable to go back to work. Normally compulsive, she did not bathe for months at a time, ate only to survive, and seldom left the apartment. After a year she finally took a job as a part-time receptionist. It was then she first went into psychotherapy. Her first therapist, a novice female, apparently mirrored her false self and Audrey soon left her in contempt. The second therapist, an African American, wanted to join her anger at whites but, according to her, could not tolerate her anger at blacks or at her father. Her third therapist, a white male, did not believe in talking about the past, she reported, so he frustrated her need to analyze and reconstruct her childhood.

## Characterological and Cultural Resistances

The concept of resistance has been used in psychoanalysis to describe a patient's unwillingness to do the work of psychoanalysis due to the negative, erotic, or even the positive transference. I refer to this kind of resistance as the characterological resistance. However, in treating Audrey and other patients in recent times I have come across another resistance, which I refer to as the cultural resistance. This is a resistance that is primarily not based on personality factors traceable to childhood traumas and the like, but instead on attitudinal trends in society. In Audrey's case, the cultural resistances proved stronger than the characterological resistances, although the two also sometimes overlapped.

In the beginning her "as if" personality showed itself in the transference. I was at times her father or older brother (whom she linked together) and at times her younger brother. At other times I might have been her mother, who would be tender and caring but who might abandon her. In either case I was an exalted figure. This meant that she idealized me and needed my approval and my permission to exist.

However, much of the time I was the white male. Since her dad did not allow her to express any negative feelings, except for anger at whites about racism, for a long time she did not express any negative feelings about me or about the therapy. Instead, when she was angry at something I had said or done, she would verbalize generalized anger at whites or males. During those times when she went on tirades about racism, I had to be very careful to mirror her point of view. It was not that I thought she was entirely wrong. Racism does exist and had affected her development in many ways. However, her narcissistic need to make racism responsible for all her problems, and the allied refusal to take any responsibility for her own contribution to her bad relationships and to minimize the contribution of her dysfunctional family, complicated the transference. Hence, from the beginning her cultural resistance was most prominent. It originated from the cultural climate in society as well as from her family history. More than anything, I became a symbol of white oppression, or of white male oppression. Because of this, occasional impasses developed during which she became so furious at me, and so convinced that as a white male I could not understand her, that she would fall silent.

My way of breaking an impasse was to insist that she see me as a human being, not as a male or a member of the white race. As simple as this sounds, it turned out not to be so simple at all. During the time of this treatment, issues of sexism and racism were prominent in America, and it was difficult for blacks and whites or men and women to see past each other's gender or skin color and relate to each other as humans. Ironically, the Human Rights Movement's obsessive emphasis on issues of gender and race only served to increase the gender and racial polarity; and the result was that females more often than not went into treatment with female therapists, males with male therapists; and blacks with black therapists. And so the same politics persisted in the therapy. Yet I plowed on.

"The only we we're going to get past this impasse is to forget about politics and concentrate on what you're feeling and what I'm feeling," I told her. "It's important for you to distinguish between your assumptions about me as a symbolic white male, and the reality of how I'm actually acting toward you in the here-and-now. Am I trying to oppress you? Is my attitude negative or demeaning? Am I making any stereotypical assumptions about you?"

"There's nothing I can really pinpoint, except for your having me lie on the couch while you sit up. It's rather oppressive. It places me in a subservient position."

"Do you feel subservient when you lie on a dentist's chair?"

"That's different. He has to have me in that position in order to do his work."

"So do I. This is the procedure that works best for me, because it's the one that brings the deepest introspection and change."

"That sounds right. But I'm still not sure I can trust you. You may just be pretending for the sake of the treatment. I don't know how you behave outside these walls when you see a black person. For all I know, you may be two-faced, like all the whites I've ever met." We had to go over this again and again as I repeatedly called attention to how I was treating her during her sessions. Although she did not give up the notion that I was two-faced, she gradually understood that all conjectures about who I was outside the office were either characterological or cultural resistances.

As we continued to explore her transference thoughts about me, she began to realize that it was she, rather than I, who had been making stereotypical assumptions. She was assuming things about me based on my being white and male. As a white, I was arrogant, spoiled, and full of unconscious hate toward blacks; as a male, I was superior, dogmatic, entitled, insensitive, and full of unconscious hate toward women. Fortunately, because of her upbringing by a white-skinned mother and black father, she could see both sides, and the transference analysis was made somewhat easier.

Resolving the cultural resistance got us past the initial impasses. For a time she seemed to understand that I was not The White Male but a human being with his own unique thoughts and feelings. We began to work on material related to her father, brothers, and mother and the many resistances associated with them. As we did this, her repression of her real feelings and memories began to pry loose. The displacement of her rage onto me and onto whites and men gave way to a more complicated picture of a myriad of feelings and memories about her father, mother, brothers, and other people in her life. At the same time, the transference toward me because more characterological than cultural, rooted in an oral-stage merger with me as a surrogate mother.

For several months we went through a typical honeymoon period. She called me, "My Dr. Schoenewolf," and would come in smiling and repeatedly affirming how lucky she was to find me. She also attributed her good feelings to a combination of the antidepressant that had been prescribed for her by an affiliated psychiatrist and the melatonin she was taking on her own to help her sleep. While the positive transference held sway, we were able to do some good work. For example, one day when I did not answer a phone call right away, she came in regretting that she had opened up to me so much. She then recalled a time during her childhood when she had opened up to a girlfriend, confiding that she hated her stepmother. The girlfriend told the stepmother and Audrey was severely punished. In this session she was able to tie together the links between her fears of depending on me to the formerly repressed, now conscious memory and the conflicts that underpinned her present psychopathology.

However, the honeymoon was brief, and gradually she shifted back into a negative transference and its accompanying resistance, in a more insistent form. The negative transference again expressed the feeling that I, a white male, was oppressing her, although now she could not be as convinced about it as she could before.

She came in one day and announced that she was sitting up and that she would be sitting up from then on. She sat in one of my chairs. She scowled at me.

"You mean you're not going to lie down ever again?"

"That's correct."

"That sounds final."

"It is."

"Can't we discuss it?"

"I'm sure we will." (Wry smile.)

I interpreted this cultural resistance, as well as the negative father transference that underpinned it, and at the end of the session she seemed to understand. There were a few sessions of positive transference. But before long she would again be just as adamant that I was simply a white male who did not "get it." Upon first refusing to lie down, she grudgingly acknowledged that she felt she was about to get in touch with some feelings, and she did not want to have any "messy sentimentalism" in front of me. It might make her more dependent on me than she already was and then I would take advantage of her. (I interpreted this to mean that I would use her in some way for my benefit, either sexually or professionally.) Later when I reminded her of this statement she claimed to have forgotten it; she just kept reiterating that she wanted to be on equal terms with me, not oppressed. In another session, when I persisted in asking for her thoughts about lying on the couch and she could come up with none, I asked her to finish the following sentence with the first thought that came into her head: "If I lie on the couch, then...?" Her reply: "You win."

At times I found myself becoming annoyed with her, and I knew this was my countertransference. I had thoughts of wanting to say to her, "If I'm a white male, then go to a black female therapist!" These thoughts were transient, and I also realized they had to do with my own childhood traumas rather than with a cultural counterresistance. I resented her because she was troublesome, not because she was black or a woman. "You're locked into a power struggle with me," I interpreted.

"It's the power struggle you would have liked to have had with your father, but couldn't because it was too threatening. In your childhood it would have been productive to resist your father, but now, as a patient, it's totally counterproductive."

By insisting that we focus on the real relationship between her and me, and contrasting it, though interpretations, with her relationship with her father, we were seemingly able to make some headway in resolving the resistance. But, like a virulent fever, the resistance still clung to her very being. We went through an extended cycle of positivity and negativity that lasted almost a year. During that year I could see progress in an inverse way; the cycles of negativity began to last longer and the negative transference took on an almost psychotic mode insofar as she was more and more stubborn about it. A point was then reached when she would no longer tolerate any interpretations. I was a white male who could not possibly understand her, and that was all there was to it. The final breaking of the fever came only when I joined her resistance one day.

She came in saying, for perhaps the hundredth time, that the therapy wasn't working, she wasn't making any progress, and I didn't understand her. She added that her friend Mary (whom she had repeatedly emphasized was a black woman) totally understood her. "It's amazing how easy it is to talk with her," she said.

Now, at last, I gave vent to the thoughts that I had hitherto suppressed. "Perhaps you should make Mary your therapist. Or go to a black female therapist."

"You sound annoyed."

"Why would I be annoyed?" I asked as calmly as I could.

"Because I keep implying that Mary can understand me better than you can."

"Did you want to annoy me?"

"Maybe. But that doesn't invalidate what I was saying. I mean, maybe you can't understand me because you're white and male. Maybe you're not aware of your own sexism and racism. Maybe I would work better with a black woman therapist."

She gave me a pointed look.

"Maybe you would."

Her expression suddenly changed. "Are you trying to get rid of me?"

"No, I'm trying to help you think things out."

She sighed and looked a bit sad. "If you want my opinion, I'd like to stay with you and struggle through this. How can we break this impasse?" she muttered. I could see she was truly hurt. "As much as I hate to admit it, you may be right about the power struggle. Maybe I am pushing you away the way I'd like to push away my father."

The following session she lay back down on the couch. "There, I'm complying, all right. But I don't like it one bit." I asked her to talk about not liking it and she launched into a diatribe about her father's total domination of her.

### Discussion

The major trauma in her life, in terms of Audrey's character development, seems to have been her separation from her mother at the age of 5. In being separation from her mother, she was in a sense separated from her self. I speculate that it was here that her sadomasochistic and narcissistic characters (the martyrdom and the feelings of moral superiority) first began. First of all, she lost the model upon whom her female identity had rested. Her mother, who had once soothed Audrey's feelings of shame, now had become an object of shame herself (a criminal). After her mother's departure, Audrey became the lone female in a house of males; this exacerbated her masculinity complex (Adler 1929), gender identity confusion, and dissociation from self and others. Her mother's departure also must have felt like an abandonment, one which she could not mourn, since her father would not allow her mother's name to be mentioned in the house. Hence she could not work through or integrate her feelings and memories about her mother, her mother's conduct (shooting her father), or her mother's departure, which again added to her alienation from her self. Then, on top of this, she soon became a pawn of her father's civil rights game, which served to reinforce her impoverishment of self.

By using her as a tool of integration, her father failed to respond to her on a human level. She became his narcissistic extension, her job being to serve his own false, grandiose self. Her mission was to act out his frustration and anger at whites. His frustration and anger was probably based both on reality and grandiosity. The reality was that there was plenty of discrimination and schools in the South were segregated and black schools were inferior. The grandiosity had to do with his mother, who according to Audrey, had raised him to believe that he was appointed by God to save blacks and that his judgments were divine. Hence his feelings of entitlement made him all the more impatient and susceptible to frustration and anger. His grandiosity was such that he saw all those around him—his children, his wife, anybody with whom he was involved—as puppets to be used at will. Since he and his purpose were divine, he could not be doubted or contradicted.

The period of bathing her father seems to have fixated her sexual development. Her inability to experience any sexual feelings in her relations with men was perhaps associated in part to the repressed memories of her emotionally incestuous relationship with her father, and perhaps to her brothers. It was probably also related to the rage that lurked in her unconscious and could never be expressed to her father, and hence to any man; it therefore had to be defended against through splitting and its associated primitive idealization and devaluation of the men she became involved with as an adult. Finally, it was related to her mother's traumatic departure and its effect on her female identity confusion.

Often in families it is the mother who clings to a daughter, preventing her from making the oedipal turn to the father. For example, Chasseguet-Smirgel, in a study of the Oedipus complexes of several female patients, concluded that they all had one common feature: "the mother was sadistic and castrating, the father was good and vulnerable" (1964, p. 132). In this case, the opposite happened; the father prevented the daughter from bonding with the mother. On the other hand, her inability to relate to women was also probably linked to the stepmother's crushing rivalry. Perhaps it was the one-two punch of the father's tyranny and the stepmother's competiveness that was the final straw of her dissociation from her self, and resulted in her own peculiar personality makeup.

"You integrated the schools," I once told Audrey, "but you didn't integrate yourself."

The additional complication in this case, as in so many cases these days, is the cross-cultural factor. Today in America people are often viewed as ethnic symbols rather than as human beings. Audrey's identity, from very early on, was tied to her role as a symbol of racial integration. Later, as an adult, radical black and feminist cultural movements reinforced her ego ideal of the morally superior black woman who must suffer and die in the world of white racism and male sexism. To try to flourish in this world, she decided, was futile. Hence, she became a prisoner of "liberation," since the very movements that promised to liberate her ended up positively reinforcing her borderline paranoid sexual and racial attitudes to the effect that "all whites are biased" and "all males are oppressors."

Treating borderlines has become an increasingly common matter in psychotherapy; treating people from various ethnic groups, who bring with them cultural resistances, has also become increasingly common. Indeed, one often encounters both at the same time, as in this case. Those with the weakest egos and the lowest self-esteem, who are full of repressed rage, are most prone to identify with a radical movement, which offers instant (though false) elevation of self esteem and an instant outlet for the expression of rage.

Increasingly today the tackling of cross-cultural issues takes up considerable time in therapy. As demonstrated in the case history, the way out of the impasses that result from such issues seems to involve focusing on the interpersonal dynamics of the therapy relationship. Here is where psychoanalytic therapy works perhaps better than any other, for it presents the opportunity to point out to the patient the difference between what she is projecting onto the therapist and who the therapist really is. The pitfall of cross-cultural therapy is the development by the therapist of a cultural counterresistance. The white therapist, for example, in treating a black patient, may have a need to prove to himself and the patient that he is not a racist and therefore develop a reaction-formation that blinds him to the patient's real psychodynamics. The black patient (especially if he or she is borderline) may then lose respect for the therapist and defeat the therapy. A similar thing can happen when a male therapist treats a female patient, especially one who uses a feminist defense. The male may have a need to prove that he is not a sexist and therefore develops a reaction formation that blinds him to the patient's use of feminism to control and defeat the therapy.

Another problem occurs when a therapist and patient share a particular ethnicity, political view, or religious view. Here the two may form a collusion of cultural resistance and counterresistance that may keep them from analyzing deeper transferential issues. For instance, a black therapist may treat a black patient, both of them subscribing to radical black ideology. The therapist may reinforce the patient's belief that all her problems stem from white racism and the treatment may then avoid transference issues entirely.

I have tried to write this in human language, as well as in the language of psychoanalysis, in order to present a visceral understanding of the case. In addition, as I am an eclectic psychoanalyst, I have referenced authors of differing theoretical positions, believing that all schools have contributed to the growth of psychoanalysis, and no school, past or present, should be dismissed out of hand. Finally, I recognize that the issues I have written about (and the fact that I am a white male writing about them) will engender controversy and criticism. I hope that there will be a few people, in this generation or next, who can hear me out.

### Postscript

The subtitle of this paper might be, "A woman in search of her mother and her self." During the course of the treatment, the patient eventually did contact her mother, but not until she had spent months working through her anger at her mother for abandoning her. At first she was still too angry for normal conversation. Once the anger had been addressed, mother and daughter began talking on the phone in a way probably similar to that of a normal mother and daughter interaction.

They talked twice a week about what was going on in each other's lives. In time Audrey came to see how much her mother had always loved her and still loved her. And in time, she recaptured a part of her self that had been lost all those years in between, a part that identified with her mother's femininity and accepted her own. I saw this as an integral part of the therapy. It still continues now, as I write these words.

**References:**

Adler, A. (1929). Problems in Neurosis: a Book of Case Histories. P. Mairet (ed.). New York, Harper & Row, 1964.

Balint, m. (1968). *The Basic Fault.* London, Tavistock.

Deutsch, H. (1942). *Neurosis and Character Types.* New York, International Universities Press.

Fenichel, O. (1945). *The Psychoanalytic Theory of Neurosis.* New York, W. W. Norton.

Grey, C. C. (1993). Culture, character, and the analytic engagement: Toward a subversive psychoanalysis. *Contemporary Psychoanalysis,* 29:487-502.

Jacobson, E. (1964). The *Self and the Object World.* New York, International Universities Press.

Jung, C. G. (1927). The structure of the psyche. In: *The Portable Jung,* ed. J. Campbell. New York, Viking, 1971, pp. 23-16.

Kernberg, O. (1975). *Borderline Conditions and Pathological Narcissism.* Northvale, NJ: Jason Aronson.

Kernberg, O., Selzer, M. A., Koenigsberg, H. W., Carr, A. C. and Appelbaum, A. H. (1989). *Psychodynamic Psychotherapy of*

*Borderline Patients.* New York, Basic Books.

Klein, M. (1932). *The Psychoanalysis of Children*, tr. A. Strachey. New York, Delacorte Press, 1975.

Miller, A. (1983). *For Your Own Good: Hidden Cruelty in Childhood and the Roots of Violence.* New York, Farrar, Straus, Giroux.

Schoenewolf, G. (1993). *Counterresistance.* Northvale, NJ, Jason Aronson.

Winnicott, D. W. (1953). Symptom tolerance in paediatrics. In: *Through Paediatrics to Psycho-Analysis.* New York, Basic Books, 1975, pp. 101-117.

# 11

# The Scapegoat and the Holy Cow in Group Therapy

---

Tolstoy once said that all happy families were alike and that all unhappy families were unhappy in different ways. I would say that all unhappy families and all unhappy groups (as in therapy groups) are also alike in certain ways. Both unhappy families and unhappy groups tend to have scapegoats and holy cows, members who are devalued and on whom everything is blamed, and members who are idealized and to whom all credit is given. This paper looks at the etiology of scapegoats and holy cows and how they may be approached in group therapy.

---

### Introduction

The novel and movie, *Ordinary People* (Guest, 1968), provides a deft portrait of a family in which one son is rejected and the other is idealized. In this family the mother is the dominant parent, so she becomes the "casting director" and decides who will play what role. Her
214

oldest son, a tall blond-haired youth, seems to represent everything that is good, bright, strong, and noble. In one flashback scene, the mother is gazing rapturously at this son, laughing and applauding and swooning at his every word. When this son accidently drowns while boating with his younger brother, the mother is overcome with grief and bitterness and blames her youngest son for his death. Long after the oldest son's death, the mother continues to keep his room, with its many athletic trophies, intact, and visits it as one would visit a shrine. He is clearly her holy cow.

The youngest son, the focus of the book and film, is apparently viewed by this same mother as representing everything that is bad, ugly, weak, and ignoble. He stutters when he speaks. He starts and quits things. He has problems academically and socially. He attempts suicide and has to be hospitalized much to the mother's mortification. In one scene in both the book and movie, his mother blames him for all the problems of their family, and when the son notes that she had not visited him when he was in the hospital and blurts out, "If Bucky had been in the hospital you would have visited Bucky!" she retorts, "Bucky would never have been in the hospital!" Clearly, this younger son is her scapegoat.

Scapegoats and holy cows are a recurring theme in many families. Some families, with several children, have one of each. Others, with only one child, will have one or the other. A combination of constitutional and environmental factors combine in shaping scapegoat and holy cow personalities. However, the most significant factor in their formation seems to be the parents' narcissism.

### The Formation of Scapegoats

The Scapegoat is an old Jewish concept. The Bible tells how long ago people who experienced plagues, famines or droughts believed that God was punishing them for a sin. Since they did not know who among them had committed the sin, they performed a ritual. A goat was brought into the center of the community and the whole community gathered around. One by one, members of the community dumped their individual sins upon the goat. The goat was then driven out into the desert, away from the community. The hope was that the goat would take on the sins of the community and put the community back into God's favor.

Early psychoanalysts hinted at how scapegoats could emerge in family life. Although Freud did not mention scapegoats in particular, he described scapegoating behavior connected with the Oedipal triangle, noting how a boy may become too close to the mother during this stage, becoming an Oedipal conqueror. Sometimes such a child is seen as an Oedipal threat to the father (Freud, 1939), and then the father scorns the child as a way of assuaging his own unconscious castration fears. Sometimes the chosen child actually has some kind of mental or physical defect which the parents then magnify and see as a sign not only of the child's, but also of their own, inferiority (Adler, 1927).

Vogel and Bell (1981), in a study of disturbed families, noted a correlation between the emotionally disturbed child and the scapegoat. In their view, scapegoated children became emotionally disturbed as a result of the state of tension that arises inside of them due to the role they are forced to play. The more they are treated liked scapegoats, the more the stress chemicals accumulate and linger inside their bodies, and the more disturbed they become. In effect, they are elected to be the object upon which the tensions produced by unresolved conflicts of parents are displaced. They are seen as the cause of all discord, the family's "problem," and are therefore punished, usually by being physically, verbally, or sexually abused (or all three). Vogel and Bell note that in families in which a child is scapegoated, the main task is to help the parents regulate marital tension. Indeed, the scapegoat is "chosen to symbolize the conflicts and draw off the tension" (p. 212).

Scapegoats serve as a conduit of all that is disowned by parents; the parents deny their own aggression, and they are quick to project it onto the scapegoat. The person who scapegoats, according to Landes (1992), is either an emotional or physical bully. Scapegoating is a defense mechanism involving projection—the scapegoat, not the parent—is to blame for everything wrong with the family. It allows perpetrators to eliminate negative feelings about themselves and provides a sense of gratification. Furthermore, it justifies the self-righteous discharge of aggression. Scapegoats not only serve as the person whom the family most hates, but also suffer from abuse on account of it. In addition, they also must be a container of all the family's guilt, anger, and anxiety

According to my research, there is often a projective identification. A chosen child reminds the parents of some quality about themselves which they unconsciously loath. They project that it is the child who possesses this quality and they devalue the child and punish him or her. Sometimes the child represents, in the transference, a parent or sibling for whom the child's parents have unresolved feelings. For example, if a mother always resented her older sister, she may in the transference scapegoat her oldest daughter. Similarly, if a mother was always in the shadows of a sister who was more attractive and felt disfavored by her father because of it, she may scapegoat her most attractive daughter and try to prevent her and her husband from forming a father-daughter bond. At other times a child may be scapegoated because he or she deviates from the family norm, as when a child acts independently when dependence is the norm, or has musical talent when athleticism is stressed.

Scapegoating may begin from earliest infancy, or it may start at a later time, due to some special circumstance, such as a new pregnancy or a father being fired from a job. Since children are in a powerless position, they can be molded to take on the scapegoat role. Designated children are seen as a problem and treated accordingly; they then act the role and actually become a problem. The problem during infancy may be bedwetting, thumb-sucking, refusing to go to the potty, or soiling; later on it might be stealing, fire-setting, using foul language, taking drugs, fighting with parents and siblings, rebelliousness, and other expressions of hostility. Over the years of childhood, their identity is formed around this role, and their self-esteem reflects it; they take this role and the lowered self-esteem into the adult world.

The scapegoat may be said to serve as the parents' externalized "ego-reject." The child somehow does not live up to the parents' narcissistic expectations. Hence scapegoats are both the products and the manifestations of narcissism. While playing their designated devalued role, they are secret holy cows, forming an ego-ideal in which they cast themselves as long-suffering martyrs whose worth will someday be recognized.

### The Formation of Holy Cows

There is no study in the literature about the development of holy cows, per se. Kohut (1971) observed various developmental lines in which narcissistic personalities may emerge. One such line has to do with a parent's making their children into narcissistic extensions of themselves, that is, into "idealized selfobjects"—which is another way of stating what Freud called externalized ego-ideals (1914). In this line, a parent with feelings of low self esteem chooses one of her children to be an idealized selfobject. The child is a selfobject because it is idealized not for its own sake or because the child is necessarily superior and deserving of such idealization; rather the child is idealized so that it can serve as a bright light that will then reflect upon the parent, who can bask in the child's glory. Hence the child serves as an object that bolsters the parent's deficient self. Similarly, Seinfeld (1991) and Shengold (1972) explored "goodness" as a defense mechanism in narcissists. Parents' narcissistic need to see themselves as all-good requires that they split off the "bad" sides of themselves and identify one or more of their children as representing all that is bad. In this case the child is made into a bad selfobject.

It is this line of development that results in the formation of what I am calling a holy cow. The holy cow is one of the extreme kinds of externalized ego-ideal personalities. Such individuals are treated as if they are sacred, as if they can do no wrong. While the scapegoat is designated as the emotionally disturbed child and actually becomes so in an obvious way, the holy cow is designated the emotionally healthy child and seems, on the surface, to be perfectly healthy. Actually, the holy cow's emotional health is superficial and fragile, and can easily break down. While the scapegoat is elected to be the object upon which the tensions of marital conflicts are displaced, the holy cow is elected to be the object upon which the parents' ego ideals are projected. Hence, while the scapegoat is degraded and abused, the holy cow is overvalued, sanctified, and pampered.

Just as the scapegoat serves as a conduit of all that is disowned by the parents, the holy cow serves as a reflection of all the family's narcissistic grandiosity. In either case, as mentioned previously, there is a projective identification. In the case of the holy cow, one or both parents' ego ideals are extended onto the designated child and he or she is accorded special treatment. The holy cow is identified as the ideal individual that the parents unconsciously believe they themselves are or could have been. Hence, a parent's frustrated ambitions can be channeled through the child.

The designation of the holy cow child depends on several factors. A particularly beautiful, talented, intelligent, or athletic child may be chosen by parents who value beauty, talent, intelligence, or athletic gifts. At other times, the child represents, in the transference relationship to the child, a parent or sibling with whom the parent experienced a similar idealizing selfobject relationship while growing up. For example, a daughter may have been a father's idealizing selfobject (her role being to reflect the father's conceit by becoming his sycophant); she in turn will unconsciously choose one of her sons to serve as an idealized object—that is, he will be projectively identified as a stand-in for the idealized father. Or if a parent was the oldest sister and was hence an idealized selfobject and had a younger sister who was the scapegoat, she may replicate that situation in her own family by idealizing her own oldest daughter and scapegoating the younger daughter. In this way, the two daughters continue to play out the original sibling rivalry, with the mother always taking the side of the oldest.

A holy cow may become a parent's symbolic lover during the Oedipal phase; hence he or she is often an Oedipal conqueror (Freud, 1939), as mentioned previously. The son actually usurps the father's place in the mother's heart, and the daughter usurps the mother's place in the father's heart, and there is often an emotionally and sometimes even a physically incestuous relationship between them. Freud (1914) believed that when a son becomes his mother's holy cow and his father's scapegoat, he may later develop a homosexual sexual orientation.

Like scapegoating, the formation of the holy cow personality may begin from earliest infancy, or it may start at a later time, due to some special circumstance. In the case of a fragmented family, where a father has appropriated a daughter and formed an alliance with her against the mother, the mother may, upon the birth of a son, immediately form an alliance with the son. In such a case, both daughter and son serve as externalized ego-ideals of a sponsoring parent, and each is touted not only to reflect the sponsoring parent's grandiosity, but also to do battle against the opposing team (mother and son vs. father and daughter). At special times, such as following a divorce, a particular child may be thrown into a role of holy cow or that role may become more significant over the years as parental difficulties mount.

### Scapegoats and Holy Cows in Group Therapy

Throughout childhood the holy cow forms an identity around this role and begins to expect this kind of treatment from others, just as the scapegoat forms an identify with and expects scapegoating. Thus both scapegoat and holy cow end up inducing the same treatment they received in their families, which results in their playing these roles all their lives.

A therapy group becomes a symbolic family and in such a group each patient brings a particular forcefield (Langs, 1973-1974). This forcefield becomes contagious and thereby induces an urge to respond in a certain way (Spotnitz and Meadow, 1976). Each group member brings to the group a particular identity formed in their families. Thus without saying a word a scapegoat may join a group and immediately become subject to attack. He or she through words or body language will emit a forcefield and present a particular identity that says, "I'm no good so kick me!" or "You'd better not kick me or I'll get angry!" or "Everybody's always thought it was my fault so you'll probably always think its my fault, too!" and thereby induce a rejecting response. Similarly, a holy cow will join a group and immediately be viewed as an exalted and sacred object. He or she will bring a forcefield and present an identity that says, "I know what I'm talking about!" or "I'm beyond reproach!" or "I'm a superior, entitled person!" and thereby induce an idealizing response from other members. The scapegoat becomes the group's externalized ego-reject; the holy cow becomes it's externalized ego-ideal.

For example, on the first meeting of a newly formed group, a young man began to introduce himself in a self-depreciating, halting tone: "My name's Mr. A, and...I just want to say I've never felt comfortable in groups....I guess that's why I'm here, so I can, you know, get some honest feedback...." Before he had gotten two sentences out a woman in the group, Ms. B, began to laugh derisively and blurted out to the rest of the group, "He wants honest feedback about as much as I want a hole in the head." The rest of the group laughed with her, and the young man, as was his custom, internalized his anger and went silent. From there, other people began to speak. The young man's scapegoat role was already set.

In this same group, the woman who had laughed at and put down the scapegoat established herself immediately as a holy cow. Whereas the young man's body language had been self-depreciating and provocative (he sat slumped in his chair, hung his head, and spoke in a halting, fearful tone), the woman's body language was self-exalting and inspiring (she sat up in her chair, held her head high, and spoke with an attitude of entitlement, and with a slight tone of sarcasm in her voice). It was apparent that she considered herself beyond reproach and felt entitled to attack others in the group, such as the young man, whom she decided were deserving of such an attack. The group rallied behind her, reacting to her forcefield, responding to her air of authority, and fearful of her sarcasm.

The task of the group therapist becomes that of providing responses that differ from the ones the scapegoat and holy cow are familiar with and expect.

Treating the scapegoat is a bit easier than treating the holy cow for a scapegoat suffers greatly because of this role. Instead of reacting to the scapegoat's induction by rejecting him or her, the group therapist responds by calling the scapegoat's attention to the kinds of messages he or she is sending. "When you keep putting yourself down that way," the therapist may say, "it makes me want to put you down as well." Or, "When you ramble on in that ditsy way, you make me want to interrupt you and reject what you're saying." Or, "When you come in with that sulky, defiant glare, it makes me want to attack you." In working with the scapegoat, the therapist must set the lead in treating the scapegoat with respect, despite the scapegoat's self-disrespect or self-defeating behavior, and must intercede when members of the group succumb to scapegoating. Other members of the group (particularly the holy cow) will at first be reluctant to give up the scapegoating, and will feel insulted that the leader is implying that the scapegoat is being in any way victimized by them (it may puncture the holy cow's narcissistic bubble).

Gradually, the therapist begins to use interpretations. "You are inducing people to be mean to you, Mr. A, because this is what you were taught to do in your family and this is the role you're accustomed to." The group has become your symbolic family and you expect this symbolic family to be the same as your real family of origin; and what you expect, you get. It's a self-fulfilling prophecy." Thus the whole group dynamic has to be analyzed and worked through. In such atmosphere of respect, the scapegoat will be able to engage in self-analysis, resolve conflicts related to self-assertion and self-esteem, and find his or her real self.

Treating holy cows presents just as much of a challenge. While scapegoats are eventually willing to give up their role, due to its painful and unpleasant nature, holy cows are reluctant—even stubborn—about doing so. If the therapist attempts to interpret or call attention to the kinds of messages the holy cow is sending to the group, he is likely to arouse the holy cow's rage and bring about a hasty, indignant exit from the group. Instead, the therapist must first serve as an idealizing selfobject in order to establish a bond of trust. "Ms. B, you really do have an uncanny insight into things," the leader may say, and he may even call on her for "authoritative" assistance at times. "Tell me, Ms. B, why do you think Mr. A doesn't really want honest feedback?" Gradually the therapist wins the trust of the holy cow, and only then may start to use other interventions. Spotnitz (1985) has demonstrated the use of emotional communication with narcissistic patients. If Ms. A uses a tone of sarcasm toward the therapist, the therapist might respond not with an interpretation, but with an emotional reaction. "Ouch!" The holy cow must be made aware of his or her unconscious sadism. This awareness will come first through this emotional communication, and later by analyzing the scapegoat and how he induces the holy cow to abuse him.

Thus, when the holy cow's relationship to the therapist changes from a narcissistic to an object transference, the leader will gradually relinquish the idealizing selfobject role and begin more and more to address the holy cow's particular form of resistance, first through emotional communication and ego-dystonic (paradoxical) joining, then through indirect interpretations via the scapegoat, then through direct interpretations of the holy cow's process. The leader may communicate an emotional response to the way the holy cow addresses the scapegoat: "You know, when you talk to Mr. A in that sarcastic tone of voice, it makes me so fearful of you that I want to agree with anything you say."

Paradoxical (exaggerated) joining prods the holy cow into seeing the other side of things. It helps her to see that she is denying her own rage and compensating for a deficient self through the erection of a grandiose self and the projective identification of her deficient self onto the scapegoat.

"Sometimes I think I ought to be a lawyer or a judge," Ms. A said during a later session. "I have this bullshit meter, and it just goes off whenever I encounter bullshit."

The therapist used paradoxical joining. "I think that's a wonderful idea. I think you ought to be a judge. But why stop there? Why not go for the Supreme Court?"

In another session, Ms. A said to the scapegoat, "You're such an idiot. I really resent your wasting the group's time with your whining."

"That's right, Mr. A, stop being such an idiot right now!" the leader echoes.

"Well, he is!"

"That's absolutely true! Mr, A, please stop being such an idiot!"

"Are you mocking me?"

"Why would I mock you?"

"Because you think I'm being too harsh on Mr. A."

"Are you?"

"I don't know. I guess."

Down the road, the leader can bring in an interpretation. "Who does Mr. A remind you of?"

"My brother."

So you're transferring your idiotic brother onto Mr. A."

"But he asks for it."

"So did your brother."

"Oh, right."

"Just because somebody asks for it, does that mean you have to give it to them?"

"I guess not."

When the holy cow's externalized ego-ideal (the therapist) exaggerates the holy cow's grandiosity and sadism, and when this grandiosity and sadism does not get its usual supportive response, the holy cow begins to question this mode of operation. At the same time, an emotional communication is a direct demonstration of the effect she is having on another person. It provides living, nonjudgmental, undeniable "evidence" to the holy cow about how she is acting out, by responding to her unconscious sadism rather than interpreting it. When this is done repeatedly, her ego becomes insulated and able to tolerate more direct interpretations.

Over time—perhaps years—the holy cow may be able to work through relevant material and realize how this role, while according the secondary gratification of being idealized, nevertheless prevents any genuine relationship from developing. The role also sets the player up for a fall. Like "Humpty-Dumpty," the holy cow's narcissistic shell is brittle. Holy cows demand and expect to be idealized by everyone, and if they do not get it--or if those they have been scapegoating get more praise then they do--they can easily crash. Their ego-strength is dependent upon their being allowed (entitled) to freely conduct themselves sadistically without reproach, and on their grandiose assumption of superiority, especially over the scapegoat. This narcissistic overvaluation, dependent on maintaining a certain hierarchy, will be disturbed if the hierarchy is disturbed. Gradually, the therapist demonstrates to the holy cow the satisfaction of genuine and respectful relationships. But this new relationship comes, if it comes at all, only after years of work, for a holy cow does not easily give up the satisfaction and power of the holy cow role.

### Countertransference

Scapegoats and holy cows each induce particular kinds of countertransference problems. Aside from the fact that both provoke strong emotional responses and impulses to act out counterresistance, each also poses problems for therapists who have themselves come from backgrounds in which they were scapegoated or holy-cowed. A therapist who was the family scapegoat may tend to protect (rather than analyze) a scapegoat patient, or become somewhat fanatical in trying to help, while reacting angrily to a holy cow. Such a therapist may at the same time give in to the impulse to attack a holy cow patient through an ego-dystonic interpretation. A therapist who was the family holy cow may unwittingly attack a scapegoat patient in the same way, while forming a twinship countertransference with a holy cow patient.

Previously (1993) I wrote about a group therapist whose narcissism made him susceptible to countertransference and counteresistance. He had both a holy cow and a scapegoat in his group. He may have been the holy cow of his own family, for he showed himself to the group and to the world as a superior, witty, and cultured man and for the most part lived up to this ego-ideal. He had established himself through theatrical presentations at numerous conferences as a wise and witty therapist, and he had an unflappable confidence in his own perceptions.

He and his holy cow patient, another man whose ego-ideal was that of a superior, witty, and cultured man, would often engage in repartee during group therapy sessions. They each served as the other's alter ego-ideal; or, in other words, they had formed a twinship transference and countertransference. In the patient's eyes, the therapist could do no wrong, and in the therapist's eyes the patient could do no wrong. They each supported and enabled one another's narcissism.

Meanwhile, there was a youngish woman in the group who

served as the group's scapegoat. She presented herself as a daffy person who would ask "stupid" questions and provoke ridicule. The therapist would generally make a show of treating this woman with respect and interpret her daffiness. However, on occasion his narcissistic need to be witty and to entertain would cause him to play off of this patient's questions the way a wise-cracking comedian might play off of the comments of a straight man. The woman might ask a question such as, "Are therapist's human?" What she meant to say was that she did not feel the therapist was giving her the emotionally corrective responses she needed. However, instead of picking up on that, the therapist would look at his holy cow patient and quip, "Let me see, are therapist's human?...James, help me out here. Daphne wants to know if therapists are human."

"You know what T. S. Eliot says about that, don't you?" James would reply, tongue in cheek.

"I wasn't aware that T. S. Eliot said anything about therapists," the therapist would say, his eyes twinkling with impish mischief.

"You're quite mistaken."

"What, sir, did he say, pray tell?"

The two lofty buddies would engage in a comical bit of repartee at the expense of Daphne. The group, although excluded from this repartee, would nevertheless get a big laugh out of it, for it would afford them a chance to release any free-floating anxiety and sadism they might be nursing (much as a comedy movie does for an audience). Hence the therapist would unwittingly encourage a group resistance. Such moments were only occasional and lasted only minutes, but they were of much impact on the group and on the holy cow and scapegoat, serving to reinforce rather than resolve their character disturbances.

As time went on, Daphne became the person people would take out their aggression on and target as the group's "problem." She was generally treated with contempt by the group, particularly James. Since James enjoyed a holy cow "immunity" he could come to the group in a state of distress and safely displace his anger onto Daphne, knowing that the leader would never criticize him but would instead support his acting out. Daphne would ramble and he would interrupt her, saying something sarcastic to her.   Others would then join in the attack, and the leader would spend time analyzing why Daphne induced this response in the group.   Daphne was blamed for any problems happening in the group, and served as the container for group tension.  For example, if any of the members of the group were jealous of the therapist's favoritism of the holy cow, they would displace the tension produced by this jealousy by attacking Daphne at opportune moments.

At first Daphne continued to play her role due to its secondary gratification of getting attention from the leader and the group.  However, eventually the anger built up  insider her and she left the group, announcing that she had entered another group where people treated her differently.   The members of the first group were derisive about her leaving and suspicious about the new group.   "Wait until they get to know her," they said.   And, they added, "Good riddance!   She was disruptive anyway."   For a while they seemed genuinely happy that she was gone, but after a while the tensions that had been contained by her erupted and the long simmering conflicts between the holy cow and other members became more apparent.

This therapist, by the way, had had many years of supervision and training, and had done quite a lot of analyzing of his own childhood, as all therapists must do.   Yet his narcissism had apparently not been adequately analyzed because it was in many ways a charming aspect of his personality and seen as a plus rather than a detriment.

### Summary and Conclusions

Scapegoats and holy cows each represent a kind of narcissistic personality.  The former symbolizes what the narcissistic parent disowns and then, through projective identification, attaches onto a chosen child.  Even though the chosen child is devalued, he or she nevertheless feels special and important, as though secretly thinking, "I am being picked on because they are jealous of my superiority."  The latter stands for what the narcissistic parent aspires to and projects onto and identifies with in another chosen child.   In their adult lives scapegoats and holy cows induce their environment  to treat them as their families did, and so they continue to play their roles in society. Scapegoats may end up as criminals, junkies, prostitutes, battered women, religious martyrs, or presidents of sinking corporations. Holy cows may end up as priests, housewives, political activists, talk show hosts, movie stars, or sports heroes.

Nearly all groups—from the smallest families to the largest societies—have both holy cows and scapegoats (one feeding off the other). In societies, one racial, religious or ethnic group may be seen as a holy cow while another represents the scapegoat. Sometimes the scapegoated group, on the basis of its long suffering, may then exalt and sanctify itself as a holy cow; it then turns around and scapegoats the former holy cow. This constitutes one of the most prominent themes in history.

A therapy group represents a symbolic family as well as a laboratory in which the scapegoat and holy cow can be studied and transformed. One of the biggest challenges of the group therapist is to deal with such characters effectively.

*References:*

Adler, A. (1927). *Understanding Human Nature.* New York, Premiere Books.

Freud, S. (1914). On narcissism. *Standard Edition.* 14:67-104.

-- (1939). Moses and Monotheism. *Standard Edition.* 23:7-137.

Guest, J. (1968). *Ordinary People.* New York, Bantam.

Kohut, H. (1971). *Analysis of the Self.* New York, International Universities Press.

Landes, R. (1994). Scapegoating. *Encylopedia of Social History,* Ed. by Peter N. Steam. New York, Garland.

Langs, R. (1973-1974). *The Technique of Psychoanalytic Psychotherapy. Volumes I and II.* Northvale, NJ, Jason Aronson.

Schoenewolf, G. (1993). *Counterresistance: The Therapist's Interference with the Therapeutic Process.* Northvale, NJ, Jason Aronson.

Seinfeld, J. (1991). *The Empty Core.* Northvale, NJ, Jason Aronson.

Shengold, L. (1992). *Halo in the Sky: Observations on Anality and Defense.* New Haven, Yale University Press.

Spotnitz, H. and Meadow, P. W. (1976). *Treatment of the Narcissistic Neuroses.* New York, Manhattan Center for Advanced Psychoanalytic Studies.

Spotnitz, H. (1985). *Modern Psychoanalysis of the Schizophrenic Patient*, 2nd Edition. New York, Human Sciences Press.

Vogel, e. F., and Bell, N. W. (1968). The emotionally disturbed child as the family scapegoat. From *A Modern Introduction to the Family.* New York, The Free Press.

# 12

# Vampire Men and Vampire Coupling

---

This study focuses on a mode of relating termed "vampire coupling," characterized by a passive-aggressive, aggressive-passive struggle in which each member of a couple frustrate each other's oral needs for nurturing. It also looks at the vampire myth, linking it to the fantasies of dysfunctional passive-aggressive males.

---

Sometimes a dream holds the key of a treatment. Such was the case with the following dream.

"I was in an ambulance and I was dead. Lying beside me was a black girl and she was still alive. I took a syringe and stuck it into her neck and sucked out her blood. She died and I came alive. Then I was at my mother's house. She was there with some of her women friends. I did the same thing to them, sucked out all their blood, and they died and I lived."

This is not the dream of a vampire, but of a patient whose childhood circumstances left him with a phobia about women's breasts. He could not stand them and he could not tolerate what they stood for—nurturing and intimacy. If there was any sucking to be done, it would have to be done on their necks, not their breasts, and the sucking would have violent consequences, as in the dream. He is one of a number of passive males I have treated who had such fantasies and dreams. All of them were involved with women who were much more aggressive than they were, whom they frustrated sexually and emotionally.

His relationship with his wife was a passive-aggressive struggle. The daily theme was one of frustration and counter-frustration. She wanted to have sex often and for long periods of time, whereas he was indifferent to it. She wanted to raise children, whereas he did not care one way or the other about marriage or children. She wanted to have long intimate talks with him, whereas he wanted to have long intimate talks with his computer. As the years of their relationship mounted, he retreated further into passivity and she further into aggression. While in his dreams he sucked her blood, in real life he saw her as a vampire who was sucking his.

During the course of his individual treatment we were able to trace his passivity and his breast phobia to the deprivation he had undergone as an infant. The nature of the deprivation and aggression by his mother had caused him to repress his frustration and accompanying rage and to develop a passive-aggressive character structure. Hence his passivity had an underlying aggressive undertow. Although he was badly in need of nurturing from a woman, he could not accept nurturing from his wife and in fact passively frustrated both her attempts to nurture and to be nurtured by him. At the same time, his passive-aggression aroused in his wife a type of response which I have previously referred to as aggressive-passive (Schoenewolf, 1996). That is, she aggressed against him in such a way as to induce passivity and make him retreat even more into his shell, which gave her the excuse to criticize him all the more and achieve the secondary gain of displacing pent-up anger from her own childhood. This process served to reinforce each of their defensive postures and keep them stuck in a duel. In effect, he induced her to behave like his mother.

His relationship with his wife became the third rendition in three generations of this kind of oral-sadistic coupling. During the course of his treatment, we found it in the relationship of his mother and father and his mother's mother and father. In each instance, the couples were apparently engaged in the same passive-aggressive, aggressive-passive duel. In each instance, a kind of vampire attitude permeated the relationship, so that instead of nurturing one another, each mate sucked life from the other. In the first two instances, the advent of pregnancy, childbirth, and nursing exacerbated the situation.

However, in the present case of "vampire coupling" when the wife of the dreamer of the vampire dream became pregnant, gave birth, and proceeded to somewhat blatantly suckle a girl child in front of her husband, things changed. His passive-aggression no longer worked, since his wife now had another object with which to satisfy her oral and emotional needs. Indeed, he not only felt powerless but also excluded (and in a sense cockolded) by the nursing child. This eventually sent him into therapy, wherein he was able to work his way out of this syndrome and break a three-generational cycle.

### From the Literature

Where did the legend come from? How did it arise? This case gave rise to a psychological investigation of the vampire story. In folklore, vampires were said to be ghosts of heretics, criminals or madmen. They returned from the grave in the guise of monstrous bats to suck the blood of sleeping persons, who then became vampires themselves. The only way to kill them was to drive a wooden stake through their hearts. In Stoker's *Dracula* (1887), the vampire slept in a coffin by day and came out at night. Vampires have traditionally been male, and their victims have primarily been innocent, virginal females. The vampire myth, looked at analytically, would seem to correspond to the fantasies and dreams of dysfunctionally passive males, and may well be an outgrowth of such fantasies. Indeed, vampires are the epitome of passive masculinity; they are so passive they are dead, and become revived only upon sucking living blood. They must kill others (turn them into vampires) in order to continue to live. In addition, through sucking the blood of innocent young women, they also attain super powers—they can only be killed in a certain proscribed way. This points to a grandiose, narcissistic component of such fantasies.

The vampire myth and dreams and fantasies that contain vampire themes have been attributed by psychological investigators to the oral-sadistic stage. Abraham writes of the vampire-like behavior of individuals whose breast-feeding was frustrated. He notes that such individuals always seem to be demanding something, and the nature of their demands has a quality of persistent sucking. Neither the facts nor the reason can prevent their pleading and insisting. He notes that "...their behavior has an element of cruelty in it as well, which makes them something like vampires to other people" (1927, p. 401). The cruel sucking behavior of which he writes not only relates to the passive male, but might also have a link with aggress-passive females in the three generations of couples in this study. He describes such people as alternately sucking like vampires and then giving out an "obstinate oral discharge." That is, they can also use cruel words as a means of controlling and psychologically killing off adversaries.

Klein drew attention to the significance of the "bad breast" in children's fantasies. She wrote of oral-sadistic fantasies of toddlers containing ideas that the child "gets possession of the contents of his mother's breast by sucking and scooping it out" (1932, p. 128). She describes an early stage of development "governed by the child's aggressive trends against its mother's body and in which its predominant wish is to rob her body of its contents and destroy it" (ibid.).

She goes on to explain that the feeling of emptiness in its body, which the child experiences as a result of lack of oral satisfaction, might be responsible for the fantasies of assault on the mother's body, since "it might give rise to phantasies of the mother's body being full of all the desired nourishment" (ibid.). Boys in particular harbor tremendous fear of the mother as castrator and their attacks on the mother's body are also directed at their father's penis, which they imagine is inside their mother's body. "He is afraid of her as a person whose body contains his father's penis" (p. 131). Ideas about the phallic woman have their origin, according to Klein's research with little boys, during the oral-sadistic stage.

Freud (1910), in a study of Leonardo da Vinci, focused on the artist's memory of a vulture-like bird that came to him when he was an infant. According to the memory, while Leonardo was in his cradle, this threatening bird came down and opened the infant's mouth with its tail and struck him again and again with its tail. Freud contended that this memory was in fact a fantasy. The fantasy conceals a memory of being suckled at his mother's breast. The fact that in the fantasy the mother is replaced by the vulture-like bird—or perhaps a hawk, according to some (Anderson, 1994)—is an indication that the child experienced this sucking as soothing menacing. Freud speculates that da Vinci was an illegitimate child, which perhaps caused his mother to cling to him all the more. This bird deprived him of a father's influence until his fifth year, and left him vulnerable to the "tender seductions of his mother," whose only solace he was. In his primitive fantasy, da Vinci saw this mother's nursing as aggressive and terrifying. At any rate, something happened during the nursing state to create in da Vinci a phobia of breasts. This memory or fantasy of da Vinci might be seen as hinting of some kind of trauma during the oral-sadistic stage.

Fenichel notes that "Oral-sadistic tendencies are often vampirelike in character" (1945, p. 489). He documents a case in which an infant was breast-fed for a year and a half, while living with a doting grandmother who spoiled him, and then was suddenly removed and forced to live with an excessively severe father. This childhood is somewhat similar to da Vinci's, with similar results. In Fenichel's case, the man became an extremely passive-dependent personality, who throughout his adulthood lived (sucked) on his father's money. He always felt his father had discriminated against him, favored his sister over him, and was convinced that life was unfair. He points out that the conflict between ingratiating submissiveness and an impulse violently to take what they think is theirs is characteristic of such types.

Other writers have focused on the type of aggressive-passive mothering that may produce a passive-aggressive male. Socarides, writing of the dreams of passive males of what he calls the "perverse" variety, interprets that their inner stress stems, among other things, from the "threat of imminent destructive incorporation by the mother" (1980, p. 249). Spitz (1965), in a study of mothers and infants in a clinic for unwed mothers, details cases of what he calls "primary active rejection" by mothers who, due to their circumstances (being teenagers who were suddenly saddled with the responsibility for a child) had an extreme distaste for motherhood. He cites a case in which a mother stiffened and looked annoyed whenever she held her baby, and Spitz remarks, "During nursing the mother behaved as if her infant were completely alien to her and not a living being at all" (p. 211). Shengold (1979) has labeled a drastic form of anti-nurturing as "soul murder." According to him, the subject of such parenting is "robbed of his identity and of the ability to maintain authentic feelings. "Soul murder," he maintains, "remains effective if the capacity to think and to know has been sufficiently interfered with—by way of brainwashing" (p. 557). Others who have alluded to the kind of early deprivation that renders children passive include Ferenzi (1933), Laing (1971), Miller (1984), and Seinfeld (1990).

A family therapist, Satir (1967) wrote of marriages in which each partner needed the other to bolster his or her self-esteem. Such people chose a mate on the basis of the mate's capacity in various ways to elevate their own self-esteem, and if and when that hope fails, they feel betrayed and angry. The feelings of disappointment toward their mate are passed on to their children; the children are treated as if they are the cause of the parents' failure. Satir notes that this kind of dysfunctional family system often results in children who reject themselves. "A child needs to esteem himself in two areas: as a masterful person and as a sexual person" (p. 54). Another way of looking at it is that the parents were unable to suck life from their mates, so they sucked life from their children.

### Vampire Coupling

John was about 30 years old at the time he had the dream reported at the beginning of this paper. He and Mary had been married for five years. As previously mentioned, their relationship had remained on a passive-aggressive level until Mary became pregnant. From the moment he found out she was pregnant, John began expressing vague feelings of annoyance and trepidation. He was not sure what he was annoyed or afraid of, until after the birth. When he caught sight of his wife breast-feeding their daughter, he discovered that what he was feeling was jealousy and rage. This jealousy and rage was brought on, first of all, by Mary's deliberate flaunting (so it seemed to him) of her nursing sessions, which he believed was her way of getting revenge for his years of frustration of her sexual and emotional needs. Second, it was aroused by a memory from the past, which had formerly been repressed, of his own oral frustration at the hands of his mother. This memory engendered a fear of reengulfment and, through the mechanism of projection, an irrational conviction that his wife's breasts were angry and dangerous things. The scene also brought back a later memory of witnessing his mother nursing his infant sister and feeling excluded from this intimacy. This in turn induced a womb-envy that was the bedrock of his later envy of, and anger at, his wife's breasts and her capacity to nurse their daughter. This theme then surfaced in his dreams.

John reported that his mother always preferred his younger sister and was hostile toward him on account of his being male. This seemed to be in part a response to frustrations she was experiencing with respect to his father, and in part due to traumas she had experienced in connection with her father (John's maternal grandfather). His mother continually complained about both men, but mostly about her husband (John's father), who would stay at work till late each night, in order, she thought, to avoid her. She complained to John, much to his chagrin, that "your father doesn't love anybody but himself," and that he not only stayed at work till late at night, but also when he came home he neglected her and his children. Often when he did come home his mother screamed at his father and the father would promise to come home later and pay more attention to her. But he never did. It appeared that the problems of John's mother and father trickled down and got displaced onto him through the manner in which his mother nursed him: grudgingly.

John noted that his mother had a problem with breast milk,

during the time she was nursing him and had to abruptly change to bottle-feeding, despite his vehement protests. And she would put the bottle in a holder rather than holding him in her arms when he sucked from the bottle. This first trauma was later reinforced when he witnessed his mother breast-feeding his sister. Although he could not put it into words at the time, he felt that she had milk for his sister because she was female, but none for him because he was a bad male (like his father). When he wanted to join in on the action (she had an extra breast did she not?) she would shame him: "You're not a baby anymore. Run along and play."

John's mother, like his wife, had apparently flaunted her nursing of John and his sister in front of the father in an aggressive-passive way. Unconsciously, she was being aggressive to produce even more passivity in her husband. The more he sank into a jealous rage and retreated into passivity, avoiding her and the kids, the more she could complain about him, scream at him and vent all the frustration she had repressed from her childhood. From the husband's side of the struggle, his passivity was unconsciously intended to provoke greater and greater aggression from the wife, so that he had the excuse of retreating further into his work world and could like an innocent victim to the children while making her look like a vampire monster.

John was forced to "swallow" everything: the oedipal guilt, the separation anxiety, the fear of maternal reengulfment, and the sibling jealousy. There was no soothing from his mother, nor a chance to ventilate or work through anything. Instead, he was made to feel that his feelings were wrong, stupid, or masculine. This constituted another layer of frustration added to the original layer of frustration during the oral stage, reinforcing the early repression.

His marriage was almost a carbon copy of that of his mother and father. He treated Mary similarly to the way his father had treated his mother. He became passive-aggress, fearing that his wife (his mother in the transference) would control and oppress him (suck his blood) rather than nurturing him. She was aggressive-passive, believing that she had to constantly nag him and shame him in order to get any semblance of love or consideration from him. And so they remained at odds, both needing nurturing, each depriving the other of it.

In the sexual sphere, this manifested itself in her being grabby and in his being withholding. She would continually demand sex and complain that he did not satisfy her—sort of like the vampire-like people described by Abraham. He would perform sex as he might perform a duty, like mowing the lawn (or, like a zombie mowing the lawn). She suffered from frigidity and blamed it on him. He suffered from premature ejaculation and blamed it on her. A huge sticking point of their sexual relations was his absolute refusal ever to kiss or suck her breasts. Almost weekly she would complain about this, and almost weekly he would refuse. He was as afraid of her breasts as he was of castration, but he did not understand any of this. All he understood is that her breasts to him were ugly. She was, naturally, wounded by this attitude and spent a good deal of effort in trying to shame him into submission.

John's mother's parents represented the third generation of oral-sadistic (vampire) coupling. For all I knew it might have gone further than that, but this is as far as we could trace it in therapy. From his mother's complaints about his father (John's grandfather), he deduced that this man too had been passive-aggressive (both at his wife and daughter), while his mother's mother had also been aggressive-passive, prone to temper tantrums that caused John's mother "to run from the house." And once again, in this third generation, the birth of a child had apparently brought about a variation in the relationship; during the grandmother's pregnancy and for a year or so afterward, the grandfather had an affair.

### The Clinical Picture

The man who became my patient was depleted of vitality and lived almost entirely in his dreams and fantasies. His fantasies were so important to him that for a long time he was reluctant to tell them to me or anybody. Indeed, the world of his fantasies was more real and more important to him than the real world. For the most part these fantasies were benign and bore no indication of the cruelty that would show up in his dreams at a later stage: trips to foreign planets where he became a heroic savior; inventions that made him famous; speeches before the United Nations that roused people to action. These fantasies—which had a Walter Mitty flavor—were indicative of his stage of narcissism, which was almost at a delusional degree in the beginning of treatment.

The therapy relationship was a replica of his relationship with his wife and with people in genera: passive-aggressive. In the beginning he was ingratiatingly submissive, giggling almost every time he spoke. If I asked him, "What are you feeling right now?" he would respond, "I don't know," and giggle. He dutifully brought in dreams, talked about his life, his work, his history, without any emotion except the giggle. At the same time, he had a great deal of problems paying me for sessions, and at one point there were ten bad checks in about twelve weeks.

Over several years, due to the working-through of the transference, his relationship with me gradually changed into a more truly cooperative one, and the passive-aggression diminished. I encouraged him to confront his wife's demands rather than retreating into his world of fantasy, and his relationship with her began to change too, as well as his relationship with his parents. Note: this change was, as I said, very gradual and moderate. He still remained passive, but the aggressive quality had gone down as he has gotten in touch with feelings.

Toward the end of four years of therapy, he had the dream recounted at the beginning. He had a number of other dreams with vampire themes. We interpreted the first dream as follows: the ambulance was a womb, and the syringe was a phallus and the black woman was his sister, who in a wish that represented a reversal to what had actually occurred, became the "black sheep" of the family. The dream alluded to both his angry incestuous feelings toward his sister and the infantile notion of a powerful phallus that could rape and kill. Later when he likewise injects his mother and her friends with his powerful but deadly phallus, it again may represent a wish for the reversal of what he felt had been done to him.

In another dream he was in a bus (another womb) and touched the thumb of a woman sitting next to him with his thumb (his phallus) causing her to tremble and die. In yet a third dream he was swimming in a rough sea, and there was a wall separating the sea from the land, and the wall had a long tunnel in it (the vagina). To get to the tunnel, he had to walk on the backs of several female swimmers ahead of him (his sister and her friends), causing them to drown. Finally he made out of the tunnel (he was born, his sister wasn't).

Aside from the vampire motif, the dreams had other layers of meaning. In the first dream he is dead, which might also be linked to his feeling that his birth wasn't wanted. The first two dreams, in which he injected a syringe into a woman's neck and touched another's thumb with his thumb, causing them to die, might also be an allusion to his womb envy or an introjection of his mother's and sister's scorn of his masculinity. In the third dream he was out in a rough sea and a wall separated him from land; this may denote his feeling of being excluded by women, separated from his mother's womb. The instances of poisonous penises in the dreams might also have been meant to assuage his castration fear. We considered all these possibilities and they all led to fruitful discussions.

I considered these dreams to be significant signposts in his therapy. They were sharper, and more emotionally tinged than earlier dreams, indicating to me that previously taboo material about the extent of his oral rage was coming to the surface. By being held up in relief, the dreams seemed to clearly show the oral-sadistic underpinning of his personality.

Prior to these vampire dreams, he had not been able to get in touch with his anger. The only person toward whom he could feel anger was his father, who happened to be the only person his mother allowed him to feel anger towards. He was misled by the mother into believing that the father had abandoned him and had chosen not to visit him after the divorce. In actuality, the mother refused to allow his visits, but the father passively accepted this refusal without putting up a legal fight. Hence John, in identification with his mother, would often express resentment toward his father: "If only he had not left, things would have been different." In addition, through a negative identification with his father, he saw both himself and his father as bad, somewhat pathetic figures.

Along with the emergence of the dreams came a release of

repression. He began to express more and more anger at his mother, his wife, and me. Much of the early work of therapy consisted in helping him individuate and separate from his mother. During this phase, he began to drop the submissive, giggly false self and to verbalize the distrust and anger underneath. He began to treat me as though I were going to latch onto him, make him totally dependent on me, and suck his blood (the mother transference). He became suddenly concerned about the fee, whereas previously he had paid no attention to it. He expressed the view that I was financially and emotionally exploiting him, that my interpretations were hostile reproaches and that the only reason I wished to keep him in therapy was to gratify myself at his expense. By verbalizing these things and analyzing them, he was able to pull himself out of the passive-aggressive, oral-sadistic defensive mode.

He was then able to explore how the same dynamics had come into play in his relationship with his wife, and to reach a state of aliveness and realness with her. He first expressed to me, then to her, his fears of her sucking his blood, and underneath this an even bigger fear of allowing himself to be nurtured by her (and become dependent and devoured by her). As he worked through this material he became less passive-aggressive. Unfortunately, his wife, who was not in therapy and was resistant, retained her aggressive-passive defensive posture. However, the changes he made helped to reduce the struggle with her. Since he was less defensive, there was less for her to fight against. This change also fostered a better relationship with their daughter.

### Conclusion

This study focused on how a certain mode of relating—vampire coupling—was passed on from generation to generation. In this mode of relating, characterized by a passive-aggressive and aggressive-passive struggle, each member of the couple frustrated the other's oral needs for nurturing. It appears this kind of coupling results in childrearing that tends to pass onto children the parents' inherent frustration and discontentment. That is to say, orally-deprived, sadistic parents tend to produce orally-deprived, sadistic children. The early psychoanalytic writing on oral sadism by Freud, Klein and Abraham still seem valid to me and allude to the vampire-like behavior of individuals who have developed certain types of fixations in the oral stage and provide some theoretical base for understanding extreme forms of orality. However, these early analysts were more concerned with drive theory and did not adequately analyze the significance of maternal aggression, paternal passivity, and its impact on the child's fantasies and subsequent development. I have tried in this paper to fill in this gap.

Regarding the vampire myth, it would seem to be an outcome of the passive, perhaps schizoid, fantasies and dreams of both males and females. The fact that it has been present in Western culture since Medieval times shows that it may be a universal phenomenon that serves as a grandiose compensation for the collective fears of humanity, fears related to castration and oral frustration and reengulfment. The myth is also perhaps an expression of narcissistic rage. This myth, like the vampire dreams, affords a symbolic enactment of some of humankind's collective fears, harking back to early oral deprivation. It may serve to dissipate some of that rage, just as dreams serve to dissipate the accumulated frustrations of the day. As such, it is a close relative of other similar myths about witches, dragons, and werewolves.

*References:*

Abraham, K. (1927). *Selected Papers on Psycho-Analysis.* New York, Brunner/Mazel, 1979.

Anderson, W. (1994). Leanardo da Vinci and the slip that fooled almost everybody. *Psychoanalysis and Contemporary Thought*, 17-483-515.

Fenichel, O. (1945). *The Psychoanalytic Theory of Neurosis.* New York, Norton.

Ferenczi, S. (1933). Confusion of tongue between adults and the child. In *Further Contributions to the Theory and Technique of Psycho-Analysis*, pp. 126-147. New York, Brunner/Mazel, 1980.

Freud, S. (1910). Leonardo da Vinci and a memory of his childhood. *Standard Edition*, 11:59-138.

Klein, M. (1932). *The Psychoanalysis of Children*. New York, Delacorte Press, 1975.

Laing, R. D. (1971). *The Politics of the Family*. Hamondsworth, England, Penguin Books.

Miller, A. (1984). *For Your Own Good: The Hidden Cruelty in Childhood and the Roots of Violence*. New York, Farrar, Straus & Giroux.

Schoenewolf, G. (1996). *The Couple Who Fell in Hate*. Northvale, NJ, Jason Aronson.

Seinfeld, J. (1990). *The Bad Object*. Northvale, NJ, Jason Aronson.

Satir, V. (1967). *Conjoint Family Therapy*, Revised Edition. Palo Alto, CA, Science and Behavior Books.

Shengold, L. L. (1979). Child abuse and deprivation: soul murder. Journal of the American Psychoanalytic Association, 17:533-560.

Socarides, C. (1980). A unitary theory of sexual perversions. In *On Sexuality*, ed. By T. B. Karasu and C. W. Socarides, pp. 161-188. New York, International Universities Press.

Spitz, R. (1965). *The First Year of Life*. New York, International Universities Press.

Stoker, B. (1887). *Dracula*. London, Hogarth.

# 13

# Child of the Full Moon

---

Should a therapist make a house visit, or does this change the therapeutic framework in such a way as to make it unworkable or unethical? This paper describes such a visit and the use of a therapeutic joining technique in order to break an impasse, which eventually revealed the lies that lurked under a family's dysfunction.

---

A while back I received a telephone call from a man who said he was having problems with his daughter. He had a heavy accent and at first it was difficult for me to understand him. However, eventually I found out he was Chinese and had been born in Taiwan. He did not know if a Western psychotherapist could help him, but he wanted to try. I told him I knew of some Chinese psychotherapists, but he said he was not interested in a Chinese psychotherapist. "They will look down on me for having problems. That is how the Chinese are," he said. He made an appointment to come to my office the next day, and he arrived about fifteen minutes early, accompanied by a teen-aged boy whom he introduced as his son.

"She doesn't speak to me," the father said in a tone of exasperation and confusion. He was a short, thin man in his 50s, but looked younger. "I don't know what to do. She's acting strange."

"How is she strange?" I asked.

"She doesn't leave the house anymore. She got fired from her job one year ago, and after she was fired she called me and asked if she can live with me. Well, what could I do? She says she no longer has money to pay for rent. So, even though my girlfriend was with me at the time, I couldn't say no. So my daughter moved in and my girlfriend moved back to her apartment. Do you understand?"

I said I understood and asked for some background information.
He told me that the girl's mother had died of a heart attack when the girl was 14. She had been acting strange ever since, and now, at 22, she never left the house and was suspicious of everybody. Only once in the last few months had she gone outside, and that was to attend a cousin's wedding. At one point during the reception, the father had introduced her to one of his friends, and again she had "acted strange." "When I introduced her as my daughter, she screamed, 'I'm not your daughter!' Then I looked around and she was suddenly gone."

"Why do you think she says you're not her father?" I asked.

"I don't know. She mentioned a few times that I gave my son, Xiao, better treatment than her. Maybe that's why."

"It's true," Xiao suddenly spoke up. He was thin like his father, but a few inches taller, and he had a thoughtful expression. "He did give me better treatment. He bought me a car, and was paying my way through
college before I dropped out."

"It's the Chinese tradition," the father interspersed.

"Also, I was mean to her," the son added. "Her name's Yueliang. It means moon. She was named Yueliang because she was born on the night of the full moon. In China there's a saying that if you're born during the full moon you'll be crazy. When we were younger I used to tease her and tell her she would be crazy. I used to call her *feng chuang*, which means crazy. I was very mean."

"It sounds like there's a lot going on in the family," I said.

"Perhaps the three of you should come in for a session—she and the two of you."

"She won't go anywhere," the father said, shaking his head.

"She won't come," the son agreed.

"Then how can I work with her?" I asked, as much to myself as to them. We all looked at one another for a moment. "All right," I finally said. "I guess I'll have to go to her."

Though I had never made a house call before in my twenty years of practicing as a psychotherapist, I recognized that in the present circumstance there seemed to be no other way, so I arranged a house visit for the following week. I made an instant assessment of the situation and decided that the daughter might be suffering from agoraphobia or paranoia. Therefore, I told the father and son it would be best if she were not told that I was coming to visit her, but rather that I was there to mediate a conflict between the father and son. We would elicit her help in working through this conflict that had become evident during this initial consultation—his spoiling of his son and the son's resentment of it. I hoped that when we began to discuss these things, Yueliang would join in and eventually we would get her to open up.

I had come to the decision to use this method of joining Yueliang's resistance because of another case I had read about. Milton Erickson (Haley, 1991) had pioneered the use of paradoxical interventions in treating patients, and one of his cases seemed similar to this one. A mother had come to Erickson to complain about her daughter because she never left the house. She was a high school student, but refused to go to school. Instead, she would stay home every day and sulk in her room. When her mother asked why she wouldn't go to school, she kept mentioning her feet. "What about your feet?" her mother inquired. She was convinced her feet were too large and other students would make fun of them. The mother cried and pleaded for Erickson to help. So he came upon a plan. She said he would visit their home on the pretext of caring for the mother, so as not to arouse the daughter's suspicion. The mother would pretend she was ill and have her daughter send for a doctor—Erickson. On the day of the visit, Erickson was led into the bedroom by the daughter and he observed that her feet weren't large at all. They were normal-sized feet. He approached the mother's bed and held his hand on her forehead, then asked the daughter to fetch him a bowl of hot water. When the daughter returned with the bowl of hot water, she stood behind him waiting for his further instructions. At that point he had decided on his intervention. He accidentally (on purpose) backed up and stepped very hard on one of her feet. She screamed, and he yelled, "Why don't they grow those things large enough for somebody to see them?" The daughter ran, mortified, out of the room.

As Erickson said good-bye, the mother whispered to him, "Aren't you going to talk to my daughter?"

"I already did."

The next week the mother called Erickson to tell him in a delighted and surprised voice that her daughter had returned to school. She was completely over her phobia about her feet and in a good mood.

Erickson is not the only person to use paradoxical methods in psychotherapy. Rosen (1962) Liang (1971) and Spotnitz (1976) have used them effectively with schizophrenic patients. Over the years I had learned that you can't use any one method with all patients. Each patient requires his or her own type of therapy, based on the circumstances. My training was in psychoanalysis, but psychoanalysis actually works with only a minority of patients. Generally it must be combined with cognitive or behavioral work, and sometimes not used at all. Patients with phobias, such as Erickson's patient, do not usually respond to psychoanalytic therapy. Behavioral interventions have been shown by research to work better with them. Therefore, since Yueliang seemed to also suffer from a phobia, I was convinced a behavioral approach was best.

On the day of the appointment I took the N train to Bay Ridge, Brooklyn, pondering the ins and outs of professional conduct. Even though I had made a decision based on research, I still had doubts. I was asking myself, "Is it ethical nowadays for a therapist to make housecalls? Am I being too manipulative by deceiving her? Will this even work? Does therapy ever work at all?" In an age in which the validity of psychotherapy was increasingly being questioned, when therapists were being accused of sexual misconduct and inducing dependence in their patients for financial gain, when the treatment of emotional disorders was becoming more and more a matter of genetics and biology and medicine, I wondered if I really knew what I was doing.

"Maybe I should give up doing therapy, and become a medical technician," I thought, having heard of recent openings in that profession. "I should do something simple, something uncontroversial, so I wouldn't have to question the efficacy of my profession and defend it from the constant criticisms of a society that seems intent on doing away with it."

I emerged from the subway feeling somewhat subdued by these winsome thoughts and zigzagged through five blocks of a run-down neighborhood. When I got to the address I had written down, Xiao was waiting for me. He waved excitedly and came forth, shaking my hand.

"She's up there," he said. "She doesn't know you're coming. She's in the kitchen in her robe."

"In her robe? Won't she feel embarrassed to have me there if she's not properly dressed?"

"No, not at all. It is an Asian custom to wear pajamas in the house, and to receive guests like that. It's normal. Don't worry."

We walked up two flights of stairs and entered the apartment. The father, still exuding the same eager and solemn manner, firmly shook my hand. He opened the door wide to let us in to the railroad apartment, and I saw that he was indeed wearing pajamas and slippers. As I walked in, I could see the daughter out of the corner of my eyes. She was on the thin side, and she wore thick-lensed glasses. Her pupils bulged through the lenses as she looked at us. I glanced at her and turned away, not wanting to convey that she was of interest to me, nor wanting her to think I was staring at her bedroom attire. She was indeed clad in a light blue terrycloth robe, which she pulled tight as I glance at her.

"Yueliang, this is a doctor. He's come to see Dad," Xiao said.

"That's right," the father said.

She said nothing, just kept glancing suspiciously, her eyes bulging at me as we set some chairs up in the living room. We sat on three of the chairs and looked at each other. There was another chair, a wooden rocking chair, placed on the other side of the circle. We looked all looked at that chair. Then we looked at each other again. We did not look at Yueliang, but we could feel her looking at us.

"So," I said. "Mr. Liu, you told me that you have been having trouble with your son, Xiao?"

"Yes," he answered, on cue. "We have had trouble for a few years. I think I must have spoiled him."

"You did," Xiao said."

"He was very wild."

We continued to focus on their relationship for a few minutes. After a while I looked around at Yueliang, who was still staring.

"Why don't you join us?" I said. "Your father and brother are trying to work out a problem. Maybe you can help."

"Who are you?" she asked. Unlike her father and brothers, she spoke without a Chinese accent. I had been told she had studied at Hunter College.

"I'm a psychotherapist."

"He's a psychotherapist," Xiao said, nodding emphatically.

"Does he want some tea? How come you haven't offered him some tea? Why is everybody acting so strange?"

"Who's acting strange?" Xiao said, strangely.

"Did you want some tea?" she said directly to me.

"No, thanks."

"I didn't know psychotherapists visited people's houses."

"They usually don't."

"Are you a legitimate psychotherapist?"

"Yes, I'm legitimate. Come join us."

"I don't think you're legitimate. You're not a legitimate psychotherapist. Legitimate psychotherapists don't make house calls."

"I assure you I'm legitimate."

"Come sit down, Yueliang," Xiao said." He's a real psycho-therapist. He is real. He came here to help."

She hesitated, then arose with a sulky, suspicious glare and slowly meandered toward us. Her father moved the rocker forward for her to sit on. But she did not sit on it right away. Instead she stood by it.

"How do I know you're a legitimate psychotherapist?" she asked.

"Here's my card?" I took a card out of my wallet and reached it toward her.

"Anybody can print up a card."

"Then how can I prove it?"

"Show me your license."

"I don't have it with me." But I'll tell you what. You can call the American Psychological Association and ask if I'm a member."

"What's their number?"

"It's in Washington. You can call information."

"I'll call them later. But even if you're a member of some organization, you can still be a quack."

This interrogation about my legitimacy went on for five minutes. Both Xiao and Mr. Liu tried to vouch for my legitimacy, but to no avail. Nothing would satisfy her. Finally, having answered all her questions as best I could, there was a moment of silence and she sat down in the rocking chair. But she did not sit back and rock in the chair. She sat on the edge and kept her eyes on whoever was speaking as if waiting for that person to say something incriminating. I resumed talking with the father and son, asking them things about their relationship. They each spoke about their relationship while she sat upright, seeming to hover above all of us, her legs folded, her fingers folded, and her eyes unblinking.

After a while, I turned the conversation to Yueliang. "What about your daughter, Mr. Liu? Do you think there's a problem between you and Yueliang?"

"Of course," he replied, looking only at me and not at her. "She doesn't speak to me. She says I'm not her father."

"Is that right?" I asked her. "You're not speaking to him?"

"That's right. I don't talk to him, because he's a liar. He treats me like a second-class citizen."

"Do you think he favors your brother?"

"Of course! Everybody knows that."

"Would you like to try to resolve your problem with your father?"

Yueliang suddenly began to laugh. She sat back in her chair and looked at me and let out a long laugh, not without some bitterness. Mr. Liu and Xiao laughed too, but their laughter had a hint of confusion to it. Then she stopped laughing.

"I thought you came here to do therapy—or whatever it is you do. I thought you came to talk with my father and brother? Why are you here?" she asked. Her eyes were bulging again through the lenses. Then she got back onto the legitimacy thing. "I don't think you're legitimate," she repeated. Then she turned to Xiao. "How did you find out about him?"

"It doesn't matter, Yueliang. He's here."

"It *does* matter. I know him," she said, glaring at her father. "He always goes to Chinese doctors. Why a Caucasian doctor this time?"

"It doesn't matter, Yueliang. Why were you laughing before? Why were you laughing when the doctor asked about your problem with Dad?"

"He always goes to Chinese doctors. As long as I have known him he goes to Chinese doctors. Not just Chinese doctors. They have to be from Taiwan. He is very particular about doctors. You know how he is about doctors, Xiao. This is all very strange." She looked around at all of us. "Why did he call this Caucasian doctor? How did you find him?"

"They found me because I put an ad in a Chinese newspaper," I couldn't help but blurt out.

"You advertise in a newspaper?"

"Yes, I did."

"Why do you advertise? Legitimate psychotherapists don't advertise in newspapers."

"He advertised!" Xiao snapped. "Why did you laugh when he asked about your relationship with Dad?"

"This is all very strange," she said.

She was like a bulldog with a bone. Once it was in her teeth, she wouldn't let go. Fortunately, the tea kettle began to hum after a while. She got up to pour herself a cup of tea and asked again if any of us wanted any. We all said and watched her pour her tea and waited with bated breath for her to return. She had a thin body, but her movements were strong and I had the feeling that she would be able to handle herself in a fight much better than her father and brother. She sat down on the rocker and carefully placed her tea on the coffee table. Only when she was sure the tea was safely settled on the table, did she look up at me. She looked at me and at her brother and father and pulled her pink Terrycloth robe tightly around her thin body.

As she looked at me with her probing eyes, I began to feel a bit uncomfortable, like I was overdressed. I wondered if I should ask them if they had an extra set of pajamas so that I could fit in better. I self-consciously loosened my tie and tried to smile.

"Anyway," she said at last, in a matter-of-fact voice, "he is not my father."

"Ah," the father spoke up at once with annoyance. "You see?"

"Why do you think he's not your father?" I asked.

"I don't think he's not my father. I know so."

"That's ridiculous!" he yelled. "I'm your father! Why do you go around saying such things! It is very hurtful for you to go around saying such things. This is what she said at the wedding. Why do you say such things? Who else is your father?"

"You think that's hurtful? You think what I did was hurtful? How about lying," Yueliang said. For the first time she raised her voice. "Is it hurtful to lie?"

"What lie?" her father asked.

"You know what lie."

"No, I don't know what lie."

"You lied to me all my life."

"What are you talking about?"

"He's your father," Xiao said.

"No, that's a lie. It's a lie," she said to me. "That's what I was told all my life. But it's a lie. I found out the truth after our mother died."

"It *is* the truth. I don't know what you found out. It *is* the truth."

"I always suspected that something was wrong, that I was adopted or something. I always suspected it as long as I can remember," she said. Her eyes were no longer bulging now. They were smaller now and sad and she was rocking slowly in her chair. "But whenever I asked my mother or him about it, they would laugh and tell me I was being ridiculous, and they'd deny it just like now. They kept saying I was crazy because of when I was born, under the full moon, but I'm not crazy. After she died, I looked through my mother's trunk and found some letters."

"What?" the father yelled. "You shouldn't do that. Who gave you permission to look through her trunk?"

"It was my job to straighten things out. I'm the only one who cleans up around here. If I don't clean up, nobody does. Certainly not Xiao. He never picks up a thing."

"Nobody said to read her letters," the father shouted.

"If you're going to yell, I'm leaving."

"I will yell if I want to. I am your father!"

"No, you're not!"

Yueliang jumped up and walked across the room. The robe wafted in the afternoon air and trailed behind her like a flag of retreat. She disappeared into the back bedroom, slamming the door behind her. We looked at one another. The room suddenly felt empty without her presence, as if some central spark had been extinguished.

"She's right," I told the father in a voice loud enough to be heard in the next room. "If this is how you usually communicate with her, then it's understandable why she no longer speaks to you. She was trying to say how she feels and you yelled at her to shut her down. Yueliang," I said, turning to the closed door. "Is this how he usually speaks to you?"

The door opened and she came back out again. "That's exactly how he speaks to me." She began walking around in the kitchen, moving pots around on the stove, washing the counter, straightening the table. "That's all he does is yell at me like I'm some animal."

"So what did you find in the trunk, Yueliang?" I asked. "Tell us about the letters."

"No. He will just yell at me again."

"He won't yell. Tell her you won't yell."

The father had fallen silent. He was looking off, vacantly.

"He won't yell," I said again. "What about the letters. Come back and sit down and tell us about the letters."

She finally returned. She stood for a minute to study her father.

He still sat gazing off. It was as if gear had snapped inside him. She sat down on the rocker and began to speak in a soft voice and there was more hurt than anger now. "I found some letters my mother had written to my grandmother when she was young, in her 20s. She wrote that she had gotten pregnant and the man didn't want to marry her. She didn't know what to do. Then in another letter she wrote that she found another man who wanted to marry her, so she married *him*." She pointed at her father. "He was in love with her, she said, and was willing to marry her and pretend the child—me—was his. And they kept pretending. She kept pretending until the day she died. I'm an illegitimate child, and that's the bottom line, as you Caucasians say. That's how he has always treated me, like an illegitimate child. Like I'm a crazy, illegitimate child. But I'm not crazy. I see things very clearly. I see through their lies."

The father and son were looking down at the floor. I asked the father if this were true.

He finally came out of his daze. "Yes, it's true. But I always loved her. I was a good father. She has no right…"

He broke into sobs. The son put his arm around the father. Yueliang stared from one to the other. Her eyes were no longer sad; they were calm and peaceful.

I decided that my work was finished for the moment and stood up to leave. "It looks like you might have more things to talk about. It might be good if you could all come to my office to talk some more. Maybe next week."

"Yes, I think so," the father said.

"I'll think about it," Yueliang said.

I walked down the two flights of stairs and heard somebody calling me. It was the father. He hurried down the stairs and handed me a check.

"How do you think it went?" he asked. He was excited and cheerful, as if he had just won a small lottery.

"I think it went well. The communication has opened up again. What do you think?"

"Yes, I think so. I think we may talk now. Thank you. Maybe we'll come to your office next week."

I called the father a few weeks later and he said that things were better. "She goes out now. We talk. It's OK. It's normal." As he told me this, I could see Yueliang in my mind's eye, sitting in her blue robe in the kitchen, with a full yellow moon peering from the window behind her. I imagined a small tear magnified through the lenses of her glasses, and for a moment I allowed myself to feel pretty good about being a therapist.

*References:*

Haley, J., Ed. (1991). *Milton Erickson, M.D.: In His Own Voice.* New York: W. W. Norton.

Liang, R. D. (1971). *The Politics of the Family.* London: Tavistock.

Rosen, J. (1962). *Direct Psychoanalytic Psychiatry.* New York: Grune and Stratton.

Spotnitz, H. (1976*). Psychotherapy of PreOedipal Conditions.* Northvale, NJ: Aronson.

# Afterward

*Psychoanalytic Centrism* is the culmination of a lifetime of research on psychoanalytic matters as well as a lifetime of my own individual psychoanalysis. Hence, I believe it represents my most mature work. I have touched the same themes in previous works, but I now regard some of these previous works as only partially successful or not successful at all. I confess, I was not mature enough as a person or as a psychoanalyst to write those books the way they needed to be written. Redemption is a word that comes to mind; it is universally accepted that people can change themselves and hence transcend whatever misguided deeds they have done in the past. Similarly, I hope it will also be accepted that a writer can reach a higher state that can transcend the errors of his past writing. This is not to say that the present work is error-free; only that it is truer than previous works.

# About the Author

Gerald Schoenewolf, Ph.D. is a New York State licensed psychoanalyst who has practiced psychotherapy for over 33 years. He has authored over 25 professional articles and 13 books on psychoanalysis and psychotherapy. His books include *101 Common Therapeutic Blunders, The Art of Hating, Counterresistance* and *Psychotherapy with People in the Arts.* He has also written and directed two feature films—*Therapy* and *Brooklyn Nights.* He lives in the Pennsylvania Poconos with his wife, Julia.

www.ingramcontent.com/pod-product-compliance
Lightning Source LLC
Chambersburg PA
CBHW070635290526
45790CB00001B/96